Assessing Open and Distance Learners

Open and Distance Learning Series

Series Editor: Fred Lockwood

OPEN AND DISTANCE LEARNING SERIES

The Open
University

Assessing Open and Distance Learners

CHRIS MORGAN AND MEG O'REILLY

First published 1999

Kogan Page Limited
120 Pentonville Road
London
N1 9JN
UK

Stylus Publishing Inc.
22883 Quicksilver Drive
Sterling
VA 20166-2012
USA

British Library Cataloguing in Publication Data

A CIP record for this book is available from the British Library.

ISBN 0 7494 2878 3

Typeset by Kogan Page Limited
Printed and bound by Biddles Ltd, Guildford and King's Lynn

Contents

Part B: Assessing learners in open and distance learning

Series editor's foreword

Ask any learner or trainee, following a course of study, to identify an aspect of his or her course that creates stress or problems, that causes frustration and anxiety and it is likely the reply will be, 'the assignments'. For many learners, in conventional teaching and training contexts as well as in Open and Distance Learning (ODL) situations, the assignments can represent a daunting prospect and one that can dominate their lives. Similarly, ask teachers or trainers what aspect of a course they are associated with and which they find problematical, that gives rise to student complaints or additional work, and it is likely that they will also identify 'the assignments'.

Calls for continuing improvement in the quality of teaching and training activities, in the accountability of institutions and progress towards lifelong learning, has focused attention on the relationship between teaching and assessment and the ways learners can demonstrate their learning. Furthermore, as the number of learners following courses in ODL contexts increases globally, even greater attention is being focused on the ways in which appropriate assessment of performance can be achieved. This book, *Assessing Open and Distance Learners* by Chris Morgan and Meg O'Reilly, will provide both a source of advice and insights, as well as an invaluable resource for those of us engaged in teaching and training, both in conventional and ODL contexts, across a broad range of ability and subject areas.

Depending on your background and interests you may decide to focus your attention on Part A of the book; a part that explores assessment issues and themes as they relate to ODL. It draws upon literature you may or may not be familiar with, but which is likely to stimulate much thought and reflection. In Part B many of the frequently asked questions associated with all aspects of the assessment process – from the design of items to advice to learners, from marking schemes to evaluation activities – are addressed. I'm sure you will find the comprehensive series of subheadings helpful in finding your way around this array of invaluable advice and comment. For those who would like an insight into assessment practices in ODL from around the world you will find Part C an invaluable resource. The collection of case studies, which include examples from the dissection of rats to evaluating photographs, from the resuscitation of new-born babies to Web design, contains ideas that I am confident you will find attractive and worthy of consideration in your teaching. The methods of assessment they illustrate, from journals to multiple choice questions, from debates to peer review, across the old and new media represent a unique resource and one I believe many will find informative.

This is a book written by practitioners in ODL for other practitioners. It is not a book that preaches at you nor one that takes the abstract high ground, but one that recognizes your likely expertise and offers concrete advice, based on evidence, and resources upon which you can reflect. I can give it no higher praise than to say I intend to reconsider the assessment strategy in the course for which I am responsible – and am likely to incorporate several of the ideas I have noted for my own benefit and that of my learners. My hope is that you and your learners also benefit.

Fred Lockwood
June 1999

Acknowledgements

We would like to thank Fred Lockwood and Martin Hayden for their support and encouragement in the writing of this book, along with our colleagues at the Teaching and Learning Centre at Southern Cross University. We would also like to thank Ann Wilson and Helen O'Loughlin for their insightful comments on early drafts.

Thanks are also due to the many contributors of case studies for the final section of this book. We would like to acknowledge their commitment, creativity and also their patience, in the face of our persistent requests for more, and yet more, information.

Finally we would like to thank Louis Davis and Jack O'Reilly for their continued support and encouragement.

Introduction

Why this book?

Why do we need a book about assessment in open and distance learning (ODL)? There are many worthy, contemporary texts and resources available on the subject of assessment that cover theories, methods and processes of assessment in considerable detail. What can we add here that hasn't already been said? Are there sufficient assessment issues that are unique to ODL to devote a book to the subject?

Interestingly, most works on assessment assume a face-to-face teaching context. Those that don't nevertheless assume that assessment issues are largely generic and equally applicable in face-to-face, open or distance contexts. Additionally, assessment does not feature prominently in the ODL literature, further underscoring the impression that there are few 'special' issues to be canvassed, or that assessment in open and distance contexts is perhaps a largely unproblematic activity for practitioners.

As course developers and designers, we understand all too well the competing demands of distance educators faced with course planning, writing and production tasks, not to mention the demands made upon us from new technologies and shrinking budgets. Amid this welter of issues, it's easy to see how assessment gets shuffled back – something to be dealt with later. It's also understandable that many teaching and training staff have a conservative view of what is achievable through assessment. While it is important to them that assessments are rigorous and appropriate, there is a tendency to stay with the known and the safer methods of assessment, which contain no surprises in terms of additional workload or administrative burdens.

A personal odyssey

A defining moment arrived for us three or four years ago when a colleague relayed to us an observation from a student that distance learners were being turned into 'essay processing machines'. Our colleague, an academic in the social sciences, had harboured this concern for some time, and had felt frustrated that while she was able to innovate freely and organically with her face-to-face classes, distance learning did not offer her the same opportunities. She felt constrained by the lack of regular interactions with her learners, and was concerned that their geographical dispersal meant inequity of access to resources beyond the learning package. By default, the essay mode – safe, academically respectable, and achievable by all students regardless of location – became the sole means of assessment for most of this undergraduate programme. By a quick calculation, we realized that learners in this programme were expected to churn out more than 60 essays during their studies.

This moment was defining because we started to see the impact of assessment from learners' perspectives. Although each assignment was sound enough in itself, taken as a whole the assessment scheme was uninspired and was not providing learners with the opportunity to demonstrate their learning in a variety of creative ways. We were also neglecting the development of important disciplinary skills such as oral communication, debate, information retrieval and research. Although we valued a broad educational experience, the unintended outcome of this assessment scheme was the message to learners: 'the only thing we value in this programme is your capacity to analyse the literature and present a well-structured written argument'.

It raised issues for us in 'openness', for although the course materials were designed and written with a great deal of sensitivity for adult learning and open learning principles, students still perceived themselves to be on a relatively inflexible treadmill. It was the *assessment scheme*, rather than the course materials, that had been shaping their learning and defining their experience. For all our efforts in developing expansive learning encounters through the course materials, we were tending to negate them through the assessment.

It also raised issues for us in distance education and our notions of 'distance'. We tended to conceptualize learners in line with a 'deficit' model of distance learning: that learners lack contact with teachers and peers; they experience difficulties gaining access to resources; they lack the opportunities of their face-to-face counterparts. This might be contrasted with an 'opportunity' model of distance learning that sees distance learners in a variety of settings and with a constellation of ideas, abilities and resources to bring to their educational encounters. Thinking within the deficit model we tend to reduce learners' assessment experiences to a lowest common denominator, in the interests of parity and achievability, given the isolation and inherent difficulties of distance learning. Thinking within the opportunity model assessment presents exciting opportunities to shape and promote learning with unique meaning to learners in their individual contexts.

As we reflected further on this situation, we saw links with a range of other issues in assessment. Our thoughts turned to questions of an appropriate assessment load. How much is too much? When does an assessment load begin to engender negative learning outcomes such as surface or survival learning? When does the treadmill begin? We considered new forms of 'holistic' or 'authentic' assessment. We also reflected on the development process, in which individual teachers design or update assessments for their own units within a programme, without reference to or knowledge of what others are doing, or the overall aims of the programme. How to foster collaboration in assessment within a culture of protected academic turf?

Understanding assessment from learners' perspectives has required us to discard, or at least temporarily suspend, our institutional perspective and our preconceptions of ODL. Within a short space of time we were trialing more challenging, interesting and diverse assessments for the programme, with the collaboration of our colleagues. For us, key questions now include:

- What opportunities are there for learners to demonstrate their learning?
- How does this assessment contribute to the development of disciplinary skills?
- How does this assessment contribute to the overall aims of the programme?
- Will it stimulate and motivate?
- How effectively do the study materials support learners' assessment goals?

There are no singular or easy answers to these questions, although a very important source is the ongoing feedback from learners, who are endlessly articulate on the subject of assessment.

To return to our original question, 'Why this book?', we would like to advance the argument that assessment in ODL is a neglected issue, and one requiring considerable critical attention. We consider that issues of 'openness' and 'distance' impact on all aspects of assessment practice, and that we need to be aware of our values about them and the variety of ways in which our assessment decisions impact upon students and their learning.

What's in this book?

The book is divided into three parts.

Part A explores issues in assessment as they relate to the ODL context. In this part we discuss theories and models of assessment from the mainstream literature and apply these to ODL. We aim to raise many more questions than we seek to answer, and hope this part will stimulate much thought and reflection.

Part B is more of a 'nuts and bolts' section, examining all aspects of the assessment process, from designing assessment items, communicating your tasks and marking, to evaluation of your assessment activities. This section is principally designed for teachers who are new to assessment of ODL and who might need some practical assistance. It will also be useful for more experienced educators who wish to evaluate their assessment activities by using this material as a yardstick, or as indicators of best practices.

Part C comprises innovative contemporary case studies from a range of educational institutions and countries. The emphasis of these case studies is: what was done, why, and how did it work. The case studies have been loosely ordered around key learning outcomes, rather than the more traditional 'assessment methods' categories. We did this because we wanted to emphasize the importance of assessment as learning, rather than simply as measurement. The case studies provide a smorgasbord of ideas and innovations and illustrate the strengths of a variety of technologies.

This book can be approached from a variety of ways, depending on your interests and needs. It can be read in sequence, or can simply be dipped into as need dictates. We hope you find it useful, stimulating and at times a little challenging.

Chris Morgan and Meg O'Reilly
Southern Cross University, Australia
May 1999
e-mail: cmorgan@scu.edu.au or moreilly@scu.edu.au

PART A

Issues and themes in open and distance assessment

Introduction

The aim of this first part of the book is to explore issues and themes in open and distance assessment. Initially, it explores some key terms in assessment that you'll encounter throughout the book. We then turn to the important relationship between assessment and learning. Since Rowntree (1977) described assessment as the '*de facto* curriculum', there has been a great deal of attention given to the ways in which assessment shapes and drives student learning. This relationship is discussed and expanded in the particular context of open and distance learning (ODL). We look at some of the unique issues of assessment in open and distance contexts, as well as the opportunities and tensions that shape our thinking and activities. We also look at some recent trends in assessment and learning as they relate to open and distance learners, particularly online or computer-based assessment, work-based assessment, self- and peer assessment, and holistic and authentic assessments.

As there are many good contemporary books and resources on assessment in higher education, we do not intend to cover quite the same ground or with the same kind of treatment as those resources. Rather, our central objective is to highlight and problematize assessment issues with which open and distance educators and learners will commonly engage. Naturally, there will be some overlap, but wherever possible we refer you to other resources if you wish to pursue an issue more thoroughly. A number of the books in this Open and Distance Learning Series, notably Alistair Morgan's *Improving Your Student's Learning* (1993), embrace critical reflection as a means of re-examining the foundations of our educational activities and practices. It is a process of questioning our assumptions and the taken-for-granted of what we do. 'Critical reflection', Morgan explains, 'is the process which enables us to become more aware of the contradictions which surround our education and training' (Morgan, 1993: 25). For example, we may be prompted to question what values underscore our assessment practices, and what experiences lead to the formation of those values. We could question our values regarding 'openness' and our constructions of distance learning and learners. In more applied terms, we can reflect upon the quality and value of particular assessments in relation to student learning, their conduct and the support we offer our learners through assessment, and the constraints that might lie in the way of changes or reform of assessment schemes or policies. During the course of this book we include many prompts of this kind, with the intention of encouraging you to critically engage with this material in relation to your own unique circumstances, values and goals as educators. It's hoped that these prompts will help you to clarify what it is you want to achieve and how your assessment activities can support your goals.

Chapter 1

Thinking about assessment

Some readers may come to this book in the belief that they are novices in the subject of assessment. You may be, for example, a new teacher or developer in higher education and training, or perhaps you are new to the field of open and distance learning (ODL). You might feel that you need to acquire a whole new body of factual and procedural knowledge about assessment in this new context.

From the outset, we would like to remind you just how expert in assessment you already are. In a sense, we are all experts in assessment, as we have all traversed the difficult terrain of primary and secondary schooling, along with many forms of adult education such as evening classes, workplace training and formal university studies. In this process, we have been endlessly sorted, tested and examined. We have generated mountains of paper. We have lived through the pressures of overdue assignments and impending examinations. We've learnt to read between the lines to figure out what was really wanted. We have been publicly acknowledged and rewarded for our perceived efforts and strengths. And, at times, our weaknesses or vulnerabilities have also been exposed to public scrutiny. Usually we've learnt about assessment the hard way.

Some may argue that their overall experience with assessment has been relatively benign and useful. Others may argue that there has been little meaning to the experience, and liken it to performing in a three-ringed circus, jumping through hoops on cue. Others still have argued that the assessment experience has been very damaging to many people – and not just to those who have failed to make the grade. Boud (1995) recounts a workshop for new university teachers in which participants were asked to write an autobiography of their assessment experience. He describes the results as 'devastating'. It was clear to him that:

> even successful, able and committed students – those who become university teachers – have been hurt by their experiences of assessment, time and time again, through school and higher education. This hurt did not encourage

them to persist and overcome adversity... it caused them to lose confidence, it dented their self-esteem and led them never to have anything to do with some subjects ever again.

(Boud, 1995: 35)

It is a damning account of the impact of assessment practices that we largely take for granted today. One wonders about the impact of assessment upon those less able academically than the above group. How many times magnified might their negative experiences be?

Take a minute to pause and reflect upon your own assessment experience. Consider both the positive and negative experiences. Do any particular experiences stand out? How did they impact upon your learning? How did they impact upon your confidence and motivation as a learner?

Negative themes

When we reflected upon our negative assessment experiences, we came up with a long list of concerns and frustrations regarding our own undergraduate experiences. Some of our common themes were:

- *Inscrutability.* Assessment schemes, or the processes by which results were obtained, were rarely explained. The whole process was largely shrouded in mystery. On what basis were marks awarded? What did markers value? What were the purposes of assessment tasks? How were final grades derived from course work results?
- *Injustice.* We recalled many examples of seemingly unfair or inequitable assignments and exams, and also a number of incidents where we were left with the sense we had been dealt with most unfairly, and without recourse. One common occurrence was contradictory feedback from markers – where one would praise and the other penalize a particular approach in the same subject. Other occurrences included exam papers that failed to assess what we had been directed to prepare.
- *Infallibility.* The status of the assessor or marker approached the infallible. There was rarely a sense of subjectivity or negotiability in awarding marks. Criteria for marking were not explained. Often marks seemed to be out of sync with the relative effort or value of the learning. Appeal or questioning of results was not a welcoming or seemingly viable option.
- *Mixed messages.* Assessment results often sent skewed messages to us regarding our relative abilities in subjects. Poor choices were made on the basis of assessment 'success', rather than our natural abilities or genuine engagement with the subject.
- *Administrative convenience.* Assessments often seemed to be devised in a manner that would most easily 'process' large cohorts of students, irrespective of educational outcomes or appropriate timing.

- *Cynicism*. Assessment seemed to be viewed as something of a game by teachers and learners alike. Success seemed to rest on one's capacity to play the game: to 'crack the code', to work out what was wanted by individual assessors, to feed back their most favoured theories, and so on. This cynicism seemed to pervade the system.

We may not have been permanently damaged by these experiences, but they have undoubtedly shaped our attitudes and behaviours in certain ways, and these attitudes have required some unpacking in order for us to think freshly about assessment. Perhaps the most damaging of these themes is the last one, cynicism. If assessment is commonly viewed by learners as a game, how must this impact upon their motivation, their self-esteem, their learning strategies, and the value they place on learning and education in general? In our case, we may have started our studies with lofty ideals in mind, but it was not long before we became schooled in the 'paper chase': the path of least resistance towards an end qualification. We wonder how many others' graduation days were as profoundly anti-climactic as our own.

Positive themes

Of course not all our assessment experiences were negative. Some of the very positive themes that arose in our reflections included:

- *Individuality*. Some of the best assessment experiences were those that encouraged our individuality as learners and the unique perspectives and insights that we brought to assessment tasks. This may have involved elements of choice, self-direction, a spirit of informed enquiry, and expansive opportunities to demonstrate our abilities and learning.
- *Acknowledgement*. When efforts in assessment were met with an appropriate level of acknowledgement and a fair reward, this engendered trust and motivation to higher achievement.
- *Relevance*. Assessment tasks that had a clear rationale and relevance, or a tangible outcome relevant to the real world were highly motivating for us. This included problem solving, project work and assessments that encouraged us to explore and find meaning within our own worlds, including our values, beliefs and professional lives.
- *Dialogue*. Assessment to us was always more meaningful when it provided opportunities for dialogue, debate and negotiation of meanings such as group work. Similarly, feedback from assignments was more useful and motivational if it sought to create dialogue and further debate, rather than simply to assess the merit of the work.

Making sense of our reflections

At first glance our lists of positive and negative themes are fairly haphazard; indeed yours may be too. Yet as we reflect further on these themes we see that they span a wide range of assessment issues and processes relating to:

- integrating assessment with overall learning aims;
- designing and communicating assessment tasks;
- communicating assessment feedback and results;
- portrayal of achievements;
- unintended consequences of assessment;
- appeal avenues and evaluation activities.

Our list also highlights a series of tensions that exist in higher education, and most particularly in ODL, where the rhetoric of student-centredness, flexibility and openness is most evident. Some of these tensions in assessment include:

- measurement and certification vs promotion of learning;
- academic skills and knowledge vs vocational competences;
- administrative convenience vs learner-centredness;
- standardized vs individualized tasks;
- openness vs academic standards.

We will return to visit these issues is some detail later in this section of the book.

We argue that it is vital for distance and open educators to have a strong reflective core to their thinking, planning and conduct of assessment activities. What do you value in your assessment experiences and activities, and why? Otherwise we are destined to unwittingly duplicate the negatives that we experienced ourselves as learners, and that are still justified today in terms of impressive but hollow statements about 'quality' and 'academic rigour'.

Chapter 2

Key issues and terms in assessment

Before proceeding too far, we would like to introduce and explore some key terms and issues in assessment that will be regularly appearing throughout the book. Many of these issues and terms are not specific to open and distance learning (ODL) although, where relevant, we have looked at the issues through an open and distance 'lens'. Initially, we'll look at definitions of assessment, as well as purposes and stakeholders. We briefly look at the issues of formative and summative assessment, and grading schemes such as norm and criterion referenced assessment. The purpose of this chapter is really to familiarize you with these commonly used terms and issues.

Explaining assessment

There are many definitions and explanations of assessment in education; let's look at just a couple of these:

> Assessment in education can be thought of as occurring whenever one person, in some kind of interaction, direct or indirect, with another, is conscious of obtaining and interpreting information about the knowledge and understanding, or abilities and attitudes of that other person. To some extent or other it is an attempt to know that person.
>
> (Rowntree, 1977: 4)

> (Assessment is) a systematic basis for making inferences about the learning and development of students... the process of defining, selecting, designing,

collecting, analysing, interpreting and using information to increase students' learning and development.

(Erwin, in Brown and Knight, 1994)

These definitions are interesting for a number of reasons. Let's look initially at what's *not* there:

- There is no mention of marking and grading. From our own experiences as learners, surely that is the driving force at the heart of assessment?
- There is very little about systems of judgement, measurement and reporting procedures – rather it is couched in more vague terms such as 'attempting to know' and 'making inferences'. Again, as students, were we not led to believe that assessment is a relatively exact science?

On the other hand, we find in these definitions a couple of significant common themes:

- Assessment is a human activity, involving interactions aimed at seeking to understand what learners have achieved. Like any social interactions, Rowntree implies, there is nothing definitive or exact about the outcome. Assessment may occur in formal or informal ways, and it may be descriptive rather than judgmental in nature.
- The primary purpose of assessment is to increase students' learning and development, rather than simply to grade or rank student performance. Naturally, one cannot grade student performance without first assessing it, but it is implied that grading is a secondary activity to the primary goal of helping learners to diagnose problems and improve the quality of their subsequent learning.

Do these definitions accord in any way with your own understanding of assessment? You might be inclined to agree with us that our past experiences of assessment have strayed somewhat from these idealized statements. For those who have been consistently assessed throughout their undergraduate years by end-of-term examinations, with little developmental feedback, this is quite understandable. Yet few issues have attracted more attention and generated more change in higher education and training in the last 10 years. Research into student learning has consistently located assessment at the centre of students' thinking: how they spend their time, what they regard as important, and the kinds of learning approaches they adopt (see Dekkers *et al*, 1992; Gibbs, 1992; Ramsden, 1992, 1997; Rowntree, 1974). We have come to reconceptualize assessment as the engine that drives and shapes learning, rather than simply an end-of-term event that grades and reports performance. Teachers and trainers who have encountered this research have been quick to find new opportunities to promote more useful and desirable kinds of learning through assessment.

Social and political pressures

Other issues have also persuaded us to reconceptualize our assessment activities, such as new pressures on educational and training institutions to broaden their educational outcomes. In the USA, for example, over the past 15 years there has been an intense examination of the quality of teaching and learning, revolving around central questions such as: how well are students learning? There has been considerable political pressure on colleges and universities to explain what they are trying to do and how well they are achieving it (Angelo and Cross, 1993). In the UK, there are similar pressures on higher education to provide evidence of student graduates with general transferable competences and enterprise skills of ongoing value to employers and society as a whole (Brown and Knight, 1994). The Australian Higher Education Council (1992) similarly called for the development in learners of generic abilities extending beyond the acquisition of a body of knowledge, such as critical thinking, problem solving, effective communications, ethical practice and so forth.

In all instances cited, there is a sense of increased accountability required by governments of their educational and training bodies, and assessment schemes and systems are often the most public face of their educational achievements. And it is to assessment that innovators have looked for ways in which to support the development of broader learning outcomes, in the knowledge that assessment will in turn drive and shape student learning.

Pressures have also been felt for education and training institutions to become more flexible and student-centred in their teaching and learning arrangements. This has arisen partly through a concern that traditional teacher-centred education has led to what Gibbs (1995: 2) describes as 'passive, bored students giving back to teachers what they have already been given in a worthless grade-grubbing way irrelevant to their future lives'. It has also grown out of the practical need for institutions to offer incentives for new enrolments, as their local and global educational marketplaces become more competitive. ODL institutions have regularly claimed the moral high ground in relation to student-centredness, pointing to their record in providing access to many who would otherwise have been denied an education through social, physical or geographical barriers. Yet apart from this important achievement, there has arguably been little that has been student-centred about the provision of much ODL. Criticism has been levelled at the kinds of highly didactic content-focused teaching materials often found in traditional ODL, encouraging learners to adopt surface approaches or 'reproducing' strategies in their assignments. This so-called 'instructional industrialism' (Evans and Nation, 1989; Farnes, 1993; Morgan, 1993) has offered little flexibility or student-centredness in critical areas such as the negotiability of content, process and means of assessment. Flexibility and student-centredness, in many open and distance settings, tend to be about choice in mode of study rather than a commitment to an open pedagogy.

Clearly there are a variety of issues of a social, political and pedagogical kind that have impacted upon our thinking about assessment. Further issues, such as increased student numbers, wider access to education and declining budgets could also be cited here as important political and social trends of recent years. How have these kinds of pressures been felt within your own educational or training establishment? Have they impacted at all on your assessment activities and if so how? Certainly you may have noticed a new rhetoric afoot, supporting 'strategic', 'holistic' or 'smart' assessments in the light of both pedagogical research and political developments of recent years. Do you see these trends as favourable to student learning and your educational practice? Let's continue with these lines of thought as we look at formative and summative assessment.

Purposes of assessment: formative and summative

Rowntree (1990) identifies two major purposes for assessing students:

1. To provide support and feedback to learners and to improve their ongoing learning.
2. To report on what they have already achieved, whether this be a grade or a written assessment.

Hence, we find the terms 'formative assessment', which helps to form and develop student learning, and 'summative assessment', which sums up what has already been achieved. These are terms that you will come across regularly in this book and in the literature on assessment. Formative assessment comprises all those activities designed to motivate, to enhance understanding and to provide learners with an indication of their progress. In traditional ODL, this has commonly taken the form of:

- non-assessable activities and feedback in study materials;
- self-assessment quizzes and tests that help learners monitor their own progress;
- feedback from assignments, or from peers, colleagues or mentors in the workplace;
- dialogue with teachers, tutors and other students;
- non-assessable tests that prepare learners for formal examinations.

Facilitating appropriate and effective formative assessment is one of the most important aspects of any educator's role, and is vital to learners' confidence and sense of progress.

The primary purpose of summative assessment is to record or report an estimate of students' achievements. These will often take the form of end-of-course exams, course work assignments that contribute to a final grade, supervised practical demonstrations, and the like. Depending on the setting and goals, it might entail awarding marks, grades, written reports of achievement or recognition of acquired competences.

In most open and distance settings, assessments usually have both a formative and summative component – this is referred to as 'continuous assessment'. Assessments are often structured so that one assignment builds upon the next, with formative feedback from the first contributing to the next, and so on. Marks are awarded for each assignment, which, taken together, form a final grade. An end-of-course examination, which has a summative function only, might also be included in the final grade.

When developed strategically to maximize learning, continuous assessment is a very sensible approach for open and distance learners, as it:

- provides some structure to learning;
- breaks down the assessment load into manageable chunks;
- is encouraging, motivating and confidence-building;
- provides a source of ongoing dialogue between teachers and learners;
- provides insight for learners into their progress, including their developing understanding and mastery of competences.

Benson (1997) notes that the pre-planning required for ODL lends itself to this strategic weaving of formative and summative assessment, and that, when the two are integrated well, it is more likely to prompt deep and relevant learning. These issues are developed further in Part B of this book when we look at designing assessment tasks. You will also find examples of this approach in Case Studies 4.2, 5.1 and 7.3 in Part C.

Assessment: whose needs?

When considering the purposes of assessment, it is important to question whose needs are being met. If we accept the definitions of assessment discussed earlier, then we might be led to believe that assessment is solely for the benefit of student learning. Yet we know that this is not entirely the case – there are a number of stakeholders in the assessment process and it meets a complex and interwoven series of needs within society. Nightingale *et al* (1996) categorize these needs into four groups as follows.

1. Students' needs

- To know how they are progressing with their studies.
- To know whether they are achieving the required standard.
- To gain certification of a level of achievement.

2. Teachers' and trainers' needs

- To know whether students are attaining the intended learning outcomes.
- To know whether course materials and teaching activities are effective.
- To be able to certify that students have achieved standards or met requirements.

3. Institutions' needs

- To provide evidence of achievement of institutional aims.
- To know whether programmes and teaching staff are effective in their stated aims.
- To make claims to employers regarding graduate qualities.
- To certify that learners can practise in specific vocational areas.
- To make judgements about access and admission to programmes.

4. Community needs

- To know whether institutions and teachers are effective and thus deserving of continued funding.
- To know whether students are adequately prepared for their careers.
- To know whether education is being geared to meet the broad, longer-term needs of society.

Hence we find a range of competing formative and summative assessment purposes which vie for our attention, and present many tensions in our roles as educators and trainers. On the one hand we are working with learners to review and support learning in a spirit of shared endeavour, and on the other hand we are making unilateral judgements regarding the merits of their achievements. In the context of open learning, these tensions are even greater because we are laying claim to a philosophy that places learners at the centre of our considerations. Whose needs come first? How do we reconcile or balance these competing but legitimate needs from all quarters? Naturally there is no formula, although teachers and trainers have responded to these issues in a variety of ways. For example, it is not surprising that many have embraced self-evaluation and peer assessment, not only as a means of sharpening these abilities in learners, but also to bring some greater balance to their roles as formative and summative assessors, and perhaps to redress some of the imbalances in the power relationships in teaching and learning as well. There are many tensions in open and distance assessment that we explore in more depth in the next section.

Assessment and the learning context

In the same way that assessment can drive active, meaningful learning, it may also promote unintended side effects. Rowntree (1977) discusses eight aspects in the design and administration of assessment that produce negative side effects in learning, such as excessive competition, excessive workload, anxiety, labelling of ability, and an excessive focus by students on forms and topics of assessment at the expense of understanding. Although these effects are unintended, they nevertheless have the same powerful impact on learning as those we do intend, and will usually lead to superficial or surface approaches to learning. An awareness of unintended side effects, and our efforts to address them, assume a willingness in the first instance to look at the assessment experience from learners' perspectives, rather than accept the outcomes of an assessment scheme at face value.

Research into the contexts of student learning and learners' perceptions of assessment tasks (for example, Marton et al, 1984) has revealed a number of major concerns. If students perceive assessment as primarily to examine content knowledge, they will tend to do little more than rote learning. If course materials are overburdened with factual content, then they are quite likely to display a poor level of overall understanding. Learners will often feel pressure to adopt and advance the views of course authors and markers to maximize their grades. Where learners feel anxious or threatened, they are more likely to adopt mechanical, surface approaches to tasks. Consistent lack of choice in subject matter or methods also points to similar results (Ramsden, 1997).

These are rather sobering findings and indicate the importance of presenting a learning context that rewards meaningful inquiry and eschews surface or reproducing approaches to assessment tasks. Although we may be very clear in our communications to learners about the kinds of responses required in an assessment, we must also look to the context of learning to ensure that there is sufficient time, support and preparation and a consistent representation of values across a programme as a whole, to increase the likelihood of deep approaches to assessment.

The grading game: norm and criterion referenced assessment

Norm and criterion referenced assessment are two distinctly different ways of awarding grades. Both methods are commonly used in higher education institutions, and debates about their relative merits and applicability have been around for many years (see Rowntree, 1977, for example). We mention them here because it is important to appreciate the distinction between the two grading methods, particularly in relation to the values they express about teaching and learning and students' achievements.

Norm referenced assessment uses the achievement of a group of students to set the standards for specific grades awarded to students. Initially, students are ranked (often using a 0–100 scale) in order of achievement among the members of the group. A predetermined institutional formula is then applied to nominate which percentage of students achieve the top grade, the lowest grade, and the range of grades in between. Hence, there are expectations upon markers that only specified percentages of any cohort are entitled to certain grades. Norm referenced assessment provides a description of where a student's achievement lies in relation to others in the group, rather than the particular qualities or competences that students individually achieve. In essence, it promotes competition between students for limited grades, rather than a detailed acknowledgement of student progress or abilities.

Criterion referenced assessment, on the other hand, uses clearly stated criteria and performance standards against which each student's achievements are judged. If the criteria and standards are met, the student achieves the corresponding grade, irrespective of how others in the group have performed or how many others have achieved the same grade. Although criteria may be used in norm referenced assessment to assist in markers' judgements, criterion referenced assessment demands that criteria are precise and explicit, and that levels of performance are linked to a grade or grades. The strength of criterion referenced assessment is that it provides a clearer focus to assessment, for both learners and markers, and a fuller description of what learners have achieved and the standard of achievement. Brown and Knight

(1994) and Hager *et al* (1994) also point to the way in which a number of occupations and professions have sought to describe their competences, which are then expressed in terms of criteria. Once adopted, these criteria impact significantly upon the curriculum, where vocational needs, teaching and assessment practices become closely interwoven.

It would be difficult to argue for the place of norm referenced assessment in open learning contexts, as it is very much the antithesis of open and student-centred learning. Rather, it speaks to antiquated notions of 'academic rigour' and 'institutional standards', and says very little about the nature and quality of teaching and learning, or the abilities of graduating learners. It continues in many institutions, one suspects, by default, due to the complexities of introducing comprehensive criterion referenced assessment schemes across programmes, discipline areas and institutions. Criterion referencing requires considerable negotiation between assessors to arrive at the agreed criteria and standards appropriate to any learning encounter. This may also entail negotiation with industry bodies, professional associations, communities and other education institutions. There are also concerns that criterion referenced assessment is inextricably linked with the competence movement, and is thereby attempting to reduce the assessment of complex professional practice into a series of discrete, observable, lower-order tasks. Yet criterion referenced assessment has been widely and successfully adopted at all levels of post-secondary education, and is often combined with holistic or integrated assessment models that seek to capture the richness of professional practice. These issues are explored more fully in later chapters of this book.

Chapter 3

Assessment in open and distance contexts

Introduction

Is assessment a generic issue, or are there unique issues facing teachers and learners in open and distance settings? On the face of it, there is little to distinguish assessment processes and practices in face-to-face and distance settings. Indeed, many dual-mode universities have policies to ensure that there is equity of treatment between internal and external students, and that all students in a subject have equitable, if not identical, assessment experiences. Yet we believe there are a range of issues that educators need to explore relating to the ways in which we conceive 'openness' and 'distance', how learners approach their assessment, and also the established cultures of distance education development and delivery. These all impact in subtle ways to make the assessment experience for open and distance teachers, trainers and learners different from their face-to-face counterparts. In this chapter we look at learners' approaches, the tensions and opportunities for assessment, and key qualities in open and distance assessment.

Open and distance learners' approaches to assessment

In open and distance learning (ODL), we have become accustomed to writing and producing volumes of study materials. They occupy a lot of our time and efforts and are often developed to a very high standard. As we move into online learning, using computer mediated communication, we are similarly challenged to devise effective learning encounters using this medium. Because of our preoccupation with shaping effective and creative learning experiences for our students, we tend to overlook the importance of assessment as the rather more powerful influence on student learning. We tend to assume that our study materials will drive and shape student learning, and that students will work through our materials more or less in the manner directed. However, research into distance learners' use of study materials (Marland *et al*, 1990; Parer, 1988) and the use of in-text activities (Lockwood, 1992, 1995; O'Reilly *et al*, 1997) suggests that there are far more complex behaviours at work. Although there are a myriad of ways in which open and distance learners approach their learning, assessment issues are nearly always pivotal to their decision making.

Picture this learner, 'Mary':

Mary is a registered nurse studying part-time to upgrade her qualifications. She has two teenage children and full-time employment that includes shift work. Her studies are important to her, but occupy third priority after family and work commitments. She has completed a handful of subjects in the programme and has a growing confidence about her study skills. She received her study materials three weeks ago but hasn't had the opportunity to open them until now. Mary has allocated four hours in her busy schedule to 'get organized'. She opens the study package and has a quick scan through the materials, registering interest in some sections, less interest in others. She turns to the assessment and reads it closely. What is expected of me? she wonders. She now focuses on the first assessment item due in three weeks. By the time her four-hour study session is up, she has devised a plan that will see her successfully complete the first assignment by the due date. She has a rough outline of what she will cover in the assignment. From the volumes of reading material supplied to her, she has earmarked a few useful sections in the study guide, and some core readings to work through. She also plans to get some help from a colleague at work for one part of the task, and will also make a visit to the hospital library to get some additional resources for the other.

In this instance, Mary has largely by-passed the carefully crafted study materials that were intended to shape and inspire her learning. Instead, she has shaped her learning around the assessment requirements and has taken a more efficient pathway to her desired goal. Mary's approach is a pragmatic or 'strategic' one (Entwistle and Ramsden, 1983) in which students are focused upon gaining the best result given their available time. Although Evans (1994) is quick to point to the diversity of open and distance learners, and similarly Morgan (1993) points to the variety of learning approaches adopted, we suggest that this is a reasonably common pattern for experienced learners who have progressed some way through their studies and have gained sufficient confidence to assert their own autonomy in relation to study approaches.

Note that we are not arguing here that ODL materials are therefore unimportant – on the contrary, they are very important indeed. However, our efforts may be wasted unless assessment tasks are closely aligned and interwoven with study materials. Lockwood's (1992) research into self-assessment activities reveals that learners tend to weigh the costs and benefits associated with activities in relation to factors such as time constraints and their study goals. For those whose primary goal, like Mary's, is to satisfactorily complete assessment tasks on time, study materials that are not closely interwoven with assessment tasks will be overlooked. Note, also, that we are not suggesting that Mary's approach is in any way inappropriate. It is one of a range of sensible and legitimate approaches to her study given her particular situation and goals. Indeed she is showing all the signs of developing independence and self-direction as a learner. Rather, it is a question of how effectively our study materials support the assessment tasks and, in turn, the primary objectives of our subject and course. We pick up this question of aligning assessment with other elements of the distance package in greater detail in Chapter 5.

Opportunities for assessment in open and distance learning

Another key distinction in open and distance assessment is the smaller window of opportunity in which to assess learners, compared to other settings. In face-to-face teaching, you come to know your students in a variety of ways – from lectures, tutorials and individual consultations. Students in face-to-face settings have a range of opportunities in which to demonstrate their learning, which aren't confined to formal assessment tasks. Their interest, motivation, questioning and interactions are all on display throughout a learning encounter. As open and distance learners rarely enjoy these varied opportunities to communicate their learning, they are much more dependent on formal assessment tasks. They have a much smaller window of opportunity to impress upon you their abilities and the value of their learning. Furthermore, they have less opportunity in which to diagnose their own errors or mistaken assumptions before they commit to a formal assessment task. For example, it may not be until midway through a semester or course, when a student's first assignment is returned, that a simple error is discovered, to the detriment of the student's final grade. While face-to-face learners can often rectify these problems long before they submit an assessment, open and distance learners do not have the same kinds of opportunities to check their understanding of an assessment task, or to compare approaches or methods with other students.

Hence distance learners are more dependent upon effective, early communication of assessment requirements, together with well-designed and cohesive assessment tasks, useful and timely support, and a transparent marking scheme that explains how judgements are to be made. They are also more dependent on rapid turnaround of assignments, so that the feedback can contribute to subsequent efforts and help maximize the valuable formative function of assignments. Assessment activities simply do not have the same level of flexibility they do in face-to-face settings – they must be thoroughly planned, communicated and managed. Although this may be viewed by some educators as a disadvantage of ODL, for learners it is perhaps one of its great strengths. With their assessment commitments clearly laid out in front of them at the commencement of a semester or course, learners are free to plan their time and make decisions about how they might best approach the tasks at hand, as we saw in Mary's case earlier.

Assessment and 'distance'

How do you conceptualize the distance learning experience? Do you essentially see learners as belonging to a 'deficit' model of distance learning: learners lack contact with teachers and peers; they experience difficulties gaining access to resources; they lack the opportunities of their face-to-face counterparts? Or at the other end of the spectrum, do you prefer to see learners belonging to an 'opportunity' model: they bring a wealth of experience, abilities, enterprise and resources to learning encounters? In the introduction to this book, we related an experience of our own that jolted us into recognizing that we tended towards the former rather than the latter model. Hence when it came to devising assessment tasks, we were often more concerned about what students couldn't do than what they could. In the interests of equity and parity, assessment tasks were often devised from the perspective of the lowest common denominator, assuming learners generally have difficulties in gaining access to resources, that they lack interactions, that they suffer severe time constraints, and so on. The result was a series of assessment tasks that were safe, achievable, academically 'respectable', yet repetitive and profoundly uninspired.

The way in which we, as educators, conceptualize the distance learning experience will impact on all of our teaching and learning activities, and most particularly the ways in which we facilitate assessment for learners. If we are thinking within an opportunity model, we are more focused on the variety of ways in which learners can demonstrate their achievements, given their unique settings, rather than attempting to homogenize the experience. Assessments are more likely to focus upon the strengths and opportunities inherent in distance learning, by encouraging learners to engage with their communities and workplaces, to create local dialogues that aren't necessarily orchestrated by the institution, and to access and harness available resources in creative ways. In addition, with the advent of computer mediated communications and the popularity of online learning, the landscape of distance education is rapidly changing. Some of the 'deficits' of the past in terms of geographical dispersal and inequity of access to resources are less likely to be an issue, requiring us to re-think our conceptions of 'distance' and the unconscious limitations we may be imposing upon assessment arrangements.

Assessment and 'openness'

Another key issue deserving of attention is our conception of 'openness' in relation to assessment. What do we understand by the term 'open' and what do we value about open education? A minimalist view of openness is that it is about increasing access to educational institutions for students who would otherwise be unable to participate in staff development or higher education. But what of the student experience once they are admitted to an institution? A more expansive view sees openness as a philosophy or approach to education where student-centred values underscore all teaching, learning and administrative arrangements.

As we discussed earlier, ODL has been roundly criticized in some quarters for its adoption of pedagogies and processes that run counter to its claim of openness and student-centredness. In relation to assessment, these concerns are focused upon issues such as:

- a lack of choice, variety and autonomy in assessment;
- insufficient use of applied, work-based and project-based learning;
- inflexible pacing of assignments;
- an over-emphasis on dissemination of content and the views of course authors at the expense of opportunities for learners to individually construct and negotiate meanings;
- an over-emphasis on summative forms of assessment, such as formal examinations;
- minimal opportunities for student self-assessment, where students are encouraged to make their own judgements regarding their achievements;
- marking schemes and processes that are inscrutable and shrouded in mystery. (Peters, 1995)

Balanced against this list of 'lapses' in open assessment, we find a range of issues and problems often raised by teachers and trainers when considering open or student-centred assessments. Gibbs (1995) raises a number of points, including:

- concerns about standards and grade distributions, as open assessments tend to produce higher average marks;
- concerns about consistency and reliability in marking, as open assessments tend to be individualized and difficult to compare;
- the additional time required to negotiate and mark individualized learning activities;
- difficulties regarding plagiarism and proof of authorship in the absence of invigilated examinations;
- higher levels of dispute, as marking methods and processes are transparent and open to scrutiny;
- learners themselves not accepting more open methods such as group work, profiles and portfolios, or alternative marking procedures such as peer assessment.

So we have some decisions to make regarding our commitment to openness. Arguably, we cannot be selectively or 'just a bit' open. Clearly, if we are to embrace open learning, we also need to be able to cast aside many of the cherished beliefs and processes of conventional education and training. We need to be able to engage critically with traditional assessment practices, most particularly where teaching and administrative convenience have supplanted learners and learning as the primary focus of attention. We need to be able to devise appropriate and rigorous solutions, or strike particular balances, in response to the sorts of concerns raised above. Moreover, we are being asked to commit more time to the assessment process, when time seems to be the most precious and scarce resource of all in higher education. The introduction of open assessments requires a clear rationale, imaginative and rigorous methods, careful planning and explicit communications to learners. An approach of selective openness, or just 'dabbling' in open methods, as Gibbs (1995) cautions, has seen courses that have been 'tripped up by problems with assessment and have reverted, chastened, to conventional techniques'.

Tensions in open and distance assessment

On a number of occasions we have alluded to a range of tensions operating in both the purposes and processes of open and distance assessment. These issues deserve some closer examination to encourage reflection on how we come to terms with the conflicting needs and stakeholders in assessment. Many of the tensions arise from our desire to be open and student-centred in our approach to assessment on the one hand, and the necessity to satisfy institutional policies, schedules and spiralling workloads on the other. Sometimes these tensions are felt more subtly, in the form of learners themselves balking at the very arrangements that were supposedly designed for their benefit. Tensions will also be felt around our notions of 'distance' and what we feel can be feasibly managed given the separation of teachers and learners. Let's look at some of the key areas in assessment where these tensions are often felt.

Certification vs promotion of learning

We have looked at some of the inherent conflicts in our roles as both formative guides and summative assessors. On the one hand we are attempting to guide and promote learning, and we may liken our role in ODL to that of a facilitator, mentor or even a colleague of learners. We may wish to shape our relationship with learners as a joint venture, or a collaboration, in which we engage in a mutually beneficial dialogue, and so forth. Yet in most instances, we are then required to make unilateral decisions about the quality of learners' achievements, sometimes in rather dire norm referenced schemes where students compete for limited grades. Our role has suddenly shifted from advocate to judge. In ODL, where formative and summative assessments are usually merged into continuous course work, it is particularly difficult for learners and teachers to separate these roles, and the use of terms such as 'learning facilitator' may be somewhat euphemistic, when you are in fact the 'subject examiner'.

How can we shape our roles as open learning facilitators, without abrogating our responsibility to certify achievement? Or perhaps it is a question of how to find a balance between the competing demands of the educator's role. One issue to consider is the way in which we balance the formative and summative functions of assessment. For example, in competence-based or mastery learning, formative feedback and support assume greater weight than summative measurement. With established performance criteria and standards at their fingertips, learners can pace themselves towards established or self-selected goals in partnership with teachers, and may improve low grades on the basis of repeated performance. Although this kind of learning may not be viable in traditional semester settings, the principles are highly adaptable, particularly the provision of explicit criteria for judgement and opportunities for learners to have multiple attempts. As in a high jump, learners can make decisions about the height they wish to attempt, while teachers advise and support their preparation. Case studies in Part C that illustrate this well include 3.1, 3.2, 3.3 and 6.2.

Contract learning provides a similar means of shifting the balance between your formative and summative assessment roles, while offering learners considerably greater autonomy in fulfilling their own particular learning needs and interests. Here the teacher's role is primarily a diagnostic and facilitative one, supporting learners to diagnose their needs, to locate resources, to shape their activities to an appropriate size and scale, to devise criteria for assessment, and to evaluate and reflect upon learning outcomes. Again, contract learning may not be appropriate in all settings and some learners may be resistant to this high level of autonomy, yet arguably self-directed learning promotes a range of lifelong learning skills that would be expected of any graduating student. As a less demanding alternative, you may retain fixed subject objectives, but introduce negotiated assessments which encourage learners to demonstrate how they have achieved the objectives in relation to their own particular interests and professional circumstances. (See also Case Studies 4.1, 4.4, 7.1, 7.2, 7.3 and 8.2.)

Another assessment strategy that teachers are adopting to promote the formative function of their role is self- and peer assessment, which involves learners making judgements themselves about the quality of their own or other learners' achievements. From a learning perspective, it encourages students to adopt a higher level of awareness and responsibility for their learning achievements, to develop skills in making informed judgements about their own and others' work, and to provide thoughtful, organized and constructive feedback where necessary. Although, from teachers' perspectives, it enhances their formative, developmental role, self- and peer assessment by no means simply devolves the responsibility of assessment to learners. There are many questions to consider regarding the negotiation of criteria, the development of learners to make judgements, the acceptance by students of the judgement of their peers, teacher moderation of marks, and so forth (Gibbs, 1995). We consider the issues of self- and peer assessment more closely in the next part, and in Case Studies 1.1, 1.2, 1.3, 4.1, 6.4, 7.3, 8.2 and 8.3 in Part C.

There may be a number of other ways in which we can negotiate this tension between certification and promotion of learning. As we can see, it usually entails some kind of reconceptualization of our teaching and assessment practices, as well as engagement and dialogue with learners to explore the ways in which teaching and learning can be more explicitly and mutually shaped as a partnership.

Academic knowledge vs vocational competences

As we know, ODL attracts adults with a very broad range of attitudes, aims and purposes. Thus we find learners with a range of orientations to education, including those which tend towards vocational relevance, intellectual and academic interests, personal challenge, self-improvement, or for social purposes (Gibbs *et al*, 1984; Morgan, 1993). When we looked at whose needs assessment serves, in Chapter 2, we found another list of competing interests and needs, including learners, teachers, educational institutions, employers, accrediting vocational bodies, and society at large. Many of these competing needs and tensions coalesce around the issue of what we assess and, in particular, what balances we strike between academic knowledge and vocational competences. Whereas technical education has always prided itself on its direct relevance to the workplace, universities have generally been valued for the broader education offered, including the exploration of disciplinary knowledge and the development of higher order skills such as critical thinking, problem solving, communication and research skills (Clanchy and Ballard, 1995, for example). Yet universities and training institutions continue to remain under pressure to be more accountable and more relevant to the workplace, and the boundaries between sectors in post-compulsory education have blurred considerably in recent years.

In ODL, we are under more pressure than ever to retain a student-centred focus, to help learners to fulfil their own learning ambitions, to develop generic and lifelong learning abilities, and yet remain mindful of the requirements of employers and accrediting bodies whose expectations will play a large part in the future lives and careers of graduates. Although we may aspire to substantial components of broad, self-directed activity, for example, failure to adhere to vocational requirements may mean that a course is largely irrelevant to the many learners who are pursuing vocational goals. On the other hand, slavish adherence to vocational requirements may produce graduates who can function in the short term, but are ill-equipped for the future, and particularly for the kinds of work transitions required of us all in a rapidly changing world. Irrespective of whether we are in a university, vocational or private training setting, there are delicate balances to be struck between the assessment of disciplinary knowledge, generic abilities and industry competences, while providing opportunities for self-directed learning.

Naturally, there is no formula or easy solution to this question. Each discipline will have its own culture and unique combination of influences and pressures to balance. Moreover, as an individual teacher, there is little you can do in isolation from colleagues across a school or programme. A meaningful balance in assessment outcomes requires a whole-of-course approach, where key abilities and competences are identified, developed and assessed in an appropriate sequence and with common purpose. Bearing in mind Rowntree's (1997) dictum that assessment is 'the *de facto* curriculum', whole-of-course planning is an important collaborative activity that provides opportunities for innovations and deeper shared understandings between teachers in a programme regarding its aims and purposes. As we have discussed, your assessment scheme is the most public face of your programme's aims, values and achievements. (Case Study 4.4 demonstrates a whole-of-course approach to assessment.)

Individualized vs standardized assessments

We have touched upon this issue already when we questioned our notions of openness, and considered how far beyond enrolment day our conceptions of openness really extend. As open and distance learners are mostly adults with a diversity of contexts, it makes sense to offer as much individualization in assessment as is possible to ensure their needs are met. Yet there are also a range of countervailing pressures that seduce us into 'processing' our students in the most efficient manner possible, given increasing workloads and competing demands on our time. There are degrees of individualization along a continuum from highly individualized tasks, such as learning contracts, to highly standardized tasks, such as objective tests and exams that test content knowledge. In the middle, we find essays and other tasks that encourage learners to relate or apply specified issues and concepts to their own settings. Individualized assessment entails some level of commitment to engage with learners' worlds, including their workplaces, their learning interests, their ideas and values, and to encourage learners to problematize practice, to make sense of issues that impact upon their worlds, and to find personal meaning in new concepts or ideas. Usually this will also entail multiple forms of dialogue fostered through the learning materials (Rowntree, 1990), course interactions (Morgan, 1993) and learners' interactions within their own contexts (Juler, 1990). Through dialogue, learners are prompted to articulate embedded concerns, to delve deeper into issues, and to negotiate their personal stances through debate and exchange. When viewed through this lens, we understand what Rowntree (1977) means when he describes assessment as an interaction aimed at getting to know your learners.

A common concern raised in relation to individualized assessment is reliability (Gibbs, 1995). When tasks are individualized, teachers will often find difficulty in comparing learners' efforts for the purposes of grading – likened to comparing apples with oranges. When there are multiple markers involved, the difficulties with reliability are potentially compounded by markers' differing values and expectations. Nevertheless, whether it is self-, peer or teacher assessed, judgements will need to be made, and so provisions should be developed to maximize reliability. Even the most open-ended assessments should have broad criteria that communicate your expectations regarding the nature and quality of student work and the manner in which it is to be presented. Markers should work closely with each other to clarify and sharpen shared understandings and expectations, and double blind marking is often employed as an additional check. Needless to say, this is a highly problematic area, despite our often misplaced confidence that we can fairly and consistently distinguish between learners' achievements (Newstead and Dennis, 1994). Part B of this book picks up on the issues of reliability and moderation in marking in greater detail.

Clearly, the time commitments of individualized assessment are considerable, yet the rewards in terms of meaningful student learning are also very considerable. It is important that we're cognisant of the time commitments we're making when opting for these kinds of tasks, so that we can do justice to their intent and provide effective support to learners. Although commitments may not always permit a high level of individualization, we need to be strategic about employing them when they are of most value to learners, and when they offer the greatest impact from a developmental point of view.

Openness vs academic rigour

ODL arrangements are sometimes criticized by those who consider them to be lacking in rigour. These claims are often advanced by those who find academic standards embodied by time honoured traditions such as formal lectures and invigilated examinations, and where the process of what is learnt, how it is learnt and how it is assessed are tightly controlled. Sometimes similar concerns might be quietly voiced by those new to open learning practice, who support the underlying principles and philosophy of openness, but are unsure of the terrain, the boundaries, the quality of learning encounters, and the give and take of these new kinds of educational transactions. Many of us have little in the way of prior experience as learners upon which we can model our open learning practice. Indeed, a lifetime's exposure to the values and practices of teacher-centred education is a rather heavy mantle to cast off.

Certainly many entrants to open learning have a history of educational disadvantage and have a very different set of hurdles to those in conventional forms of education. In Part B we include a long list of considerations for those developing open and inclusive assessments relative to learners' diverse educational and social backgrounds and financial status, sex, power imbalances, and the widely differing interests based on whether learners are working, retired, or studying for leisure (Evans, 1994). Depending on your viewpoint, these considerations can be interpreted as reasons why open learners can't quite 'cut the mustard', or alternatively, they can be used as a basis upon which we develop considered support and sympathetic strategies to ensure that they do. Tensions will be felt in the way we prepare learners for assessments, such as the pace at which learners opt to progress, the balance of formative and summative assessment, and where we (or learners) may choose to set goalposts at various points in their pathway.

Yet open assessments need not be any less rigorous, disciplined or challenging for learners than for their counterparts in more traditional forms of education. Certainly any suggestion to the contrary would be insulting to most learners themselves, who are unlikely to be angling for an easy way to get a qualification. The sheer expenditure of time, money and energy, and the sacrifices willingly made by so many, more than dispel these claims. To the contrary, many in open learning would claim that open assessments provide the potential for learners to achieve well beyond the limits of the course, as these limits are perceived by us. The challenge is to come to terms with our own traditionalism, and to devise assessment schemes that 'enable us and our students to be genuinely unconstrained by prior expectations of what the syllabus does or should contain and what the study of a particular (subject) should entail' (Cowan, 1996: 60). Therein we find new dimensions of quality and rigour in learning.

Key qualities of open and distance assessments

From our discussion to this point, we can now draw together some desirable qualities of all open and distance assessments. In the previous section we looked at a range of tensions that pervade open and distance assessment. In this section we hope to suggest some ways in which to balance these competing pressures. The following discussion draws on the work of Gibbs (1995), Rowntree (1977) and Boud (1995), adapted somewhat for the ODL context. Six key qualities are offered for consideration.

1. A clear rationale and consistent pedagogical approach

From the very outset, it is important to be clear about what you are hoping to achieve through your subject and associated assessments, including the elements of openness you wish to introduce to the subject and why. As we have seen, there is a spectrum of open assessments, from highly self-directed forms such as learning contracts to more moderate levels of openness, such as projects or negotiated essay topics. As Gibbs (1995) points out, your decisions regarding assessment should be informed by a rationale for the course or subject, rather than a general commitment to student-centred learning. Assessment tasks will drive learning, so ensure that they are meaningful tasks and develop the qualities and abilities sought. Similarly, your pedagogical approach should be consistent and closely aligned with your rationale and assessment choices. For example, there is little meaning in opting for highly self-directed assessments if your study materials encourage learners to passively reproduce the ideas of course authors. Your pedagogy should explicitly support assessments, in this instance, by encouraging a spirit of self-directed inquiry and active construction of meanings by learners.

2. Explicit values, aims, criteria and standards

The values that underpin your assessment design and the criteria by which you make judgements about student achievement should be clearly communicated to learners. We referred earlier to traditional assessment schemes that are shrouded in mystery, where learners have difficulty explaining the purpose of tasks and understanding how marks are awarded and terminal grades derived. Once learners understand your values and intentions, they are more likely see the learning experience as a joint venture and be better able to make decisions about how best to approach their learning. As Gibbs (1995: 8) argues, 'students need to be on the inside of the logic of the course, believing in its rationale, not tagging along, feeling bewildered and jumping through hoops'.

3. Authentic and holistic tasks

Bearing in mind the variety of work contexts and life experiences open and distance learners bring to their learning, authentic assessment tasks are particularly appropriate as a means of encouraging learners to engage with 'real life' issues and problems in their own worlds and workplaces. Authentic assessment tasks also help us to make judgements about whether learners are able to demonstrate higher order abilities such as problem solving and analytical thinking in applied settings. However, as we discussed, reliability is a question with these kinds of open-ended assessments, although Rowntree (1977) provides balance to this issue when he advises us to 'not strive for unnatural consensus among assessors, especially when complex objectives and profound qualities are being discussed'. At the same time, he suggests we 'resist the temptation to concentrate on (the assessment of) qualities and abilities that are more routinely measurable and less likely to provoke disagreements among assessors' (p 242).

Similarly, holistic assessment (Boud, 1995; Hager *et al*, 1994) strives for integrated and meaningful ways of assessing wide ranging student attributes and knowledge, avoiding the fragmentary assessment of atomized competences. An holistic approach to assessment creates opportunities for open and distance learners to engage in rich, applied assessments such as case studies, scenarios and projects, which can be tiered to allow for formative feedback points during their development.

4. A facilitative degree of structure

This is a phrase that Gibbs (1995) employs to describe the fluid balance we seek in open and distance assessment between structured tasks and learner self-direction. Arguably, self-direction is not an innate quality in learners, particularly given the many years of teacher-centred experiences that have tended to socialize learners in the reverse direction. Rather, it is seen as a quality that can be fostered in learners by a progressive shift from teacher to learner control throughout a programme of study, as learners incrementally acquire competence in information retrieval, goal setting, critical thinking, self-management and self-evaluation (Candy, 1991).

Thus, a 'facilitative' degree of structure in ODL is one that develops these abilities purposefully with the explicit goal of self-direction, and seeks a balance between structure and self-direction at any given time which is 'optimally helpful' (Gibbs, 1995: 8). For example, early encounters may be quite structured in relation to learning outcomes and means of assessment, although they may offer flexible pathways towards end goals. As learners progress, learning outcomes and assessment become increasingly negotiable. As discussed, pre-packaged course materials with a tendency towards content dissemination will work against this end goal, as they leave little room for personal exploration or construction of individual meaning.

5. Sufficient and timely formative assessment

Because of the separation of teacher and learners, formative assessment is at a premium in ODL. Formative and summative assessment should be strategically interwoven to motivate and provide some structure to learning, to create a source of dialogue, and to help learners gain insight into their progress. Formative support and dialogue can also be promoted through a range of additional sources, including peers, mentors and work colleagues. As discussed, teachers may reshape their pedagogy in a range of ways to maximize their formative role as facilitators of learning, rather than simply examiners of achievement.

6. Awareness of the learning context and perceptions

Thoughtful planning of open and distance assessments will include an awareness of learners' contexts beyond the subject at hand, including competing assessment commitments in parallel subjects and prior learning experiences and knowledge that are brought to the learning encounter. Ramsden (1997) also alerts us to students' perceptions of assessment tasks, which may vary considerably from our own, and which may prompt surface approaches to learning despite our most careful designs:

> If students feel that there is insufficient time to study the examined topics properly (perhaps due to the demands of other courses), or if they have experienced inadequate teaching, or if they are given high marks for reproducing lecture notes, or if their previous knowledge within the area is insufficiently developed, then they will feel constrained to use surface approaches.
>
> (p 216)

Hence open approaches to assessment may founder if only existing as a small pocket within a larger conventional assessment scheme with conflicting values. Deep approaches in ODL need to be developed and rewarded through assessments that promote consistent goals and values, and that are equitably weighted across the programme as a whole.

Chapter 4

Online technologies in open and distance assessment

Introduction

We have argued that, despite the range of innovations associated with traditional open and distance learning (ODL), assessment activities have tended to remain somewhat static. While new generations of multimedia and telelearning technology have had major influences on the design and delivery of ODL, we have tended to remain with traditional forms of assessment, such as invigilated examinations and written assignments. It is not suggested that distance teachers are less innovative or creative than their face-to-face counterparts. On the contrary, distance educators have traditionally struggled with a range of logistics, such as the geographic dispersal of learners, the difficulties in facilitating interactions at a distance, and the inequality of access to resources, to name a few. In the interests of parity, learners have been assessed within comparatively narrow parameters and with a relatively limited range of methods. Through a combination of a lack of resources and inherent constraints, there has been less opportunity for variety in assessments and a limited scope for development of professional and disciplinary skills. Although essays are a very efficient vehicle for developing learners' abilities in critical thinking and written communications, any graduating student would be expected to demonstrate a far wider cache of generic skills such as a variety of communications skills, technological literacy, problem solving skills, team work, and so forth.

As online learning moves into the mainstream of ODL, many of these hurdles are being rapidly overcome, and it is worth questioning how these new opportunities in teaching and learning at a distance will impact upon assessment. Questions that now arise include:

- What kind of new learning and assessment opportunities can be created through online learning?
- What kind of pedagogies can be employed to support meaningful online assessment?
- What are the losses and gains of this medium for teachers and learners in open and distance education?
- Do traditional models of assessment readily translate to the online environment, or do we need new ways of explaining the purposes and forms of assessment?

Opportunities presented by online learning and assessment

New opportunities using online technologies include a level of immediacy and a range of interactions that were not regularly available to the traditional off-campus student. Studying online means students can now access the course anywhere, anytime (although progress through the course may not be so flexible). The rapid turnaround capabilities for comments and discussion in the online learning context mean that learning can be supported in an incremental, tailored and iterative way, so that learners develop and build upon their own tangible and continuing successes. In the previous chapters of this book we have discussed the significance of linking formative assessment to summative grades. Online technology is showing itself to be a quick, effective and, at the basic levels of e-mails, listservs and quizzes, almost a seamless mechanism for supporting this kind of scaffolded learning. The case studies in Part C include examples of the use of small, incremental online assignments based on the discussion and reflection that students develop and nurture over the study period.

Online assessment is an innovation that takes many forms, all of which require design, development and teaching time. When teaching online, your availability to students closely approximates the on-campus situation where you can leave the door wide open or post consultation times on a closed door, allowing yourself dedicated periods for other work. Online students may expect a response from the teacher within 24 hours unless otherwise informed. In the same way that you announce your times on the office door, online students need to be told clearly about the planned turnaround period for all interactions. The constancy of demand from students throughout the study period will also depend on the structure and design of the study experience. Generally you can expect and plan for some peaks and troughs in the teaching schedule, the majority of your work being reserved to support students' assignment preparation, to mark assignments and provide rapid feedback to individuals, groups or teams. Online learning that is interactive, collaborative, social, self-directed and reflective in nature may also remove some pressure to facilitate discussion continuously. Managing online discussion is important when considering workloads, teaching and assessment time. When discussion is graded, archives of individual and group submissions make this task easier.

Examples of all these features are included in Part C.

In addition, the online environment affords a level of privacy and a more democratic context not necessarily possible in the face-to-face or traditional distance encounter. This has the potential to enhance the development of shy and less confident students. You may recall the discussion in earlier chapters of the book about power imbalances between teachers and learners and how this impacts upon assessment. Such a power differential is directly affected by the virtual nature of relationships in the online environment where assessment can rest much more within the learners' control. It is therefore not surprising that peer and self-assessment practices are being increasingly explored by the online teaching community. The potential for enriching the learning experience through encouraging international perspectives and cross-cultural dialogue is also very exciting. With the current expansion of global education, cross-cultural approaches to self- and peer assessment as well as all kinds of collaborative projects are also now emerging for attention.

Before moving on, let's take a closer look at a few of the new assessment opportunities provided by the online environment including:

- peer and self-assessment;
- teamwork and collaborative assessment tasks;
- online dialogue and debate;
- simulations and role plays;
- problem solving;
- online testing;
- digital scrapbooks and portfolios.

Peer and self-assessment

As we have mentioned earlier, the ability to reflect upon one's own work and that of one's peers is an important ability of any adult learner. These reflective assessment methods have at times been implemented in traditional distance education where some face-to-face elements are included in the off-campus programme. For example, where residential schools, workshops and community-based events can be structured to allow live presentations or demonstrations to a critical audience of peers, students have traditionally been able to give an assessment of each other's achievements according to stated or agreed criteria. But peer assessment is not usually possible in many off-campus programmes where the facilities and infrastructure do not permit face-to-face arrangements. Through computer mediated communications students now have the ability to preview or review the work of their student peers, and in addition to this, the online medium can also efficiently support the iterative and usually confidential process that peer and self-review require.

With regard to self-assessment, it is a common perception that students are either the harshest judges of themselves, or they tend to have an inflated perception of their own capabilities. For this reason, the ability to reflect upon one's own understanding or performance is as much a learning process as it is an assessment process

(Boud, 1986) and is greatly assisted by the use of guidelines, criteria or standards that support learner self-assessment. Elements of self-doubt or unrealistic perceptions of self-esteem can be somewhat attenuated through the use of these rational and constructive approaches to self-assessment. Students are usually relative beginners in terms of marking academic work – both their own and that of their peers. It is therefore crucial to make explicit the complete approach to marking to be used, providing the instructions/checklists, agreeing with students on the criteria and the allocation of marks, structuring anonymity and providing an opportunity for reflection upon the marking process (Habeshaw *et al*, 1993).

As with all innovations, when introducing peer or self-assessment 'students must be prepared to investigate, or be persuaded of, potential benefits accruing from peer support' (Johnston, 1997: 71). Where online class sizes are large or where flexible entry means that students progress according to their own study programme and not necessarily apace with their peers, these methods of assessment can become too problematic to structure.

Teamwork and collaborative assessment tasks

Until the emergence of the Web, the concept of teamwork and collaborative assessment in open and distance contexts had been restricted to those situations where an on-campus, residential or community-based component was possible to facilitate. In the past, these methods were more commonly introduced into residential schools where group skills were seen as core to the discipline area. Although traditional distance contexts may have incorporated preparatory or follow-up communications between students using the postal or telephone services, the possibilities for hands-on teamwork were clearly limited to the period of time when students were physically together.

In the online environment, the possibilities extend to all sorts of text-based and multimedia styles of teamwork and collaboration. Team-based activities and projects can now be employed using e-mail and discussion forums. With the provision of clear guidelines for students as to their team structure, roles and tasks, the online environment allows for small and large group work in problem solving, debate, collaborative authorship and the design and development of prototypes and models. This can be done either synchronously (ie in real time) or through asynchronous messages. Mutual support among students can also be developed as a feature of an online course. By acknowledging of the diversity of student backgrounds and their prior knowledge and experience, it is possible to encourage the development of a community of learners and the sharing of knowledge and resources. Through the development of a 'frequently asked questions' file, a data bank of questions and answers may remove the need for many routine queries.

Assessment of teamwork comes with its own issues of how to allocate grades – collectively, individually, by negotiation or a combination of methods. Habeshaw *et al* (1993) and Gibbs (1995) discuss these issues in considerable detail.

Online dialogue and debate

Clearly the usual deterrent for distance students, that of isolation from resources and from their fellow learners, is the feature most effectively addressed by appropriate communications strategies for online learning. For example, it has long been acknowledged that computer conferencing has many advantages that outweigh whatever problems or disadvantages may also exist in this medium (Mason, 1990). On the one hand, with freedom from any synchronous demands of communication, e-mail or conference-style discussion can allow a student the time for deeper reflection, critique and analysis before contributing to online dialogue. On the other hand, in self-paced programmes, where learners are not part of a cohort, archived discussion combined with one-to-one dialogue can ensure that students have a sense of being part of a community of learners. Whether discussion is synchronous or asynchronous, electronic archives are useful in providing access to past papers, previous discussions, databases and model answers (Mason, 1995).

The availability of text-based dialogue through online communications has greatly diversified the interaction possibilities for open and distance students because the dialogue itself can be structured in a variety of ways. Paulsen (1995) has synthesized a summary of four overviews of computer mediated communication techniques, including Harisim's (1991, 1992) work and presents 11 learning techniques for effective online communications. This list is presented here as a good selection of possibilities for structuring assessable interactions in the online medium:

1. seminars;
2. small group discussions;
3. learning partnerships and dyads;
4. small working groups (problem solving, research projects, etc);
5. team presentations/moderating by learners;
6. simulations and role plays;
7. debating teams;
8. peer learning groups (including co-authorship of assignments);
9. informal socializing: the online café;
10. mutual assist for help;
11. access to additional educational resources.

To create dialogue in an online learning community requires a common focus and a willingness to be part of a dynamic group where the content is fluid and the process is both reflexive and negotiable. Dialogue can be a source of data that students draw upon and refine for submission. Journals, critique, case study or literature analysis and reflective commentary are all styles of online discussion commonly used as the basis for assessment. Part C illustrates many such approaches and includes one example of an online debate. Debate is a specific form of communication that conforms to accepted rules of procedure. With asynchronous means at our disposal, debates can occur across national boundaries and time zones; they can support cross-cultural and cross-disciplinary perspectives and they can further students' analytical thinking, communication and research skills. Assessment of debating skills would consider students' abilities to formulate ideas, develop an argument and defend or critique positions and counter-positions.

Another possible form of dialogue is through videoconferencing. Although it has been found to support students' progress through their project work and to provide useful formative assessment of conceptual understanding, it has also been reported as presenting problems with bandwidth and the level of technical support required for successful implementation (Laffey and Singer, 1997).

Simulations and role plays

Simulations are representations of real-life contexts in which scenarios are developed either by individual students or by students in response to others. There has been little or no exploration of this in traditional distance education. Use of telephone and videoconferencing might have gone some way to facilitate real-time events, but the effect of geographic dispersal and the need for videoconferencing systems at both ends of the communication has militated against the extensive adoption of videoconferencing for simulations and role plays in distance education.

Simulations can be constructed in a pre-programmed way on CD ROM or dynamically online with students playing out their roles. Students can become participants in a scenario, gathering information to make decisions and seeing the consequences of their choices. Simulations and role plays are suited to online learning due to the social potential of online discussion and the dynamic processes in searching for and accessing information. Multimedia can enhance the online role play context, as can videoconferencing or some other component of live interaction. Linking CD ROM resources with Web-based interaction is a useful approach to simulations (see, for example, University of Sydney, 1998).

Assessment in this context is commonly weighted towards elements of factual correctness, feasibility and the solution of a problem. Where dynamic scenarios are developed, credibility of role and contribution to the outcome of the simulation can also be assessed (Alexander and McKenzie, 1998).

Problem solving

Individual and work-based or community-based problem solving were once the only possibilities in traditional distance education, limiting the scope and development of students' problem solving skills. Through print, and at times supported by television, problem solving has also been carried out by students for submission by post. In the online context, it is now possible to facilitate collaborative problem solving exercises and problem-based quizzes and enable rapid feedback to learners. Case studies in Part C demonstrate examples of these. As with the discussion on simulations above, online problem-based scenarios can be delivered either as multimedia and text-based components prepared in advance, or through the facilitation of problem-solving communication processes. Either way, it is the process of coming to the solution that is important for students, rather than the solution *per se* (Siegel and Kirkley, 1997). Processes of problem solving using online technologies require clear facilitation initially by the teacher or trainer, and could be delegated to selected teams of students later.

Online testing

A new opportunity brought about by online technologies is the capacity for students to undertake examinations at home, rather than in invigilated examination rooms. Online testing cannot on its own address the development of higher order skills that are required of students in tertiary programmes; however, it is particularly useful for quick return of formative feedback. No doubt it is suited to certain discipline areas more than others (O'Reilly and Patterson, 1998).

The development of online testing, quizzes and exams has implications for security and authentication. How do we know who is completing the exam and under what conditions? There are some who have taken the plunge to administer timed online exams in their course (see the case studies in Part C), while others in the teaching community have greater reservations about the security, the technical reliability of online testing, and the value of this assessment strategy in relation to the broader goals of their programmes.

Digital scrapbooks and portfolios

Scrapbooks and portfolios are not, strictly speaking, recent innovations in distance education assessment. This item is included here because of the level of enhancement that has been brought to this well-used method. Due particularly to the rapid turnaround of feedback, scrapbooks and portfolio assessments can now be viewed by teachers and student peers more easily in various stages of development, and can be more effectively supported over time. Since scrapbooks and portfolios can be submitted incrementally, the link between the formative and summative features of assessment is again maximized (Habeshaw *et al*, 1993). Feedback can provide development of reflective practice and action learning-style cycles. In the online environment, scrapbook and portfolio styles of assessment can readily be combined with peer and self-assessment due to their developmental focus.

Potential losses

Despite the exciting range of new opportunities that online assessment presents, our enthusiasm should be tempered by some caution, as we may be unwittingly undermining many of the existing features and strengths of ODL. We need to be alert to both the losses and gains in online learning and assessment, and make strategic decisions based on an understanding of their implications. Issues worthy of consideration are outlined below.

Access

If the online medium becomes the principal or sole vehicle for learning and assessment in a programme, we may be denying access to learners in remote and non-technologically serviced areas, to people who are unable to make the necessary investment in contemporary desktop computer equipment, and to those who do not have the necessary technological literacy or confidence. Although we may be buoyed to some degree by the enthusiastic adoption of Internet technology, we need to remember ODL's traditional desire (or mandate) to provide access to those with social, physical or geographical disadvantage.

Learning needs and styles

Learners' success in this medium requires a facility with Internet technologies and an inclination towards screen-based learning. Although this will rest to a certain degree on the level of support and preparation offered by educational institutions, as well as the appropriate design and development of Web-based programmes, it will also depend on learners' enthusiasm to embrace this style of learning in preference to, or at least in concert with, more familiar forms of linear, print-based learning. While many 'early-adopting' students have energetically embraced online learning, the vast sea of learners in their wake will be rightly questioning what exactly it is we are offering that will make this effort worthwhile. Will it offer an enhanced or more meaningful learning experience? Will it save time and effort, relative to traditional forms of delivery? Will I have to develop a different style of learning? Open learning seeks to place student needs, concerns and preferences at the forefront of decision making, yet if the central impetus for development of Web-based programmes is the desire to expand enrolments and forge new educational marketplaces, student-centred concerns may become a secondary question.

Autonomy

Many early examples of online pedagogy have tended to mirror the face-to-face rather than an open and distance experience. With the new learning opportunities (and obligations) associated with online learning, open and distance students are likely to have more paced and structured encounters, more closely aligned with scheduled weekly classes. While there are some obvious gains associated with this, learners may no longer enjoy the autonomy of devising their own approach to assessment tasks and scheduling their progress in relation to semester or course time-frames. Similarly, collaborative work can promote excellent learning outcomes, but makes a range of new demands upon learners, and may particularly aggravate those who mostly prefer to 'go it alone'. Opportunities for interaction are sometimes resisted by students, when the idea of dialogue, teamwork and collaboration seem unrelated to their core purpose of study. Thus learners may be required to 'attend' synchronous discussions and virtual events and to participate in a range of scheduled activities that present certain tensions in relation to autonomy and openness, and may provoke considerable conflict for learners who have elected to study at a distance because they are already juggling a range of work and family commitments.

New technology – old practices

A challenge of online learning is to use the qualities of the medium to advantage, rather than replicate existing teaching, learning and assessment practices. Distance educators moving to the Web may simply want to mount their printed study materials, with 'enhancements' such as hyperlinks and discussions lists, but keep the traditional forms of assessments and general distance experience intact. In this way, Web-based learning is employed more as a new delivery method than as a new rich learning context that requires fresh conceptions of aims and objectives, pedagogies and assessment activities. To take advantage of the medium, we need to harness new opportunities for interactions, dialogue and debate among open and distance learners, and to create assessments that promote the value of these learning processes. While it is argued that assessment strategies such as multiple choice testing and end-of-term exams, with accompanying pedagogies that emphasize dissemination of content, have less relevance in these settings, many of these strategies now flourish with greater technological wizardry than ever.

Reconceptualizing our pedagogy

Our discussion of online pedagogies and accompanying assessment strategies assumes certain changes to the teaching and learning environment. There is a new learning context (an interconnected community rather than a series of individual learners), a new rich medium for learners to explore (the World Wide Web, listservs, e-mail, course delivery tools), and new ways of going about their learning (high levels of interaction and collaboration). In such a new environment, we cannot assume that our old methods and thinking regarding teaching and assessment will still apply. During the course of developing this book, we collected a range of case studies illustrating innovative assessment using the Web. Some of the most stimulating and successful cases entailed quite a radical re-think by teachers of past practices in the light of new opportunities presented by the medium. This re-think often includes:

- *Aims and objectives.* Do I still have the same objectives to assess, or are there new objectives to introduce, such as learners' team skills or participation in online dialogue and research? What opportunities does the medium offer that allow me to achieve my broad aims more effectively? What new opportunities can be provided to allow learners to achieve their own aims?
- *Approach to knowledge.* Given the new ease of access by learners to Web sites and library databases, do I have the same role as 'content provider'? Can I enable learners to adopt a more self-directed approach, and to engage more actively in

constructing knowledge and meaning through their interactions and inquiry?

- *Teaching and learning environment.* How should learning be facilitated? What degree of structure is required? What new learning activities should be introduced? What new abilities require developmental support in this new environment? What tools are available to support these goals?

- *Assessment.* What new forms of assessment will most effectively support and promote these new objectives and learning arrangements? How can I maximize formative feedback? Are there ways to achieve more authentic or holistic assessment experiences? Upon what criteria do I now judge student achievement? Are there worthwhile opportunities for peer and self-assessment?

If our teaching and assessment practices are not reconceptualized in this way, we are not likely to gain the benefits of the medium, nor are we likely to persuade learners to make the leap to online learning when there are no tangible benefits or enhanced opportunities compared to print-based learning. Certainly, it presents a major challenge to educators who are already struggling with larger student groups and shrinking budgets, added to which are concerns about equity of access to the online medium. We don't believe that teachers lack the imagination to create powerful online learning experiences, but for most it entails a major upheaval of established, tried-and-true methods, and comes at a time when they may feel ill-equipped to fully embrace these new opportunities. These initial tentative efforts in online teaching usually represent a first phase of development, in which both teachers and learners are able to familiarize themselves with the landscape and explore the opportunities and losses it presents in their discipline areas.

The notion of 'community' has been raised a number of times in this chapter, and seems to encapsulate much of what we are striving for in open, online encounters. The kinds of virtual learning communities that can be created include not only teachers and learners in a specific cohort, but participants in other related programmes, librarians and resource experts, vocational or professional groups, community and interest groups, government departments, international scholars, and so forth. The idea of community is only limited by one's imagination, and can be fostered by teachers and learners for a variety of purposes, using strategies such as discussion and debate, reflection, peer and self-assessment, collaboration and cross-cultural exchange and dialogue. As we move into an era of education without borders, teachers and learners will also be challenged to develop additional abilities in intercultural communication, to negotiate difference, and to address cultural and racial stereotypes. We address the issue of developing a community of learners further in Chapter 8 of this book.

PART B

Assessing learners in open and distance learning

Introduction

Do open and distance learners have special needs when it comes to designing, developing and supporting assessment tasks? In Part A we argued that distance learners do not enjoy the same opportunities as face-to-face learners to demonstrate their learning. They have a smaller 'window of opportunity' to impress upon you their abilities and the value of their learning. Furthermore, they have less opportunity in which to diagnose their errors or mistaken assumptions before they commit to a formal assessment task. In this section, we argue that it is critical to design, communicate, support and manage assessment in a realistic and sympathetic manner for open and distance learners. A successful assessment scheme in a face-to-face setting may not necessarily translate well to an open and distance context. As we know that assessment is paramount in the minds of distance learners, that it shapes much of their learning, and that assessment opportunities are more limited and often more condensed than in face-to-face learning, we need to maximize opportunities for considered and meaningful learning through assessment.

In particular, we argue for a focus on clearer communication of assessment requirements to learners, ensuring that the purposes, tasks and criteria for marking are transparent and clearly laid out for them. We also argue for a more considered approach to formative assessment – ensuring that feedback to students is timely, relevant, developmental and supportive of formal assessment tasks. Finally, we stress the importance of appropriate student contact and support, which promote interaction and dialogue among their peers and teachers.

The chapters in this part include:

5. Designing assessment tasks
6. Communicating assessment tasks
7. Marking and grading
8. Creating dialogue through assessment
9. Managing time

10. Developing assessment policies
11. Evaluating your assessment practices

We have sought to avoid replication of material from other books on assessment in conventional settings. Rather, we have focused upon assessment issues that we believe are particularly relevant to contemporary open and distance settings, and have referred you to other texts for more detailed coverage of issues of a more generic kind. There are many ideas represented here, only some of which may be applicable in your particular setting or discipline area. We encourage you to read this material critically, rather than simply consider it as a recipe for successful assessment practice. We hope you will find it stimulating and that it prompts many ideas of your own.

Chapter 5

Designing assessment tasks

Introduction

Designing assessment tasks is a key activity in the earliest stages of subject design and development. If you are a writer or developer of open learning materials, it is easy to forget assessment issues, because we are so focused on developing and writing the course materials. Anyone who's written open learning materials understands the exhaustive efforts involved, and the ongoing debates about what to include, how to approach particular subjects, how to sequence the concepts, what resources to draw on, and so on. It is understandable that assessment issues are often sidelined – something to be 'picked up later'. In our mind's eye, we envisage the way in which students will work through the material as directed, guided by our thoughtful prompts and supporting commentary. Open and distance learners, however, may have other intentions. For many of these students, learning revolves around the set assessment, rather than directions provided in the study materials.

With their study materials and assignments laid out in front of them at the commencement of term, open and distance learners are free to make strategic decisions about what they need to do in the light of assessment requirements. This is particularly the case with learners who have progressed through the early stages of their studies and are now feeling more confident. Learners will make strategic decisions about whether to complete in-text activities, how to progress through materials, whether to skip sections, or even by-pass the study materials altogether, based upon their perceptions of assessment requirements. This is not necessarily a problem – indeed, from an open learning perspective, it is highly desirable to encourage these independent and lifelong learning skills. Rather, the question is whether the assessment really engages the learner with the main bodies of knowledge and skills development as intended. In other words, does the assessment meet the aims and objectives?

Aligning assessment with objectives

In making decisions about what to assess, it is helpful to have a clear statement of the *aims and objectives* of your subject or unit of study. Your assessments should be designed to allow students to demonstrate their mastery of these objectives. Aims are usually a broad statement of intention from the point of view of the teacher. Objectives, on the other hand, are written from the point of view of the learners and what they should be able to do on completion of the unit. Objectives are usually introduced with verbs denoting academic or practical activities such as 'to critique', 'to demonstrate' or 'to explain'. These verbs are important because they help to identify the level or standard at which students are expected to perform. Clearly there is a difference between 'describe the three major theories of adult learning' and 'analyse and critique the three major theories of adult learning'. This would call for quite a different level and style of assessment. A broad statement of aims and a clear list of objectives are very useful starting points in developing your assessment, but they are not essential. Many prefer to devise their assessments and assessment criteria first, and then write objectives. Others still may start by developing a list of content areas to be covered, or teaching and learning strategies to be used. The most important thing is to have a plan or blueprint of how the elements of your subject will be aligned. For example:

aims and objectives = content = teaching and learning activities = **assessment**

This is a simple equation that underscores most subject development activities. At the end of the equation is assessment – it is the culmination of all your teaching and learning activities. The closer the elements are in alignment with your assessments, the more effective your assessments will be.

Consider this example. If your aims and objectives stress analysis and problem solving, it is most likely that you will structure your content in an ordered way that helps students to sift through the facts, recognize issues, make judgements, and apply their reasoning to given problems. Your teaching strategies will be aimed at developing the requisite skills in analysis and problem solving, and might take the form of applied activities that step them through these processes, with supporting feedback to enable them to diagnose errors and sharpen their skills. Assessment options could include a case study or problem scenario that provides opportunities for students to demonstrate their developing capacity to analyse the facts, apply them to a lifelike problem, and argue a case for its resolution.

Taking this example further, what would happen if the assessment tested only their recall of the facts, or simply required them to describe and relate the issues? Because assessment requirements are such a potent influence on what students actually learn, the aims and objectives of the subject will be undermined. Not surprisingly, students will focus their efforts on memorization rather than analysis or problem solving. Many will make strategic decisions to by-pass much of the course materials and will probably adopt a surface approach to their learning. At best, it is a lost opportunity. Worse still, it may cause students much frustration and anxiety.

Misalignment between subject objectives and assessment is surprisingly commonplace in open and distance education, particularly where the assignments are updated each year but the materials remain largely unaltered. Here's what one lecturer says on this issue:

> Though we have very good rules about relating assessment to objectives, it's been my experience that many lecturers do this as an afterthought. Too often the assessment is tagged onto the end, then lecturers try to perform whatever contortions are necessary to match the assessment to the objectives. I know this to be true because I did it myself in my early floundering stages of teaching at a tertiary level without guidance from my peers. Because assessment is often done at the last minute, well after the learning materials have been written, what is offered is yet another essay.
>
> (Carson, 1997)

Assessment changes are often made in haste and with only scant reference to original intentions. New teachers, with preferences for other methods of assessment, replace the old. Class sizes increase, and so teachers seek easier or more automated forms of marking. There are many reasons why assessment changes may be needed from time to time, but if they are not made with close reference to the existing objectives, content and teaching and learning strategies, there may be unintended and undesirable learning outcomes. Course materials may need to be significantly altered to support a new assessment scheme.

The equation presented earlier will not be appropriate in all learning encounters. In more self-directed forms of learning, the student's objectives become central to the equation. In some cases, content can be de-emphasized or removed from the equation, as the focus is more upon learners' active construction of meaning rather than the presentation of an organized body of knowledge. In competence-based programmes, assessment criteria may be the central, governing factor in the equation. Although the equation may change according to the nature and goals of the learning encounter, a well-planned and aligned subject is more likely to promote deep learning. This is because it sends consistent and unambiguous messages to learners about what is expected of them. There are no hidden agendas about what is or isn't valued. Furthermore, the study materials support student learning in a relevant way, and lead meaningfully into assessment tasks.

Selecting methods of assessment

There is a wealth of assessment methods commonly used in open and distance learning (ODL) – again, the challenge for teachers is to devise the most appropriate ones for your subject and your particular objectives. A number of factors will vie for your attention when thinking about assessment. For example:

- *What are the desired outcomes of the course as a whole?* Are your selected assessment methods working consistently with the 'big picture' aims? Do your assessments offer diversity or do they simply repeat assessment methods used over and over within a programme? (Recall our discussion of how some courses turn students into 'essay writing machines' or 'examination junkies'.) Is there a strategic approach to assessment in your course, or is each subject an island of individual academic activity?

- *What are the aims and objectives of the subject at hand?* As discussed earlier, the aims and objectives provide us with a clear picture of the knowledge and skills learners should be able to demonstrate and the required level of performance.

- *What generic higher education skills could we be developing?* Society, and particularly employers, has come to expect certain skills and abilities of any graduating student, regardless of his or her degree or institution. Consider thinking skills such as analysis, critique and argument, or communications skills such as writing, listening and speaking, and, importantly, information retrieval and research skills such as using libraries and online databases, analysing data, forming hypotheses, and so on. Are we equipping open and distance learners with skills for lifelong learning and a capacity to adapt to change?

- *What specialist disciplinary skills should learners be equipped with as they move into their vocational fields?* For example, in your disciplinary area there may be specialist forms of communication, such as report writing and particular types of oral presentation. Specialist research skills may include laboratory work, interviewing skills, project management and budgetary responsibilities. Thinking skills could include specific kinds of data analysis, problem solving, planning and so forth. Framing assessments to include these vocational skills gives them a lifelike disciplinary context and provides increased motivation for students.

Naturally, you will not be able to include all of the above considerations in the context of a single subject, although we hope they will spark ideas. We argue for a considered and whole-of-course approach to the planning and selection of assessment methods to maximize the variety of skills developed by learners, to increase motivation and to ensure vocational relevance in a rapidly changing world. There are many bold claims made by training and educational institutions regarding the qualities of their graduates – commonly based on the quality of facilities and teaching staff. Although these are by no means unimportant, it is probably the effectiveness of their assessment schemes that speaks most eloquently of graduate qualities.

Which assessment methods are appropriate for open and distance learning?

Traditionally ODL has relied heavily on 'pen and paper' assessments such as essays, journals, projects, or invigilated and take-home exams. However, with the relatively recent explosion of information and communication technologies, there are very few methods used in face-to-face learning that cannot be readily adapted for distance settings. We are now seeing more frequent use of group work, debates, performance, discussions, role plays and other interactive and collaborative assessments that had previously been difficult or impossible to facilitate at a distance. Part C of this book contains a number of case studies of innovative and successful open and distance assessment methods, many involving the use of communications technologies. Rather than being listed by method, the case studies are organized around key *student learning outcomes,* which are considered desirable across any programme of study within higher education (Nightingale *et al,* 1996). Although these are explored more deeply in Part C, let's take a glance at them now.

1. Thinking critically and making judgements

Open and distance education has traditionally been very effective in assessing intellectual activity of this kind as it is generally best assessed by pen-and-paper methods such as essays, reports and journals.

- *Essays* focus on the development of a sustained argument supported by a critical evaluation of appropriate evidence.
- *Reports* require information to be represented cohesively, highlighting issues and problems, together with recommended solutions or actions.
- *Journals* call for personal reflections on critical incidents, events or issues and record the learning achieved as a result.

As these activities require substantial individual effort, they are relatively easy to facilitate effectively at a distance.

2. Solving problems and developing plans

Although this kind of activity may be assessed effectively with learners working in relative isolation from each other, it is clearly enhanced by group work, discussions, brainstorming and other face-to-face techniques. Electronic discussion lists and bulletin boards are very useful ways of bringing these activities alive for distance learners. Assessment methods include *problem scenarios or simulated events,* which may unfold during the course or semester with increasing levels of complexity. Ideally, individual or group responses are progressively assessed with rapid feedback provided electronically. They require learners to discern significant information, use theory to interpret facts, generate ideas, seek consensus and plan actions. Self-selected issues or problems from learners' own workplaces may also be the subject of a similar process, and are particularly effective if learners work collaboratively with colleagues to create lasting outcomes.

3. Performing procedures and demonstrating techniques

Teaching and assessing procedures and techniques at a distance have often been difficult, unless residential schools or face-to-face sessions are organized for the purpose. *Videos* are often employed both as a means of teaching skills and assessing student performance at a distance, although in some instances this can be cumbersome for students and unreliable from the assessor's point of view. *Workplace mentoring and assessment schemes* have gained considerable popularity in recent times – the learners appoint an appropriately skilled mentor/assessor with whom they practise procedures and techniques in their workplace (or lifelike setting) until they have achieved the standards specified by the educational or training institution. Upon verification by the mentor, students receive an ungraded pass, to avoid issues of reliability between assessors. The success of these schemes has rested largely upon the availability and goodwill of mentors, the level of support and detailed information provided to them, and sufficient flexibility within the workplace. Abilities assessed using these methods include using equipment, following detailed procedures and protocols, putting theory into practice, and communication skills.

4. Managing and developing oneself

This category contains a wide spectrum of self-management skills and abilities aimed at helping students take responsibility for their own learning and development. They are commonly assessed at a distance by the use of reflective journals, portfolios, autobiography and learning contracts.

- *Journals* are a means whereby students identify their own values, attitudes and beliefs underlying their reactions to situations and how these may impact upon their professional life.
- Similarly, *autobiography* encourages learners to relate specific incidents in their lives to their sense of values and identity, and how in turn this might impact on their professional lives and judgements.
- *Portfolios* are collections of what learners themselves judge to be the most meaningful representation of their learning in a subject. Learners choose their own means of representing their learning and may include a number of small pieces of work, or a couple of larger ones, with explanations as to their relevance. Although traditionally used in the creative arts, portfolios are now increasingly used in science, social sciences and humanities.
- *Learning contracts* are also excellent ways of promoting self-management. They are commonly used in many disciplines and usually take the form of self-directed small projects in which learners define and articulate an issue or problem, design and carry out a learning project around it, analyse information and differing points of view, reflect on project outcomes, and evaluate their achievement according to self-determined criteria. It is a 'contract' in the sense that the project proposal is initially negotiated with the teacher, particularly in relation to its scope and rigour. Learning contracts are generally highly appropriate for experienced open and distance learners, who have the maturity and self-motivation required for this level of self-directedness.

5. Accessing and managing information

These abilities are developed in learners to encourage and foster important information retrieval and research skills, which will be drawn upon by many learners for the rest of their professional lives. The focus is usually upon the process and methods of accessing and managing information, rather than an end product. They are assessed at a distance by a variety of methods that may be tailored to particular disciplinary needs. For example, *annotated bibliographies* are widely used as a means of assessing students' ability to selectively scan and analyse relevant information or a literature base. In disciplines such as law or political science, where there are complex searching procedures, *tasks or problems* may be set that step learners through exploratory processes. Collaborative assessments may be devised where students develop a *database* of information pertaining to a subject, while sharing methods and sources of information. Usually assessments of this kind are introduced early in a subject or programme. Their primary purpose is a formative one, aimed at providing a common platform of skills that will be built upon by learners throughout a programme.

6. Demonstrating knowledge and understanding

This broad ability is often assessed in companion with other activities of a higher order such as critical thinking and problem solving. Demonstrating knowledge is often not viewed as an end in itself, unless it is applied or critically examined. Skills developed within this category include identifying, describing, relating, recalling and reporting. When assessed in isolation to other abilities at a distance, it often takes the form of invigilated *written examinations*. For distance learners, these are mostly facilitated through local study centres in accordance with institutional arrangements. Computer mediated assessment has sometimes replaced the need for invigilated exams, with the added advantage of rapid handling and turnaround of results. Exams may include multiple choice, true/false, matching, short answer and long answer questions. The principal weakness of this kind of assessment is that it provides little in the way of formative feedback to learners. While testing higher order skills, *reports and essays* are also common ways to assess knowledge and understanding, although with less emphasis on memorization and recall.

7. Designing, creating and performing

These abilities are often assessed in the disciplines of architecture, engineering and the visual and performing arts. *Projects and portfolios* are the principal methods of assessment, bringing together elements of aesthetics, creativity, theory, problem solving and technical disciplinary skills. Assessments tend to be substantial and applied in nature and require detailed assessment criteria, particularly in relation to any aesthetic and artistic judgements. In the case of performance, *videos* are used to assess student work at a distance. The video is often accompanied by an oral or written rationale of the performance and might also include theoretical links, reflection and self-evaluation. Presentations at residential schools or conference events are other ways in which these kinds of assessment may be facilitated.

8. Communicating

This category of skills and abilities includes written, oral and visual communicating. Virtually all assessment work is an exercise in communicating, using a variety of genres. Written and visual communicating is assessed at a distance through submitted written material such as *reports, journals and essays*. Although the emphasis is usually upon content, marks and feedback are usually awarded for logic of argument, linking of ideas, correct use of genre, clarity of expression, presentation and layout. Teachers may decide to place additional weight on these activities in the early stages of students' studies and put considerable effort into formative feedback of these important developing skills. Oral communication skills are often assessed at a distance through the use of video, demonstrating *oral presentations, role plays* and *workplace communications*. *Debates* may also be facilitated at a distance through postal communications, although more effectively through e-mail and discussion lists. Visual communication may be assessed through *posters* and presentations using computer software such as PowerPoint.

How much assessment is sufficient?

If you accept our argument about the powerful influence of assessment on learning, then you may be persuaded to increase your assessment load. Before taking such drastic action, consider first the dangers of over-assessment. Too much assessment in a subject creates similar problems for learners to those of misalignment – anxiety and a surface or 'survival' approach to learning. While some teachers believe that extensive assessment provides the necessary rigour to a subject, it's actually having the reverse effect upon learners. It is also impacting on learners' capacity to meet assessment requirements for other subjects they may be studying at the time, creating inequities between subjects.

There is no universal formula for judging the appropriate amount of assessment per subject, although often there are agreed standards within an institution or faculty. To begin, you should have a reasonably clear idea about the total time to be spent by students doing each of the various activities, such as reading, doing formative activities and undertaking assessment tasks, and this should be communicated to students. Naturally each student will differ according to abilities, prior learning and time availability, to mention just a few variables, but an approximation is a useful guide for you and learners alike. Chambers (1992, 1994) discusses the issue of workload in ODL, and suggests that 14 hours' study per week would be the maximum time allocation for part-time students, given their usual range of commitments. She offers a system to measure learner workload by making estimates of the average time it would take to read all course material and complete the activities as directed. Although this is still only an approximation, and it assumes that learners use materials in the manner intended by the course authors, it is nevertheless a sobering activity for any course author or developer to undertake.

Some teachers are prone to over-assessing their students because they believe they have to assess everything in a subject. The challenge for teachers is to determine what really needs to be formally assessed, so that you are getting a balanced sample of the subject as a whole, but not creating a treadmill for students. Another strategy is to consider holistic assessments, which broadly assess many topics in the one assignment. Examples of holistic assessments include portfolios, projects, reflective journals, oral examinations, workplace projects, problem solving activities, and so forth. These are all excellent ways in which to sample student learning across a spectrum of topic areas. Bear in mind that, when postal services are used, open and distance learners often experience a considerable delay in receiving feedback on assignments. In order to maximize the valuable formative function of assessments, a smaller number of holistic assessments are of far greater value than a series of little ones.

How long should an assessment be?

Most programmes of study contain benchmarks in terms of word lengths of assignments, and they will also vary according to the level at which students are working, the number of student hours spent on the subject, and so forth. You will also need to exercise your own judgement regarding the size of assignments – is each component of the assignment achievable within given limitations? Clearly, big is not necessarily better. Assignments with large word limits will often encourage long-winded and rambling responses from students. Keep your assignments as short as is reasonably possible, thus encouraging students to be rigorous and tight in their answers.

How should the assessments be spaced?

Ideally, students should have the benefit of feedback from one assignment before they commence another. Failure to ensure a rapid turn-around time in marking and feedback is one of the most common complaints made by open and distance learners. From a student's perspective, it is understandable that they are reluctant to begin a second assessment until they have the benefit of some feedback. Was I on the right track? What can I do to improve my grade? Did I miss something significant? These questions are milling around in the minds of learners, and the appropriate timing and adequacy of our response to them are at the heart of learners' concerns. Failure to return assignments on time denies learners this vital formative function of assessment.

What value should be placed on each item?

The value that you place in percentage terms on each assessment item will influence learners' decisions about how to spread their time. The respective value of each item should reflect the time, effort and importance of each item in relation to the objectives as a whole. Inappropriate weighting will send the wrong messages to learners.

Some teachers like to weight earlier assessments more lightly, to ensure that learners have the benefit of feedback and the opportunity to improve their overall grade on a more heavily weighted final assignment. For example, if there are two assignments per subject, the first might be weighted at 40 per cent of the overall mark; the second at 60 per cent. A single, holistic assessment, such as a project, may be broken down or tiered into two submissions in this way.

Is the assessment practicable?

In an ideal world, we could assess distance learners in all sorts of creative and innovative ways, but there are a range of practical issues that must also be considered, both from the students' and the teacher's perspective. First, consider carefully what you are asking learners to do. For example:

- Will distance education students in more remote locations, or in international settings, have equity of access to the necessary resources to fulfil requirements?
- Will learners be required to have an Internet connection to successfully complete their studies?
- If students are being asked to interact with others or work with a specialized mentor, how accessible are these people, and what kind of obligations are being created?
- If students are expected to interview others or collect 'people' data of some kind, there is an accompanying set of responsibilities. Are people or organizations being approached in the right way? Are there ethical or privacy issues regarding data gathering?

From the teacher's perspective, there are also a number of questions to ask. You will need to ensure that you have adequate resources and time to give to marking assignments. For example, if you are asking students to submit a video of a role play, ensure that you have adequate marking time to properly view and comment on the work. Likewise, reflective journals or learning logs can be quite time-consuming to read. Be clear about what you will be looking at and providing feedback on. Do not set assignments that you cannot adequately 'service'. Consider factors such as allocated marking time per assignment, and the number of students enrolled in a subject.

These are just a sample of the sorts of practical questions you will need to think through. However, if the assessment goal is important enough, then it is worth working to find solutions or fall-back positions for occasional students who may be disadvantaged by a particular assessment method or task. As one of the basic tenets of ODL is to provide access to those who may be denied an education or training through traditional means, it is important to ensure your assessments maintain a high level of openness and choice. This issue is considered further under the heading 'Are your assessments open and inclusive?' below.

Are your assessments valid and reliable?

'Validity' and 'reliability' are terms commonly used in educational measurement. Put simply, validity poses the question: are we really measuring what we are supposed to, as detailed in the objectives? We have already touched upon this in some detail when examining the alignment between objectives and assessment. For *validity* to be high:

- the assessments must sample students' performance on each objective (although you clearly don't need to have a separate assessment for each objective);
- an appropriate mix of assessment methods should be used;
- the assessment should provide the truest picture possible of the particular abilities being measured. We need to seek the truest or most lifelike conditions for performance of an ability. For example, if our objective is to test learners' oral communication skills, we clearly don't set a written essay to fulfil that objective.

Reliability is about the consistency and precision with which the assessment item measured the desired objective. In theory, a reliable test could be administered to the same student on two or more separate occasions producing the identical result. In reality, of course, this would be difficult to achieve as there are all sorts of other factors that could intervene to affect student performance. The key component in determining reliability of an assessment is consistency in marking. There is always the opportunity for human error, particularly when more than one marker is assigned to a batch of student assignments. For example, Newstead and Dennis (1994) provide us with a sobering study on the surprisingly high level of disagreement between markers as to the relative merits of a piece of student work in undergraduate psychology. Accepting that we don't live in a perfect world, the goal for educators is to strategically minimize inconsistency in marking.

Some of the following strategies are employed to strengthen reliability:

- write assessments that are clear and unambiguous, with detailed and high quality marking criteria;
- ensure that marking occurs at a time and place where you are not frequently interrupted and are able to concentrate fully;
- develop model answers and checklists of things to look for in student work;
- work closely with other markers with occasional double blind marking, to ensure agreed standards and consistency of approach.

We'll be examining many of these issues in greater detail when we look at marking practices in Chapter 7.

Are your assessment tasks authentic?

In order to make judgements about students' acquisition of higher order abilities – particularly when there is a complex blend of skills, knowledge and attitudes – 'authentic' or 'integrated' assessment tasks are often required. These are tasks that are usually drawn from the working world and require students to identify issues or problems, draw upon their knowledge to carry out solutions, respond to contingencies as they arise, and evaluate their results. These assessments support learners in developing vocational skills and experience and provide an applied context for their learning. An authentic assessment is often the culmination of incremental skills development and acquisition of knowledge over time, with the benefit of formative feedback. Computer-based simulations, with in-built feedback, are becoming increasingly available in some disciplines to support development of this kind.

As many open and distance learners are already working, there are rich opportunities for authentic, integrated assessment, which can also be tailored by a learning contract to meet individual needs. Most workplaces offer teachers and learners a variety of issues and problems around which valuable learning may be structured. Workplace problems usually have the additional benefit of being complex and poorly structured, and so offer excellent opportunities for learners to demonstrate a blend of higher order skills, knowledge and attitudes in their responses.

Authentic assessments have high validity, although they may suffer problems with reliability. As they entail complex tasks with potentially many variables, judgement of student achievement is more likely to be open to interpretation than smaller, discrete tasks. The challenge is for teachers to articulate marking criteria that are sufficiently broad to cover most situations, yet detailed enough that they are useful and provide guidance to students. The challenges of marking criteria are considered in more detail in Chapter 6.

Are your assessments open and inclusive?

Concern for equity issues and inclusiveness will naturally pervade all thoughtful ODL encounters. Courses are commonly developed with concern for issues of sex, ethnicity, disability, and so forth. Inclusive language and non-stereotypical representations of people are, by and large, common policy in educational and training institutions. Yet when it comes to assessment, inclinations towards openness or inclusivity are often subsumed by concerns about industry standards, vocational requirements, disciplinary traditions, and vague declarations about academic rigour. Sometimes openness in assessment is simply dismissed as a 'soft option'.

In another book in this series, *Understanding Learners in Open and Distance Education*, Terry Evans (1994) illustrates the diverse issues, needs, concerns and worlds our open and distance learners inhabit. It is deceptively easy, he argues:

to develop courses on the basis of taken-for-granted assumptions about students' circumstances, such as their access to libraries or study centres, spare time to study, reading and writing abilities, interest in the subject, physical abilities, etc… there are many possible variations, some of which will render the assumptions incorrect and counterproductive for a number of students' learning.

(p 126)

Teachers in ODL will need to steer a course through this difficult terrain, weighing vocational and disciplinary objectives with the variety of needs and differing circumstances that will arise in any cohort of learners. Evans (1994) suggests that we should challenge our taken-for-granted conceptions of who our students are and what counts for good teaching in open learning environments. Particularly, he argues, we need to understand what our learners value as openness, as they progress and develop throughout their studies.

What are open and inclusive assessments? From our discussion above, it seems clear that there are no hard and fast rules. It is more a process of listening to and understanding the implications of our students' unique situations, combined with a willingness to negotiate arrangements where the most positive learning outcomes are achieved for individuals. Evans (1994) outlines some of the main themes or issues likely to influence open and distance learners. Let's look at these briefly through the lens of assessment.

1. Learners' social and educational backgrounds

In most programmes of study we are likely to encounter learners from vastly differing worlds and social backgrounds, ranging from those who have successfully interwoven work and study for most of their lives, to those who are making their first tentative forays into higher education or training. In addition, the existing cultural diversity of our student population grows as our programmes are delivered beyond our own shores. How do we design assessments for such diversity? Consider the following:

- Is there sufficient formative assessment to support all learners?
- Are the challenges set through assessment reasonable ones in relation to the differing learning curves students are on?
- Is there choice and diversity of assessment? Is there negotiability?
- Do assessment tasks have meaning and cultural relevance to all students?
- Could students negotiate differing levels of achievement within assessments?
- Are high achieving students being held back by 'lowest common denominator' assignments?

2. Money

Although many school leavers are often at least partially supported by their parents, this is less likely to be the case with open and distance learners, who must bear the cost of course fees and texts in addition to their living costs. Moreover, as computer mediated communications and online delivery of programmes become the norm in ODL, additional expenditure may be required, entailing considerable sacrifice. For some, it might be out of reach entirely. The prompts below are only a sample of the questions that may need to be asked:

- Are students notified well in advance of any expenditure associated with their completion of assessments in a programme? Are they given sufficient time to plan and budget for such contingencies? Does your institution offer advice and assistance with planning?
- Do any of your assessments require unusual financial expenditure, such as field trips, projects, travel, etc? Can satisfactory alternative arrangements be devised for those who are unable to meet these costs?
- Do your assessments advantage those who are more able to afford resources or equipment? Can this advantage be ameliorated by borrowing arrangements? Can you make other suggestions to help learners maximize their access to resources?
- For those who cannot yet afford to make the leap to online learning, are there other equitable delivery and assessment arrangements available? Could alternative access arrangements be made?

3. Sex

Much worldwide recognition and political support has been given to ODL on the basis that it is successfully redressing inequality of educational opportunity for women. Certainly it has created options for many women with parenting responsibilities, who may otherwise feel trapped by their circumstances or highly limited in future employment. Evans (1994) argues that in the context of ODL, understanding gender is not so much about matters of balance between the sexes, or eradicating sexist language and practices from courses, as important as they are. Rather, it is about 'recognizing the power and depth of masculine and feminine meanings and practices in our culture' (p 52). He found that the learning worlds of men and women are very different, particularly regarding the support they receive. Whereas it was common to find men who are fully supported by their partners as a matter of course in their studies, women could not take the same support for granted, and often sought to balance hopelessly irreconcilable commitments. Many of the pressures experienced by women returning to study will manifest around assessment, particularly the difficulty of finding the required span of undisturbed time to complete an assessment item. Although these may seem like tokens in relation to the larger problem, consider:

- whether your assessment items are spaced with a reasonable lapse of time;
- whether you are sufficiently flexible and approachable by students seeking extensions when circumstances such as these apply;
- what other kinds of support you can offer in individual cases. It is also worth reflecting upon our own experiences in times of struggle with study. The timely and practical support of a teacher can be critical in decisions on whether to continue.

4. Power

As teachers and trainers we can hardly fail to acknowledge the wide power we hold over the lives and affairs of our students. Nowhere is this more apparent than in the rites of assessment. To some degree, ODL abrogates that power by enabling learners to study in the own time, place and pace, within certain parameters. In other ways, control over student learning is magnified by the way that knowledge and values are pre-packaged in many learning materials, allowing little in the way of self-directedness or negotiation of meanings. For adult learners who usually have their own 'ways of knowing', this can easily lead to alienation or a cynical surface approach to their learning. When formulating assessments, consider whether:

- you encourage students to engage critically with the learning materials, or whether there is a 'correct line' which students must follow in the assessment tasks;
- learners are encouraged to find their own meanings and relevance in the subject content, and whether assessments relate to their own worlds;
- there is sufficient choice in assessments to enable students to focus on areas of particular interest, or self-directed activity;
- your assessment tasks encourage students to demonstrate *their* learning, or only what *you* want them to learn;
- you are willing to learn from your learners.

5. Work, leisure and retirement

People engaging in ODL do so for a variety of reasons. Some are motivated by their desire for professional development or career advancement. Some see study as a source of understanding, self-esteem and personal competence. Others may find it a source of leisure in retirement. Usually learners' motivations are not fixed – rather, they are fluid and may change over the span of a course, depending on the nature of the subject matter and other temporal factors in their lives. Evans (1994) makes the distinction between those who see study as leisure and those who see it as the loss of leisure; each with their own implications for use of time, competing interests and effects on study. While educators assess and judge students by given criteria, ultimately learners will be their own judges as to successes and failures, as well as the value and merits of a programme. Our challenge is to consider the extent to which there is a mismatch between our own objectives and the likely aims, attitudes and motivations of our learners. It is similarly challenging to set aside our own attitudes and values about study and support learners on their own unique pathways.

Conclusion

As there are nearly always institutional pressures that undermine openness in assessment, it is usually left to individual teachers to advocate greater openness in their programmes. This is not always easy, as there may be many countervailing forces such as administrative systems and accrediting requirements that teachers must ultimately satisfy. We argue in this chapter that, for all their diversity, open and distance learners share a large reserve of prior knowledge and experience, a generally high level of motivation, and a series of unique stresses and strains. Evans (1994: 124) likens it to the night sky:

> Previous homogenous conceptions of *the student* are exploded into a galaxy of individual, unique students. The more one finds out, the more one realizes there remains to find out. It is rather like settling down to sleep under the stars in the Australian desert on a moonless night. As one's eyes become more accustomed to the dark, the stars between the stars between the stars become clear.

Our capacity to understand our learners, to recognize the complex dynamics in their worlds, and to help them shape these from deficits into strengths, is the key to maximizing their learning.

Designing assessment tasks – at a glance

Aligning assessment with objectives:

- Is your assessment clearly aligned with subject aims and objectives, content and teaching and learning activities? A well-aligned subject is more likely to prompt a deep approach to learning.

Selecting methods of assessment:

- Consider broadly the knowledge, skills and attitudes that can be developed through assessment. Aim for diversity in methods that encourage the broadest range of vocational and disciplinary skills.
- Choose methods that are appropriate to desired outcomes. Think creatively about perceived difficulties – just about everything can be assessed at a distance.

How much assessment?

- Remember the maxim, 'More is not necessarily better'. Over-assessment prompts anxiety and surface learning – the reverse of what you intended.
- Sample student learning, or take an holistic approach, rather than trying to assess everything.
- Keep word limits for written assignments as short as is reasonably possible. Encourage tight, rigorous responses.

Spacing assessment:

- Spread assignments to ensure that feedback from one is available before learners commence another. Maximize formative feedback.

Determining the value of assignments:

- The weighting or value of each assessment should generally reflect the desired effort, time and importance of the assignment in relation to the subject objectives as a whole.
- First assignments could be weighted lightly to emphasize their formative role.

Are your assessments practical?

- From learners' perspectives: is the assessment achievable? Are any special resources or activities required? Will anyone be disadvantaged? Do special provisions need to be in place?
- From teachers' perspectives: is the assessment serviceable? Do not set items that you do not have adequate time or abilities to support.

Is the assessment valid and reliable?

- Do your assignments provide the truest picture possible of the particular abilities being measured?
- Can your assessment items be marked with a relatively high degree of consistency and objectivity – particularly if other markers are involved?

Are your assessments authentic?

- Do your assessments have a lifelike or 'real world' quality? Are you adequately preparing learners to enter their vocational domains, or to develop their existing professional expertise?

Are your assessments open and inclusive?

- How well do you understand the complex dynamics of your learners' worlds?
- What support and flexibility can you offer learners to overcome barriers relating to sex, socio-economic status, education backgrounds, age, and so forth?
- Are your assessments designed to engage students who have varied motivations, prior experiences and knowledge, interests and work contexts?

Further resources

There are many useful resources on assessment methods and procedures you might like to explore, especially if you wish to examine a particular method in greater detail than is covered here. Below are a few recommendations:

Brown, S and Knight, S (1994) *Assessing Learners in Higher Education*, Kogan Page, London

Gibbs, G (1995) *Assessing Student Centred Courses*, Oxford Centre for Staff Development, Oxford Brooks University, Oxford

Habeshaw, S, Gibbs, G and Habeshaw, T (1993) *53 Interesting Ways to Assess Your Students*, Technical and Educational Services Ltd, Bristol

Nightingale, P et al (1996) *Assessing Learning in Universities*, University of New South Wales Press, Sydney

Chapter 6

Communicating assessment tasks

The communication of assessment tasks is another important and sensitive aspect of open and distance learning (ODL). It doesn't matter how innovative or motivating your assignments are, if you fail to adequately and concisely communicate your tasks, their effectiveness as a means of promoting learning is lost. The impact upon learners can be quite considerable – confusion, anxiety, waste of scarce time, and thoughts of discontinuance are common results. The impact upon the teacher is almost as bad, as you are likely to be deluged with queries from concerned students. Worse still is the plight of students who are reluctant to make contact, and are left to stew in their own confusion.

The problem with poorly communicated assessment tasks is that teachers don't realize there is a problem until materials are in the hands of students. No one sets out to write a poor assessment task – but often they may be hurriedly prepared and, unlike face-to-face or online teaching where problems like this can be swiftly rectified, once ODL materials are printed and mailed it is rather more complicated to fix. This chapter covers three areas that will help ensure that assessment tasks are clearly and purposefully communicated to students:

1. Communicating sufficient and clear information.
2. Developing marking criteria.
3. Moderating assessment tasks.

Communicating sufficient and clear information

How many assessment items have you seen that look something like this:

> *Culture is the blueprint for human behaviour, which can be a significant determinant of human thought and action.*
>
> Critically analyse this statement with reference to relevant literature. (Length: 2,500 words.)

It is common enough as a form of assessment item in higher education – direct, no-nonsense, and often admired for its rigour and lack of 'spoon-feeding'. Yet, from a learner's perspective, there are a number of problems immediately apparent, particularly for open and distance learners. For example:

- What is the point of this assignment? Why am I doing this? How does it relate to the overall aims of the subject, or the course?
- How do I approach this assignment? Is there a 'correct line' I must adopt? Can I admit my own views? Will I be rewarded or penalized for developing my own argument? Can I use 'I statements'?
- What does the term 'critically analyse' mean? Does it mean the statement is wrong and I have to criticize it?
- What does the marker want? How much of the literature should I refer to? What would be the standard of a very good answer as opposed to a mediocre one?

Through a process of trial and error, more experienced students may have already worked out the answers to many of these questions. Gradually, they become encultured in their discipline area, with all the often unwritten conventions and expectations that go with it. After a while, they also get to know individual teachers and markers, and their particular whims, likes and dislikes. This 'cue-consciousness', identified by Miller and Parlett (1974) is a common characteristic of students, particularly those who are motivated by pragmatic or 'extrinsic' reasons. Cue-conscious students negotiate the assessment system by seeking cues from teachers about how to maximize their grades, what to focus on in examinations, and so forth. There are parallels to Entwistle and Ramsden's (1983) findings of a 'strategic approach to study', Lockwood's (1992) 'assignment focused' learners, and also Laurillard's (1979) research, which concluded that students adopted differing approaches to an assignment, based upon their perceptions of the task.

Without the benefit of face-to-face interactions, of course, it takes much longer for open and distance learners to pick up on these cues. In the absence of face-to-face interactions, students have to read between the lines of their study materials for clues to what is expected. Alistair Morgan (1993), in his book in this series, *Improving Your Students' Learning: Reflections on the experience of study*, makes a case that dialogue between teachers and learners is the most effective way for students to understand what is required of them:

> Sussing-out what is required in study is a major part of being a student... In distance education and open learning it can be a difficult and slow process, hence the importance of local tutorial support. (p 109) ... The function of dialogue seems to play a unique role in helping students construct meaning from

the course material and at the same time enabling them to grasp what kind of learning is being encouraged by the university.

(p 110)

In the absence of local tutors, however, opportunities for dialogue become more difficult, relying on telephone or computer mediated communications. It seems there is an added onus on open and distance educators to ensure that the kinds of discussions that are commonly conducted in face-to-face sessions are offered in various forms to open and distance learners. When communicating your assessment tasks, consider some of the strategies discussed below.

1. Provide a rationale

The rationale for an assignment is something that is usually taken for granted by a teacher, but rarely communicated to learners at a distance. It provides a broad statement of the purpose of the assignment, what is being sought in learners and how it relates to the subject as a whole. Let's follow through with our original essay question, but now adding a rationale:

Rationale

This assignment has three aims. First, we want to check your understanding of some basic terms and concepts you have worked through so far. Secondly, we want to develop your skills in constructing an informed argument using the essay form. Thirdly, this assignment aims to develop your skills in analysing arguments put forward in the literature, identifying strengths and weaknesses, and making judgements about their relevance to your argument. We encourage you to take your own stand on the question, but it also must be supported by firm evidence, rather than just your own experiences. The assignment relates to Objectives 2 and 3 and is covered in Topics 4, 5 and 6 in your study materials, and Chapter 3 of your textbook.

A clear rationale of this kind immediately communicates to students your intent – indeed, it helps to clarify your own intentions! A clear rationale has the capacity to answer many of the questions and concerns students commonly raise.

2. Explain terms

The language of assessment is sprinkled with specialized terms denoting types of required academic activity, such as to 'analyse', 'critique', 'evaluate', 'discuss', 'compare and contrast', etc. These terms are often used imprecisely or interchangeably, and are rarely explained in any detail to learners. If teachers are unsure of the difference between, say 'analyse' and 'interpret', or 'evaluate' and 'critique', it is rather unrealistic to expect learners to be much the wiser. Appendix A contains the meanings of a number of terms commonly used in assessment to assist you in clarifying your understanding. As there is always some variation in usage, make sure you explain *your* interpretation of these terms to students. To follow on with our earlier example:

Terminology

'Critical analysis' has two interrelated tasks. To analyse is to separate the whole into its parts so that you discover their nature, function and relationship. To criticize is to express your judgement regarding the correctness or merit of the factors being considered. Hence, 'critical analysis' requires you to first break down the given statement into its component parts, examine each part and the evidence both for and against, then express your judgement of the merit of the statement in the light of your analysis.

---

3. Offer suggestions for methods of approach

Most experienced open and distance learners have devised successful strategies for developing and writing assignments, usually by trial and error. Often students strike upon successful strategies which, once established, become cherished and reflect their own styles of learning. Although in most cases it would be inappropriate to impose particular strategies or methods on adult learners, most new learners are very eager for this type of support (Morgan *et al*, 1998). While discussions often take place in tutorial settings about suggested methods of undertaking an assignment, distance learners are often left to their own devices. Naturally, methods will differ according to disciplinary requirements and the nature of the assignment, but any constructive support and timely advice that can be offered learners could prove invaluable, and form the basis of a sound long-lasting study approach. Here is some advice we could offer learners approaching the assignment above:

Suggested approach to this assignment

1. Define and explore the argument. What is the author's central argument? What evidence is used to support the position?
2. Differentiate between descriptive and evaluative key terms. Which terms are value-laden and which are not? What are the author's underlying values?
3. Locate your own position. How do you stand in relation to the values expressed? What do you have to make decisions about? What further data do you need?
4. Build a thesis. How is your argument developing? Have you explored different perspectives? Will you argument withstand scrutiny?
5. Structure the essay. How will you best structure and represent your argument? What is your central thread? How will you marshal your arguments and data? Can you synthesize results into a conclusion?

Each discipline has its own conventions, with accompanying microskills that combine to support disciplined knowledge building. How explicitly and effectively are they communicated to learners?

4. Familiarize learners with disciplinary discourse

Students are often required to adhere to a range of disciplinary conventions regarding style and tone, referencing and the manner in which knowledge is constructed and arguments advanced, to name but a few. Yet often these conventions are not explained to students in any detail, and are almost like a secret code which learners are left to crack by trial and error. Moreover, learners are expected to master a range of genres, from the formal essay to reports and more personalized reflective journals. When we add in the differing expectations and quirks of individual markers, we really start to get a picture of how difficult and frustrating it is for learners to establish a clear and consistent picture of what is expected in their discipline. We need to unpack these issues far more effectively for learners by explaining the mechanics and processes of the discipline and offering samples of best practice in a variety of genres that illustrate the conventions we value. This can't be done within the context of a single subject – rather, it is something that needs to be strategically developed from the earliest stages of a programme.

5. Use clear, plain English

This seems a rather obvious point, and yet it is surprising how many grammatical errors and ambiguities manage to find their way past writers and editors into the hands of students. For example, did you notice the ambiguity in the quote used in our exemplar earlier? Is it 'culture' or 'human behaviour' that can be a significant determinant of human thought and action? In most cases we can sort out ambiguities from the sense of the surrounding sentences, but for students this can be unnerving and is quite unnecessary. In our own university, a memo was recently circulated from the examinations officer complaining about the increasing frequency of errors and ambiguities in examination papers that were placing considerable strain not only on students at a vulnerable time, but also on invigilating officers in exam rooms. While this might be a product of increasing workloads and declining budgets, it is nevertheless a critical responsibility of teachers to ensure the clarity and accuracy of their communications.

6. Information overload

Care should be taken not to overload your assessments with too much supporting information. The strategies discussed above may be useful in some instances and not in others and should be used selectively. First-year students may need a great deal of support along these lines, but you should exercise your judgement regarding the staged acquisition of skills such as essay writing and the amount of supporting information you provide. In the context of one subject, there is only so much you can achieve – ideally it should form a part of a larger whole-of-programme approach to assessment and skills development.

Developing marking criteria

Well-developed marking criteria that accompany assessment items are perhaps the most important of all supporting information. Marking criteria establish a framework for your evaluation and grading of student learning. It is here that you communicate to students what you value in their work and how you exercise your judgement as a marker. The objective of marking criteria is to make the process of assessment as open, as fair and as defensible as possible, particularly if there are multiple markers in a subject.

Marking criteria often contain:

- criteria upon which the assignment will be evaluated, such as:
  - understanding of key concepts,
  - argument,
  - structure,
  - presentation;
- details of what is valued or sought for each criterion. For example, argument may have a series of subheadings such as purposeful introduction, sound use of references, reasoned and persuasive argument. Presentation may include components such as appropriate layout, bibliographic conventions, and attention to grammar, spelling, punctuation and so forth;
- percentage weighting or actual marks apportioned for each aspect of the task, and/or corresponding standards for the total mark (eg credit, distinction).

Consider some of the following examples, which offer a variety of ways in which marking criteria can be communicated:

Example 1
In this example there are three main criteria. The marks have been assigned to each category in percentage terms out of 100 per cent.

Content:	evidence of reading, well developed argument, sound analysis, understanding of key concepts	50
Presentation:	introduction, body and conclusion, logical flow of paragraphs, clarity of expression, layout, style	30
Technical features:	bibliographic conventions, referencing, grammar, spelling, punctuation	20

Example 2

This example sets out individual tasks required of students, with an accompanying explanatory key to the mark allocated for that task. The criteria can be used as a marking guide that is returned to students.

Key:				
Not at all	Not really	Yes	Yes, well	Yes, very well
(0 marks)	(1 mark)	(2 marks)	(3 marks)	(4 marks)

1. Have you provided clear headings using report format? 0 1 2 3 4

2. Have you provided a clear explanation of your plan   0 1 2 3 4
   including methods?

3. Have you anticipated any possible barriers and   0 1 2 3 4
   strategies for the same?

4. Have you provided effective evaluation strategies?   0 1 2 3 4

5. Evidence of clear expression and neat presentation?   0 1 2 3 4

Total mark for this assignment: ___ 20

Example 3

This example identifies another way of distinguishing between five grade levels. It can be used in an holistic or impressionistic way by asking which category each essay seems to fit best, or can be used more analytically by addressing each individual item in the five categories. The marks shown are percentages.

High distinction (85–100):	Consistently high-level synthesis of ideas and argument; original and thought-provoking ideas; evidence of systematic and creative use of sources, extremely pleasing prose.
Distinction (75–84):	Understands and systematically compares theories and concepts; evidence of wide use of sources, makes critical comment, sustained argument, stylish composition.
Credit (65–74):	Concepts and theory well applied, some useful insights, reasonable use of sources, reasonable argument, although could be improved.
Pass (50–64):	Readable; descriptive rather than analytical, a limited use of sources, seeks to address major issues; acceptable although major improvements possible.
Fail (below 50):	No significant grasp of concepts, irrelevant material included, incomplete, unreadable, misunderstands the topic, little evidence of significant effort.

Example 4

This example demonstrates ways in which various standards of achievement can be chosen by the students, based on their level of skill or commitment. It consists of a core activity then a series of extension activities that earn additional credit. This is particularly appropriate in some competence-based activities where core tasks may be relatively easily achieved by some.

Minimum requirements for pass (10–12 marks)

- Complete and submit all laboratory tasks as specified in workbook
- Complete all assessable workbook activities
- Submit all results to challenge tests with workings.

Credit level (13–14 marks)

- Complete all tasks for a minimum pass, and
- Undertake and submit extension activities provided at the end of each topic with workings.

Distinction level (15–16 marks)

- Complete all tasks for a minimum pass, and
- Submit a learning log, recording your reflections on issues, problems and major learning outcomes for you during semester (1,500 words).

High distinction level (17–20 marks)

- Complete all tasks for a minimum pass, and
- Design a work-related project, which seeks to apply some of the key principles discussed to a real-life problem in your workplace. The project should identify the issue or problem, relevant principles and concepts and proposed strategies for addressing them (2,000 words).

As you can see from the variety of examples above, different types of assessment tasks will call for differing kinds of criteria. It's an area in which you're free to innovate and devise your own way of communicating to students about what you value in their work and how you will assess it. There are many more examples of marking criteria contained in the case studies in Part C of this book.

Moderating assessment tasks

Now that you have designed and drafted your assessment items and accompanying criteria, are they ready to be despatched to students? Possibly they are, but as you're no doubt very close to them at this stage, it is difficult for you to stand back and re-assess them. Given the array of difficulties arising from ambiguous or incomplete assessments for learners and teachers alike, it is worth investing a little more time at this point. Moderation of assessment tasks by colleagues is an excellent safeguard against errors and ambiguities as well as ensuring that the tasks are fair and appropriate for learners. One way of moderating assessments is for tasks to be devised by a group of staff. This way, you will benefit from fresh ideas and the collective experiences of the group. Alternatively, you may choose to draft the tasks yourself, then have them reviewed by colleagues. You could seek input along the following lines:

- To which objectives does each assessment task relate?
- Is each assessment task appropriate?
- Do the assessment tasks reflect a suitable sample of the unit content?
- Is the number of assessment tasks appropriate?
- Is the spacing between each assessment task reasonable?
- Are the tasks set at a suitable level?
- Is each assessment task and the accompanying criteria stated clearly?
- Where students are provided with choices, are the choices comparable in terms of difficulty?

Needless to say, most assessment items benefit from a re-draft after initial testing. Refer back to the summary section 'Designing assessment tasks – at a glance' at the end of the previous chapter for a fuller checklist of issues for review. Moderation is also a useful strategy in marking, which is considered in the next chapter.

Chapter 7

Marking and grading

Introduction

Having drafted your assessment items and accompanying marking criteria with care and in considerable detail, the tasks of marking and grading become immeasurably easier. Yet with increasing numbers in training and higher education, marking loads are often where pressures are most sorely felt. As their briefcases bulge with assignments, teachers and trainers often feel inundated with marking commitments and treat them as something to be completed as quickly as possible. From learners' perspectives, however, assessments are often a labour of love, involving weeks of time and effort. Less experienced learners mail their assignments into what may seem like a void, unsure about their abilities to succeed and whether they have responded adequately to the tasks set them. Assignments may represent the only form of communication between a teacher and a learner at a distance. It is incumbent upon us to really ensure that we engage thoroughly with students' work and to maximize the invaluable formative function of assessment by providing detailed, supportive feedback. This is one of our most important and sensitive roles as open and distance educators.

Marking practices

The governing principles in marking are fairness and consistency. While we all aspire to these principles, it becomes a little more difficult in practice, with the regular interruptions and busy schedules of teaching and training. We need an ordered and methodical approach to the task of marking, with a series of built-in strategies to reduce errors or inconsistencies. Consider some of the following suggestions.

Divide your marking into manageable portions

Given that marking can rarely be completed in one sitting, you need to be reasonably organized about finding regular blocks of time where marking is controlled and has your full attention. If you're grabbing a few minutes here and there between classes, it is difficult for you to maintain an overview of standards and the consistency required to fairly assess each student's work. At the other end of the spectrum, some teachers find themselves in long sessions of marking late into the night. This has obvious problems as well, as your abilities to assess effectively are diminished through fatigue.

Avoid interruptions

Set aside an organized, quiet place away from phones and other distractions that might prevent you from giving the job your full attention. If your workplace is too busy, don't try to do it there. Work at home or any other quiet place where your concentration can be maintained. Given the effort that students have generally put into this work, it is inappropriate to give them any less than your best.

Set benchmarks and review marking

It is advisable to browse through all assignments in a batch to get a feel for the range of quality in the responses. Although your marking criteria will specify standards in some detail, in many pieces of assessment, particularly those that require a degree of individuality or creativity, your own judgement is constantly called upon. You might also like to select some benchmark assignments that represent certain standards as specified in your marking criteria. As you progress through the assignments, refer back to your benchmarks and compare their particular qualities against the one at hand. To ensure consistency and fairness, it is important that you maintain an overview of the standards by which your are judging each piece of work, or you may experience a 'drift' of the standard as you progress.

Moderation in marking

There are a number of useful moderation strategies that can be used to enhance fairness and consistency in marking. For example, 'double blind' marking is sometimes employed, where assignments are reviewed and marked separately by two markers, and then the result is averaged. Rarely, of course, will our time-frames and budgets support double blind marking as the norm, but if random samples are double marked from time to time, it's an excellent way of prompting dialogue between teachers seeking shared understanding about standards and quality. It is also invaluable as a development tool for new teachers seeking some monitoring and feedback on their marking activities.

Where multiple markers are used in the one assignment, and marking criteria are open to interpretation to some degree, moderation is essential. There are a number of strategies that may be employed, the practicability of which will depend on the particular context, for example, the number of markers and whether or not the markers are able to meet for a briefing and possible follow-up sessions. If possible, markers should meet to discuss the criteria, preferably with the aid of some sample responses. Some sample double blind marking may also be usefully employed here. If markers are geographically dispersed, contact by electronic means may be sufficient. Another moderation strategy where there are multiple questions is to assign a particular question to each marker, thereby aiming for consistency in the way in which each question is marked across the different students' assignments.

It is important to have moderation strategies in place early in the semester or course, and that other markers are aware of these processes. It is much more difficult to address the problems after the event if significant differences in the pattern of marking occur.

Marking guides

Marking guides have already been discussed in the context of marking criteria, although it is worth mentioning them here as they are another important way in which to promote consistency and fairness in your marking practices. Marking guides are sheets attached to student assignments that enable you to provide a detailed response to students' efforts regarding each criterion being assessed. Example 2 in the previous chapter demonstrates the way in which they might be designed and laid out. The more detailed and precise, the more transparent your marking practices become, and hence the more valuable they are to students. Refer to Appendix B for a further example of a marking guide.

Feedback on assignments

Written feedback on assessment items may be the only communication open and distance learners have with their teachers. Although this is less than an ideal situation, it is still the reality for many distance learners who do not have ease of access to electronic communications or the services of a local tutor. So written feedback on assignments becomes a critical point for dialogue between teachers and learners. Providing useful, constructive feedback to learners about their work is one of the most important abilities of a good marker. Constructive feedback:

- creates a dialogue between teacher and learner;
- helps learners to identify areas in which they can further develop;
- teaches the learner new skills;
- prompts reflective and self-evaluative thinking.

Speaking from our own experiences as distance learners, poor or minimal feedback from assignments – those things that we'd put so much effort into – was one of the most frustrating aspects of being a distance education student. There's nothing more demotivating than putting a good deal of effort into an assignment, only to receive an abbreviated comment like 'good work'. How was it good? How could it have been better? One rightly questions whether the marker has engaged at all, or just skimmed through the paper to find some key words to tick.

Rowntree (1990: 328) makes the following suggestions to improve written feedback on assignments:

- Draw the learner's attention to facts they have overlooked or misinterpreted.
- Suggest alternative approaches or interpretations.
- Suggest new sources (eg other people) from whom learners might get feedback.
- Draw attention to gaps in the learners' reasoning.
- Suggest how learners might present their ideas more effectively.
- Offer comments that will help learners sharpen their practical skills.
- Ask for further explanation of muddled answers.
- Demonstrate useful short-cuts in procedure.
- Help learners reflect on how a piece of work might have been improved.
- Point out relationships between the learners' present work and their earlier work
- Commend the learners for any unexpected insights, special efforts or improvement in competence.

If you heed Rowntree's advice as above, then you are doing three important things:

1. you are *teaching* rather than simply 'marking';
2. you are entering into a *dialogue* with learners rather than simply communicating their results;
3. you are encouraging learners to *reflect upon and evaluate* their own achievement, rather than relying on you as the sole arbiter.

These issues are important in open and distance learning (ODL), as your comments may be the most significant – or perhaps the only – interactions you have with learners. From our own experiences we might add a few more to Rowntree's list:

- Engage with learners' arguments or points of view – are they persuasive? Are they sufficiently supported?
- It is just as important to give detailed feedback to those doing well as for those who are struggling.
- Write neatly! Don't leave your students staring blankly for hours at your illegible scribble.
- The online medium supports rapid, formative feedback to learners and should be used wherever possible, rather than unnecessarily relying on postal services.

Finding the right language and tone

While it is generally easy to praise good work, it can be quite difficult to make critical comments. Although frank and honest feedback is a good general rule, be careful not to annihilate your students with a barrage of negative comments, regardless of whether you feel they are justified or well-intentioned. You are not judging their intelligence or worth as learners; rather, you are judging the effort they have made in this instance. Too much negative comment – or indeed sarcasm – does nothing to enhance learners' understanding of a subject or their confidence. Even if there is very little to be positive about, try to build some rapport, as you would do in a face-to-face encounter. You may strategically decide to focus on only one of a number of problems – perhaps the most significant one – as the subject of your detailed feedback, rather than overwhelm a learner with too much information. Broad statements are not particularly helpful unless you point to specific examples of the problem. Similarly, your advice and support should be grounded in the student's own work. You might end on a personal note, encouraging the learner to make contact with you if he or she doesn't understand or is still struggling with the problem.

Open and distance learners are usually their own harshest critics. High standards and high expectations of themselves, fear of failure and lack of confidence are commonly cited issues in studies of ODL and student discontinuance (Garland, 1993, for example). Constructive, engaging feedback is a very important source of support and motivation for learners and one of the most demanding and sensitive tasks that teachers are required to perform.

Audio, video and telephone feedback

A range of other media can be used to enhance student feedback on assignments. Audiotapes are a simple and lively way to communicate your feedback, and enable you to expand the teaching component of your interaction with learners. In addition, tapes add a personal touch to your communications, and enable you to make critical comments in a softer way with more explanation and support. Teachers who use this feedback medium find it particularly useful for borderline or vulnerable learners, where they want to say a lot more than can be written on an assignment. Telephone feedback is also useful in this way, with the additional benefit of two-way communication, although it is advisable that you agree a mutually suitable time with the learner. Audio feedback is usually employed in conjunction with written annotations and comments, rather than as a substitute.

Video feedback has been trialed in some distance teaching institutions with considerable success (Hase and Saenger, 1997). Learners were able to put a face to the name, they felt more connected to the institution, they found it easier to make contact, and they enjoyed the spontaneity of the medium. Teachers found it particularly useful to present concepts and complex explanations for those who really needed help, and also to present themselves as people – thus opening the way for further interactions. New developments in computer mediated communications will enable audio and video feedback to be recorded and delivered with comparative ease and minimal expense from the teacher's desktop.

Marking turnaround time

The time and effort you put into providing feedback on assignments will need to be balanced against another competing pressure: the need to return assignments quickly to students. If assignments are not being returned to students in time for them to gain the benefit of feedback before they commence their next assignment, then much of its formative value is diminished. Effectively, the assessments are only performing the summative role of graded performance.

There is no benchmark time for return of assignments – it will depend on a number of variables such as the length of the subject, the timing of other assessments, the competing commitments of markers, and whether assignments are returned via the post or electronically. Considerable planning will be needed to ensure that you're able to respond as quickly as possible, given these factors. Consider some of the following strategies to save time while maintaining the quality of your feedback.

1. Group feedback

In many assessments it may be appropriate to supply generalized feedback to all learners in the group, in addition to specific comments to individuals. This may be in the form of a letter or an attachment to your assignment sheet, outlining how the assessment was handled in general terms. It could include a discussion of areas that were consistently handled well, common problems or issues needing attention, and pointers for the next assignment. It could also give an indication of the range of student marks so that individuals can see how they fared in relation to the cohort. This may well save much time in making comments repetitively on many assignments.

2. Model answers or worked solutions

In some instances you can supply model answers or worked solutions that will save you the time of closely annotating each assignment. This is particularly appropriate in assignments where student responses are relatively fixed and finite. Where multiple markers are involved, this has the added advantage of promoting greater consistency in marking. It is not suggested that these strategies be used as a substitute for individual feedback, but as a way of removing some of the more laborious and repetitive components of marking.

3. Computer mediated communications

Open and distance learners can benefit enormously from the rapid turnaround available through e-mail and discussion lists. This could take the form of a small assessable posting from individual learners, or assessable discussion between learners around key concepts, or small-group work based upon an issue or problem to be resolved. This works particularly well in the early stages of a subject, as a first assessment item, providing learners with the benefit of early and rapid feedback on key concepts and issues. It also prepares them for further more weighty assessments, and encourages them to get connected with other students in the group. *Small* is emphasized in this instance, as the assessment purpose is primarily formative.

4. Review administrative procedures for receipt and despatch of assignments

Turnaround of assignments can sometimes be significantly improved by a review of your administrative procedures:

- Do your assignments languish for days in somebody else's tray before you receive them?
- How rapidly are they despatched once your marking is complete?
- Are there quality systems in place for rapid handling of assignments?
- Is there policy in place (for example, a guaranteed two-week time-frame from receipt to despatch)?
- Are administrative staff aware of the importance of this activity? Is staff development required?

Awarding grades

We have already discussed in some detail the process of awarding marks for students' work and some strategies for ensuring consistency and fairness. What then happens to those marks? Usually, they are tabulated in some form to provide a final grade for a subject. By itself, a grade may have little meaning to students unless it is contextualized and explained in some way. In Part A of this book we looked at norm and criterion referenced assessment schemes. These are two common examples of the ways in which institutions seek to grade students and communicate those results. Put simply, *norm referenced assessment* grades students on the basis of their performance in relation to each other. Raw marks are distributed along a 'normal distribution curve' to adhere to pre-determined institutional quotas. So regardless of the tally of their raw marks, only a certain percentage will obtain a final grade of high distinction, distinction (or A, B), and so forth. Similarly, at the other end of the curve, only a certain percentage is permitted to fail. Below is an example of such a scheme:

High distinction	allocated to	0–3 per cent of group
Distinction	allocated to	0–12 per cent
Credit	allocated to	10–35 per cent
Pass	allocated to	40–80 per cent
Fail	allocated to	0–15 per cent.

Norm referenced schemes are usually in place to 'protect the standards' of the institution, although they have been roundly criticized for many years by teachers who feel that students are being unnecessarily pitted against each other for limited quotas of grades, that they do not reflect individual performances, and that they assume that all cohorts of students perform to a similar standard. With *criterion referenced assessment* there is no predetermined distribution of grades. There are clearly stated criteria against which each student's performance is judged – if the criteria are met according to set standards, then the student achieves the relevant grade. As we have discussed earlier, the success and reliability of criterion referenced assessment depend on the consistency and precision with which the criteria are developed, communicated to students and interpreted by markers. The tally of marks for students' work may be represented as an overall grade, using schemes such as the following:

High distinction	85 and above
Distinction	75–84
Credit	65–74
Pass	50–64
Fail	below 50.

These schemes may vary considerably between institutions. Alternatively, in competence-based assessment, a grade of pass/fail (or 'competent'/'not yet competent') may be awarded, depending on whether complete mastery of a competence is required, or there are degrees of skill that may be correlated with grades.

Arguably, norm referencing schemes have no place in open learning systems, where the needs and interests of learners should eclipse institutional rhetoric about standards. Although most individual teachers will have little choice but to follow the policy of their institutions, it is important that teachers be aware of the implications of these grading schemes. It is also vital to inform students of the way in which their grades are derived, and to make the system as transparent as possible. The mysteries and sleight of hand associated with marking and grading systems are not only a major source of frustration to learners, but support an antiquated power differential between teachers and learners.

Ungraded or pass/fail assessments are useful in certain circumstances, where it is desirable for the competition for grades to be removed, allowing for more open-ended exploration of the subject matter, or where criteria are difficult to determine. They also may be employed effectively to avoid negative side effects of assessment such as excessive competitiveness, anxiety or heavy marking workloads (Habeshaw *et al*, 1993). Ungraded assessments, of course, have their own side effects, such as the impact upon student motivation and learning approaches, so all these factors should be weighed, and ungraded assessments should be used strategically. In many instances, learners themselves will be unsatisfied with this approach to grading as they want more feedback than this about the level of their achievement.

Authentication

Authentication – the ability of teachers to verify that a student's work is not that of another – is an issue that has long bedevilled distance educators. How do we know whose work is being submitted for assessment? If our learners are no more to us than a name and a student number, as is unfortunately often the case, then this indeed can be a problem. Some distance educators respond by instituting a regime of invigilated examinations in their courses, not so much for reasons of pedagogical appropriateness, but for the grim task of verifying the identity of the student. In online contexts, where objective testing methods such as multiple choice and short answer questions have become popular, the issue becomes even more thorny. Colleges in the USA, which use this kind of testing frequently, have resorted to photographic capture of the keyboard operator, and even iris scanning, as a means of authentication. These kinds of surveillance methods tend to reflect the thinking that all students are 'born cheats'. Yet those small numbers of students who manage to cheat usually stay a step or two ahead of us and our capacity to detect them. As our repertoire of teaching, learning and assessment methods expands, so too do the options for those on this creative but unrewarding pathway.

To bring balance to this issue, it is worth remembering that we are working largely with adult open and distance learners whose reasons and motivations for study are such that cheating is anathema to them. We need to examine our own thinking and values regarding students and cheating, and whether they continue to apply in ODL contexts. In the process of providing for authentication, are we limiting or undermining the learning experiences of the vast majority? What balances should be struck? Benson (1996) offers some practical suggestions to minimize the problems of authentication:

- Link assignments so that each one builds upon the former, preferably with some application to individual student circumstances.
- Individualize topics as far as possible with use of students' own workplaces, lives and values as the source of discussion.
- Use self-directed forms of learning such as learning contracts.
- Use work-based mentors, supervisors or assessors to report on work-based learning projects and performance-based assessments.
- Use video- and audio-based presentations as an alternative to print.
- Undertake oral assessments by use of the telephone.
- Adapt or change assignment topics regularly (but without losing the alignment between objectives, content and teaching, and learning activities).

These strategies represent an important part of the process Rowntree (1977) describes as 'knowing' our learners. Assessment is an interaction between teachers and learners that aims at getting to know our students and the nature of their learning. If learners remain anonymous numbers to us, then authentication will probably remain a problem, and sizes of cohorts in some instances do not help this situation. If, however, we come to know our students by assessments that engage us with their worlds, then authentication is far less likely to be a problem.

Chapter 8

Creating dialogue through assessment

In an earlier chapter we looked at the kinds of dialogue that can be created between teachers and learners through assignment feedback. This is only one of a series of strategies you may wish to develop to engage with learners through assessment. In this chapter, we would like to focus on some different forms of dialogue that prepare learners to undertake assessments. Some of these interactions may involve a teacher or tutor leading discussions with students, some may involve an equal two-way exchange of ideas. Others may not involve the teacher at all – rather, they are initiated by students in their exchanges with peers, mentors, coaches, work colleagues, family and friends. Exchanges can occur using tele- or videoconferencing, electronic means such as e-mail or Web-based discussion lists, residential schools, or through face-to-face sessions in students' local contexts. Whether you are the mediator of these sessions may not matter very much. What is important is that learners have the opportunity to express and debate ideas, to expand their thinking and understanding around topics, to check their interpretation of assignment tasks, and to generally deepen their approach to assessment. As a teacher, you are in a unique position to shape these encounters and, indeed, encourage learners to shape their own interactions as their needs arise. We know that open and distance learners are diverse in their needs, so not all learners will necessarily embrace the same forms of dialogue. Some will have preferences for certain kinds of exchange, some may only require intermittent contact for specific issues. Others will seize any opportunities available, particularly if they are inexperienced learners and assessment issues are the focus of discussion. It is hoped that this chapter will spark some ideas about how you can encourage and support interactions that deepen students' approaches to assessment.

Facilitating dialogue in open and distance learning

Although seemingly innocuous concepts, 'interaction' and 'dialogue' have been forcefully debated in the open and distance learning (ODL) literature for over 20 years. For example, Daniel and Marquis (1979) expressed their concern that too much interaction or contact with students will undermine their independence as learners. They stressed the need to find the 'right' balance between the two. Writing some 10 years later, Evans and Nation (1989) reject Daniel and Marquis' conception of distance education as 'going it alone', with only limited or regulated contact. They argue that there is no inherent contradiction between independence and dialogue – on the contrary, enhancing dialogue is a way of promoting independence and autonomy in learners, and challenges power relationships in teaching and learning. Juler (1990) furthers this debate by suggesting that interactions are complex, multifaceted, and should extend beyond the teaching and learning environment to include peers, colleagues, other learners, family and so forth. Much of the debate has stemmed from Evans and Nation's concern that ODL has been dominated by 'instructional industrialism' – that the mass-produced teaching texts, encouraging one-way transmission of knowledge, have become the primary vehicle for learning at the expense of learner autonomy through dialogue. This is even further entrenched by assessment systems that encourage students to uncritically reproduce the views or particular constructions of course authors (Peters, 1995).

The following sections look at some of the ways in which interaction and dialogue can build confidence and motivate learners, encourage them to exchange ideas and negotiate meanings, and help them to develop assessment responses that are personally meaningful and represent a deep engagement with the issues.

Making contact

Making contact with learners early in the course or semester helps lay the foundation for a teacher–learner relationship, and can set the tone for the remainder of the course or semester in relation to learners' engagement with the subject. Ideally, a one-to-one communication is the most effective, although this will depend on the size of your group, communication options available, and so forth. Timing of communication is also important. Most learners welcome contact in times of high activity such as the weeks preceding an assignment submission, when they are more likely to have queries or issues with which they're grappling. Try not to structure these interactions too much – allow the agendas and concerns of learners to emerge.

Many open and distance teachers provide welcoming information in their study materials, with contact information, on the assumption that learners will initiate contact themselves if required. This is often done by teachers in the belief that they are encouraging learners' independence and self-management. Yet many learners are very reluctant to make contact, unless they have no choice. Let's hear from some adult distance learners on the subject of making contact by phone.

'Catherine', aged 48, is the manager of large aged care facility:

I find it very hard making contact by phone to a lecturer. For starters, I'm doing it from work. I'm busy, another phone is ringing, someone's knocking on the door. The lecturer's busy, you can tell they are by the tone in their voice – you've just got to get it all out as quickly as you can. Unless you know the person, or you're really articulate and assertive, it's really quite difficult. I think you could speak to a whole range of people who are studying and they'd all agree that it's quite unnerving to be ringing (the university) and not knowing what sort of reaction you're going to get. I avoid it. It's a last resort. If I do, I'm usually in deep trouble!

How can we explain that a worldly, mature and otherwise confident business manager would have these difficulties in making contact with academic staff? While adult education theorists have argued that self-direction and autonomy are the natural domain of adults, there is also little doubt that we have been socialized by our past educational experiences. Consider the traditional stereotype of the academic – the wise all-powerful sage. Add to this the quite real power differential between teacher and learner, the former having the capacity to determine almost all aspects of a student's success and progress through a programme. As educators we all need to reflect on our own attitudes towards our position and our relationship with learners. Implicit in the word 'dialogue' is a relative degree of equality and symmetry. How can we hold a dialogue or exchange meanings with learners if we place ourselves on pedestals of superior knowledge and status? Recall our discussions on the unique bodies of knowledge and prior experience that adult learners bring to a programme. How can we acknowledge and value this?

Communicating empathetically

In order to create the kind of dialogic relationship we have mentioned with and between your learners, you will need to have a certain level of empathy with them. Empathy is a heightened awareness of others' feelings and the capacity to see things from others' perspectives – to be able to put yourself in their shoes, so to speak. The willingness of learners to make contact with you, or to respond to your invitations to engage in dialogue, will depend on a variety of factors including:

- what's happening in their day at the time you're making contact;
- what's happening generally in their lives at the time, relating to family, work and study commitments;
- their prior experiences of interactions with academic staff. Were their calls ever returned? Are they cynical? Intimidated?
- their progress through their studies, and their relative confidence as a learners.

Race (1989) has identified three stages a learner goes through and the accompanying feelings:

- *Stage 1* – at the beginning – feeling excited, apprehensive, curious, exposed and vulnerable, inadequate. (Can I really make the grade?)
- *Stage 2* – mid course – feeling fed-up, intimidated, pressurized, alone. (Should I really have started this?)
- *Stage 3* – towards the end – feeling fatigued, stressed by examinations. (Will I manage it?)

The foundation of good interactions with your learners is your capacity to understand and relate to their experiences, particularly as the pressures of assessment compete with the other demands in their lives. Good communications with tentative learners at the beginning of a programme can significantly alter the course of their studies and their approach to learning. When fatigue sets in, you may be able to provide the encouragement for them to keep going. On the face of it, these are simple common sense courtesies and good practice in teaching. But it is surprising how we can lose sight of these things in ODL contexts, as this learner 'Richard' describes:

> There was one academic I found particularly hard to deal with. He seemed like such an ogre – gruff, like I was intruding upon his time by phoning him. When I met him finally – it wasn't until I actually graduated – I discovered that he was really quite a warm and friendly guy. The image I had built up of him on the phone didn't correspond at all with who he actually was in person.

It may be that this teacher excelled in face-to-face contact with learners, but devalued his role as a distance educator. Or perhaps he hadn't thought through some of the basic issues about his role in distance teaching and dialogue. Phone communications, it seems, are simply not part of his teaching repertoire. Indeed, many would share his attitude that phones ringing in the workplace are an intrusion upon the 'real' business of the day.

Communication breakdown

What happens when contact breaks down entirely? Let's hear again from a distance student, 'Lizzie', aged 42, mother of three and part-time student:

> I was really concerned after I got my first assignment back. There were some things that I had... I didn't understand. It was going to have a big impact on my next assignment. I rang to speak to the unit co-ordinator but she wasn't there so I left a message. No reply. Left another message. Then there was a reply on my answering machine: 'Returned your call.' Rang again, left another message. No reply. After two weeks of this I was frantic... The assignment was looming, I was at a loss. Should I have a go at it? I started the assignment, tore it up. Rang again. No reply. I couldn't believe it – I only needed three or four minutes of her time! In the end I dropped out. I felt angry, and defeated and... I don't know... I drafted a letter of complaint to the university, but I never sent it.

Lizzie's account provides us with a sobering reminder of our responsibilities to maintain contact, and to offer more support and dialogue around assignments than that contained in the course materials. Studies of attrition rates in ODL commonly point to difficulties of this kind as a major factor in student drop-out. For example, Brown's (1996) study revealed that insufficient support from tutors and difficulties in contacting them were the two major contributing factors to discontinuance for 67.7 per cent of the sample. These should be compelling statistics for teachers who are content to leave distance students to 'go it alone' in the mistaken belief that they are prompting self-directed learning. As Lentell (1994: 50) reminds us, 'however splendid the printed texts, and however refined the quality measurement tools, it is the relationship between the tutor and the learner that determines success or failure'.

Encouraging self-management and self-direction

As we have discussed earlier, encouraging self-directed learning does not mean abandoning students to 'do their own thing'. Quite the contrary: skills in self-management and self-directedness in learning are usually acquired gradually and with ongoing support and encouragement by teachers through dialogue. For example, if learners are required to undertake a self-directed project or negotiate a learning contract, there will be a number of relatively complex issues with which they will grapple, including:

- reflecting on their learning needs in order to devise a substantial and meaningful activity relating to the programme's objectives;
- shaping the activity to an appropriate size and scale;
- defending or negotiating the proposal with a learning facilitator;
- managing and conducting the activity within a time-frame, including information retrieval, resource location, presentation of findings, etc;
- reflection upon outcomes, self-evaluation.

Given the array of challenges learners are presented with, it is important for teachers to be able to offer timely support, to be a sounding board for ideas, to make useful suggestions, and most importantly, to encourage less experienced learners to believe they can successfully tackle these kinds of assignments.

Developing communities of learners

Dialogue, of course, does not simply involve teacher–learner communications. In face-to-face settings some of the most important exchanges are between students – checking their understanding of an assignment, comparing approaches to an essay, exchanging tips on library resources, debriefing after an examination, and so on. How might this dialogue be made available to open and distance learners? In Part A of this book we referred to the notion of a community of learners in ODL, an ideal that has proved difficult to realize using traditional means. With the expansion of online learning, however, tremendous opportunities are becoming available to teachers and learners to foster peer relationships, team skills, collaboration, group problem solving and debate, as well as less formal or structured communications between students and their wider professional communities. Through online learning and assessment, we have the opportunity to further a culture of shared endeavour, critical and reflective thinking, and democratic and negotiated processes. Below we consider some of the pedagogical principles that could underpin the development of a community of learners.

1. Discussion

Opportunities for discussion have rapidly developed through the use of course discussion lists that encourage exchanges of both structured and unstructured kinds in relation to course content and assignments. Taken further, we find more ambitious activities such as debates, forums and virtual conferences. Klemm and Snell (1996) argue for the use computer conferencing to 'raise the intellectual level of group discourse by requiring student groups to produce tangible products, not just opinion comments'. Ideally, computer conferencing is well integrated into the subject, and will also be of greater purpose to students if it is assessed (Day, 1998). Ideally, the role of the teacher or moderator in online discussion is peripheral rather than central, and should aim at facilitating and supporting discussion between students, not directing it (Holt et al, 1998).

2. Reflection, peer and self-evaluation

Arguably, graduating students need the ability to reflect on events and actions, to evaluate the quality of their own work, and to make considered judgements of others' work. Traditionally, self- and peer assessment have not been practised widely in ODL, although online methods now make these activities more achievable. For some discipline areas, such as creative and visual arts, peer assessment is not only a necessary skill but is a positive enhancement in terms of motivation and a sense of community. Self-assessment is clearly a valuable life skill and is important in any discipline; it also tends to encourage learners to take greater responsibility for the quality of their work. Key issues in peer and self-assessment include ensuring the context is appropriate for this approach, the validity of students' judgements, shared understanding of assessment criteria and reliability. There are a number of sources such as Gibbs (1995) and Habeshaw et al (1993) that offer practical advice on facilitating peer and self-assessment.

3. Collaboration

Collaborative activity is only limited by your imagination and energy, extending from group projects, problem solving, shared decisions and solutions, to development of prototypes and model building. These kinds of activities are relatively new to ODL, as students have generally worked alone and produced individual assignments. Indeed, collaborative assessments may prove challenging to distance learners who prefer to work alone. They also provide challenges to traditional notions of 'openness', as students working collaboratively will have a number of additional time constraints within their groups. Yet the benefits of collaborative activities are substantial in terms of learners developing shared purposes, and are more likely to reflect real conditions in workplaces, where team skills such as negotiation, sharing knowledge, dealing with conflict and a broad repertoire of interpersonal skills are essential.

4. Intercultural dialogue

New opportunities for international dialogue and collaboration have also emerged from Internet technology (indeed, they were the driving force behind its inception). Students now have opportunities to learn directly about other cultures through shared learning tasks in such areas as politics, media and business (Alexander and McKenzie, 1998). Collaboration between students from far-flung institutions around the globe can considerably enrich the experience and broaden the contextual perspectives of each participant (Day, 1998). Learners will be challenged to develop skills in intercultural communication, to negotiate difference, and to confront cultural and racial stereotypes.

Mentoring

Apart from electronic networking, there are a number of other ways in which you can support the development of a community of learners. Students' workplaces and local communities are enormously rich sources of knowledge, experience and skills, and may offer excellent opportunities for dialogue and support. Learners should be encouraged to see their workplace as a resource, and to critically review theory in the light of workplace experience. There are a number of successful open and distance mentoring schemes that operate to flexibly meet the needs. The following two examples are currently in place at Southern Cross University, Australia.

Example 1. Student–student mentoring at a distance

In this scheme, experienced distance students volunteer their services as mentors to new distance learners. Mentors and mentees develop a supportive relationship and communicate with each other mostly via phone and e-mail. They are not necessarily from the same discipline area, as the principal goal of the mentoring activity is to familiarize new learners with being a distance learner, including time management, accessing resources, making contact with the university, developing self-confidence, understanding what is expected, and so forth. While supporting new learners, mentors also undertake study in mentoring theory and practice. This is an accredited unit that enables them to explore the role and reflect upon their developing expertise. Many mentors are aspiring human resource development professionals and can apply this expertise within their chosen career.

Example 2. Community and workplace mentoring

This scheme seeks to link distance learners with mentors in their own communities and workplaces, and is designed to:

- develop disciplinary skills in an appropriate and safe setting;
- assess learners' developing skills and competences;
- test and apply concepts in real-life settings;
- provide experience of the culture of learners' chosen disciplinary practice;
- create new forms of interaction and decrease the isolation of distance study.

The scheme has been operating in the discipline areas of clinical nursing, counselling, social welfare and acupuncture. Distance learners select expert mentors from their community or workplace to practise the required skills and abilities in a safe setting. Mentors provide on-the-spot feedback, document the learners' progress, and provide input to learners' formative and summative assessment. The mentor/mentee relationship is shaped considerably by learners themselves, and can be expanded to include study skills support, vocational experience and even future employment. One strength of this scheme is that it enables the university to offer programmes at a distance which otherwise could only be offered in face-to-face settings. It also provides access for part-time adult learners to programmes normally not available because of geographical, work or family constraints.

Conclusion

In this chapter we have made a number of suggestions for creating dialogue at a distance, and for the kinds of support that help learners to engage deeply with their assessments. Implicit in these suggestions is the idea that learning is a social activity, and that in ODL we need to think carefully about the opportunities for creating learning relationships that extend beyond the printed page. We ask you to think not only about the teacher–learner relationship, as important as that is. We also ask you to think about the possibilities of creating more expansive learning communities through which students find meaning and shape their own learning.

Chapter 9

Managing time

So far in this part of the book we have given you many prompts and suggestions for innovative ways to assess and support your open and distance learners. While we hope they are useful and timely suggestions, we also realize that your time is becoming increasingly limited. The phrase 'more with less' seems to capture the general tenor of training and higher education in most countries around the globe. Unless you are in the relatively luxurious position of setting up a new programme with adequate time and funds to realize your plans, then you are most probably working within an existing programme where redevelopment may occur sporadically and resistance to change may also be a significant factor among colleagues. If you are new to higher education or training, then you could be on a survival pathway, lurching from one course or semester to the next with little time to contemplate change. Questions raised in this chapter include:

- How do we reconceptualize and implement our assessment practices within the limited time available?
- How do we manage an assessment load including activities such as marking, learner support and facilitation of discussion?
- How can we support learners to manage their own time effectively?

Finding the time to make change

Although many of the suggestions in the earlier parts of this section are time-consuming to develop, they are designed to save you time in the longer term. For example, detailed marking criteria, use of marking sheets, and 'front-ending' your assessment tasks with detailed supporting information are all time-saving investments when it comes to student queries and problems during the course or semester. In many ways, a well-organized, detailed and transparent assessment scheme is infinitely easier to administer and support than one that is patched together with string and sticky tape. The latter variety tends to unravel at short notice, resulting in a sea of student inquiries, and requiring urgent circulars and amendments to be sent to students, blanket extensions granted as a result of errors or insufficient information, and so on. Those who have experienced this kind of crisis management of assessment know how stressful it is for teachers and learners alike.

More substantial changes to assessment schemes may require the collaboration of colleagues. This is particularly the case when you are looking at issues such as the assessment mix across a whole programme, policies regarding assessment load, or marking practices. In such instances it is advisable to recruit like-minded colleagues to form a discussion group or working party. This will help you pool a wide spectrum of ideas and will also help if you require support for reform in wider circles. Given time limitations and other constraining factors that may impede your progress, consider the following strategy:

1. *Prioritize* your proposed changes from the most to the least urgent. Some changes need to occur in tandem with others, whereas some can take place over a longer period.
2. *Support your argument* for proposed changes using examples or case studies from other institutions, with detailed reasons for change, proposed outcomes, and benefits for students and staff. There is a burgeoning body of literature on assessment in training and higher education from which you can draw.
3. *Pilot and monitor* the progress of changes you have made and their impact on learning. Gain feedback from learners. Reflect upon your own experiences. Compare notes with others involved in similar activities and learn from their experiences.
4. *Advocate* among colleagues for further or wider-ranging redevelopment as necessary, using evidence gathered, as above. Recruit support from other like-minded colleagues.

Managing an assessment load

It is vital that you can confidently manage and support your assessment schemes. It doesn't matter how innovative and relevant your assessments are, if you don't have sufficient time to support them well, they will probably attract negative responses from students. The key to effective management of your assessment load, as always, is planning. If you teach in more than one subject, try to avoid due dates for assignments falling at the same time. Do a semester or course plan, plotting key assignment dates, marking time-frames, optimal student consultation times, and key interactive times on discussion lists. There may be other important events, like meetings with other markers, student tutorials, residential schools, and so forth. If you can capture all your commitments on the one schedule, you are more likely to be able to diagnose problem areas in advance, to prepare for times when you are overburdened, or to justify your request for additional support.

Supporting learners to manage their time

Unlike their face-to-face counterparts, open and distance learners are not paced by scheduled weekly classes. With their study materials and assessments laid out before them, they are usually free to strategically pace themselves, within certain constraints such as semester or course lengths and assignment-due dates. For busy adult part-time learners, this is both one of the joys and the great challenges of open and distance learning. Learners can organize their study around other more pressing commitments in their lives, such as family, children, work, recreational and social commitments. They may work in bursts as time permits, and then put their books aside when it does not. The other side of this coin is the time and effort required to catch up when assignments are due. Sometimes learners feel they get too far behind and choose to discontinue.

There is no doubt that time management is one of the essential skills of being a successful open and distance learner. Although most busy adults will be reasonably adept at managing time within their lives, part-time study is a very taxing additional commitment. When commencing studies, the learning context and culture may be quite foreign to them, and they may not have previously formed successful study habits. Usually they are learnt the hard way, by trial and error. How can we help learners to develop vital time management skills? If we provide learners with detailed and well-communicated assessment tasks, which are closely aligned with subject objectives, content and learning activities, then this is a very good start. In addition, we need to support them to plan their available time in the light of assessment commitments, with the provision of sample study timetables, such as the one shown in Table 9.1.

Note we use the term 'sample' timetable, as clearly most open and distance learners' lives do not necessarily work quite this neatly. There will be weeks when learners may not be able to do any work at all, and other weeks where large strides are made. The primary purpose of sample timetables is to prompt learners to do their own planning, using the supplied timetable as a guide. It is particularly helpful for inexperienced students who are only beginning to learn how to manage their time effectively. The development of sample timetables is also an interesting and revealing exercise for teachers, as we are mapping out our expectations from a learners' perspective. If we have incorrectly paced our activities and assignments, or if we have overloaded students with work, it is most likely to be revealed here.

Table 9.1 *Sample study timetable*

Week	Activities	Due dates
1.	Scan through study materials. Study assessment requirements. Plan semester commitments	
2.	Work through Topic 1. Reflect on outcomes of Activity 1.4	Join discussion list. Discuss Activity 1.4
3.	Work through Topics 2 and 3. Begin literature search for Assignment 1	
4.	Complete Topic 4. Start drafting Assignment 1	Optional teleconference
5.	Complete work on Assignment 1	Assignment 1 due end week 5
6.	Commence Topic 5. Work on problem scenario	Join discussion list. Team problem solving
7.	Work through Topics 6 and 7	Submit team results to forum
8.	Work through Topic 8	
9.	Work through Topic 9	
10.	Complete Topic 9 and prepare for Assignment 2	
11.	Complete Topic 10, continue work on Assignment 2	
12.	Complete work on Assignment 2	Assignment 2 due end week 12

Chapter 10

Developing assessment policies

Most training and educational institutions have a raft of assessment policies dealing with all manner of issues such as conduct of examinations, marking and grading, provision for disabilities, special consideration, plagiarism, cheating, and so forth. Much assessment policy, such as appeals procedures, may exist at an institutional level, whereas other policies, such as the granting of extensions to assignments, may be left to the discretion of individual teachers or trainers. To what degree are these policies tailored for open and distance learning (ODL) contexts? How sympathetic are these policies to the ideals and philosophy that underpin open and student-centred learning? Open and distance assessment policy should be developed with more than a token understanding of the range of issues and concerns of part-time, adult learners. Policies reveal values – how we value student learning, the relative emphasis we place on formative and summative assessment, the degree to which we place students before institutional convenience, our preparedness to be flexible, and so on. This chapter briefly looks as some key assessment policies affecting open and distance learners.

Whole-of-course approach to assessment

What can you confidently say are the graduating qualities of your students? Although you might claim that much is taught to students, the assessment scheme in your course is the only solid evidence of the knowledge, abilities and attitudes your learners have acquired. We have already discussed the importance of a whole-of-course approach to assessment, to ensure that the key graduating qualities are consistently developed. In competence-based programmes, or vocational courses with direct industry links, assessments and broad learning outcomes are likely to be closely linked. However, in more general university courses where individual academic turf is often carefully guarded, the nature and worth of graduating qualities are very much more open to question. As we discussed, ODL has traditionally taken a relatively conservative assessment path, tending towards repetitive written assessments such as essays at the expense other forms of research, thinking and communication skills development. The worst case scenario is that learners have only acquired segmented pieces of knowledge and the limited range of abilities that have been easy to assess at a distance.

A whole-of-course approach to assessment assumes a high level of collegiality among teachers in a programme, a shared vision about the qualities of graduating learners, and a willingness to explore integrated assessment approaches and new assessment methods to achieve those aims. It also implies strong leadership and policy to support these aims, and to avoid the drift into separate islands of assessment activity.

Student appeal procedures

What appeal procedures are available to students who wish to query or appeal against their allocated grades? What opportunities exist for students to re-draft and re-submit assignments rather than fail a subject? Both these issues are critical in terms of open and student-centred learning, as they reflect attitudes about student achievement and also our willingness to interact and negotiate with students about assessment and grading issues. Indeed, these kinds of questions challenge our foundations of openness and our ability to relinquish some elements of our power and control over the assessment process.

Consider also how well the steps and processes of appeal are outlined to students. Is it a difficult process or one that is likely to be intimidating? And how do we respond to appeals lodged against our own marking? Are they a hassle or an affront, rather than a normal part of the assessment process? Are there various avenues of appeal? Is there appropriate mediation involved?

Appeal procedures are usually part of an institutional assessment policy, and may be beyond your immediate realm of influence, although you should be aware of the policy and ensure that it is well communicated to students. If you believe the policy to be inadequate or unfair, take it up with an appropriate senior academic member of staff.

Extensions to assignments and special consideration

What is your policy on granting extensions for assignments? The same principles that underscore your marking and grading activities should also govern your actions here: fairness and consistency. When considering your policy, you need to bear in mind that your students are adult learners with a range of other pressing work and family commitments. Clearly there are a range of unforeseen factors, such as illness, that may affect students' capacities to meet deadlines from time to time. Some teachers feel that assignment deadlines are more of a formality rather than a necessity in open learning, and that students should be granted extensions as a matter of course, without having to explain themselves. On the other hand, time management, as we have seen, is an important professional skill and is part of the discipline and rigour of academic study.

Your policy on extensions should take into account both sides of the issue, and should be sufficiently detailed that it can accommodate most incidents and requests. This eliminates unfairness in treatment that may arise due to factors such as the mood you're in when approached! Ideally you should have a high level of consistency with other colleagues in your programme. Share and discuss your policy with colleagues, as well as any particular instances that posed difficulties for you. Ensure that you make known to learners your policy on extensions at the commencement of study.

Marking practices

Some marking practices are sufficiently important in relation to ODL that they should be instituted as policy, in pursuit of quality management and student-centredness. Consider the following.

Marking turnaround times

As we have discussed, there is no absolute standard in relation to marking return times – it will vary according to factors such as the length of the subject, size of assessments, numbers of students, the medium used for submitting assessments, and so forth. However, it is important that you set a maximum time for return of assignments that is both realistic in terms of administrative and marker workload, and also sufficiently rapid to ensure that the valuable formative function of feedback from assessments is not lost to learners. If policy is developed with the involvement of stakeholders in this area, it may have a very welcome effect upon the clerical and administrative systems that handle the movement of assignments. Although this is rarely done, marking turnaround times should be published to students at the beginning of the course or semester so they can plan their assessment preparation times effectively.

Occasional double blind marking

Where multiple markers are working on the same assignments, occasional double blind marking is a good policy to promote consistency and reliability between markers. Although budgets will rarely extend to double marking as the norm, strategic double marking is often a necessity, particularly in large cohorts of students where drifts in standards are experienced. It also presents an excellent staff development opportunity for new markers to be inducted into the shared standards and values of the marking group.

Sex bias in marking

While many would not consider sex bias to be an issue in their marking, Bradley's (1993) UK research indicates that, irrespective of the sex of the marker, examiners tend to award higher or lower grades to men, and middling grades to women. These trends were not apparent when students' names were not identified. Habeshaw *et al* (1993) suggest a procedure of allocating numbers to all students, which then appear on students' assignments instead of names. Only when all results are concluded are the numbers translated back into names.

Plagiarism

Policy regarding plagiarism – the act of passing off another's work as one's own – is usually dealt with at an institutional level. It is generally regarded as a serious breach of academic principles and practice, and therefore an important policy for you to be aware of. In open and distance contexts, most learners are adults who are not interested in cheating or taking the work of another. Many technical breaches of the rules of plagiarism result from ignorance of the appropriate methods of citation. Ensure that methods of acknowledgement of others' work are clearly explained to learners, and that feedback that reinforces appropriate methods of citation is given wherever possible in assignments. This will be most important for newer students who are still grappling with these skills. Some new learners mistake normal academic discourse for plagiarism, and hence err on the side of caution by not referring to the work of others. Learners should be encouraged to distinguish clearly between the two, and be encouraged to draw upon and cite a wide range of sources without fear of penalty.

While we may never entirely eliminate plagiarism, strategies for minimizing it include:

- regular review and modification of assignment questions;
- publishing thorough explanations of plagiarism to students and detailed advice on referencing methods;
- a signed declaration by students on each submitted assessment, certifying the work to be their own, except where indicated. An example of this might read:

I certify that although I may have conferred with others in preparing for this assignment, and drawn upon a range of sources cited in this work, the content of this assignment is my original work.

Signed...

- a proactive student support and marking facility, which is alert to sudden shifts in performance of individual students, or suspicious similarities in work, with an accompanying range of appropriate counselling strategies.

Chapter 11

Evaluating your assessment practices

This chapter looks at the variety of ways in which you can explore the effectiveness and efficiency of your assessment practices. Evaluation is an activity with which you are undoubtedly engaged on an ongoing basis – assessment is but one of a series of issues that open and distance educators will wish to explore, including the quality of the learning experience, effectiveness of the course materials, student and administrative support, and teacher–learner interactions. Ideally, evaluation is planned from the very beginning, and is a regular activity that provokes thought and nourishes the teaching and learning environment, driven by questions such as what's happening and why. At its most basic level, it may take the form of reflective sessions with colleagues, where assessment experiences and observations are shared and problems are identified and discussed. More structured forms of evaluation include the collection and analysis of data from a variety of perspectives such as teachers, learners and administrators to develop a broad picture of a situation. In almost all instances the objective of evaluation is to create more effective and meaningful ways of doing things.

Evaluation in open and distance settings

Thorpe (1988) argues that while there are a range of commonalities between evaluation in conventional settings and those of open and distance learning (ODL), there are some important issues that set the latter apart. The similarities exist in both the processes (goal setting, design, data collection, analysis) and purposes (the quality of learning, effectiveness of materials and services, suitability of courses for learners' needs). Differences include the following:

- ODL tends to be less open to inspection compared to face-to-face settings, which can be observed and evaluated directly.
- There is more to evaluate, due to the team effort entailed in the development and provision of ODL. There is also a wider variety of options and pathways for open learners to go about their learning.
- There is a greater range of learners in terms of age, reasons for studying, employment circumstances, competing commitments, and so forth. Students have differing criteria for success, and this leads to more complex data regarding issues such as drop-out, course completion, and approaches to learning and assessment.
- ODL is still an innovatory approach to educational provision, particularly with respect to the use of new technologies. There is much that we still don't know about what we're doing or trying out.

Purposes of evaluating assessment

In assessment, the main objective of evaluation is to find out whether your assessment tasks are supporting appropriate kinds of learning. Under this broad objective, there are a number of things we could choose to look at, such as:

- The appropriateness of assessment items within a subject, including:
  - size,
  - frequency,
  - diversity,
  - alignment with objectives,
  - relationship to programme objectives as a whole,
  - validity,
  - authenticity.
- The response by students to assessment items:
  - How did learners perceive the tasks required of them?
  - Were they motivating, stimulating, inclusive, relevant, well explained?
  - Did they offer sufficient scope to demonstrate learning?
  - Did they allow students to apply learning meaningfully?
  - Were there any unintended side-effects from assessment schemes and accompanying support?
- The nature and quality of the feedback provided on assignments and its contribution to student learning:
  - Was the feedback timely, relevant, supportive, encouraging of dialogue, prompting further thought?
- The nature and quality of administrative and tutorial support:
  - Was the right kind of support available at the right time?

You will see from the above list that *learners' perceptions* are critical to our evaluation activities. Gone are the days when the terms 'evaluation' and 'assessment' were virtually synonymous, where the achievement of behavioural objectives was the measure of the success of a programme. Assessment results are useful to the degree that they provide a measure of learning outcomes, but they explain very little and lead to hasty assumptions about learners, such as 'low achievement' equals 'low ability' or 'poor motivation'.

More recent research into student learning has emphasized that the students' context and perceptions of assessment tasks significantly affect their approaches to learning (for example, Entwistle and Ramsden, 1983; Laurillard, 1979; Marton et al, 1984). How assessments are regarded and tackled, from learners' perspectives, provides us with stark evidence of the effectiveness of assessment schemes. If learners are persistently adopting surface or survival strategies to get through, if they are engaged substantially in rote learning for the purposes of feeding back content on cue, if they are experiencing consistent difficulties in reading the intention of tasks, or if they see no real value or reward in engaging deeply or meaningfully with issues, then clearly there is a problem with the assessment rather than the learners! Indeed there may be a number of issues to revisit in these instances, including a review of the programme objectives, workload, teaching and learning resources, tutorial support, and so on.

In recent years, evaluation activity has become closely linked with the quality assurance movement, and Morgan (1997) notes the tendency for evaluation in ODL to rest largely upon student satisfaction surveys. While there is an appealing simplicity to casting our students as consumers and seeking their approval of our educational 'products' by the use of rating scales, it only provides us with a small part of the picture regarding the nature of learning experiences and the qualities of graduating learners.

Types and methods of evaluation

There are commonly two types of evaluation – formative and summative:

- *Formative evaluation* includes all the ongoing evaluation activities that might answer questions such as: How are we doing? What do we need to change to make it better? It collects data that helps to make changes while the project is in progress, or before it has even commenced, such as a pilot.
- *Summative evaluation* collects data with the aim of summing up the effectiveness of a programme once it is complete. It will answer questions such as: Did we achieve our aims and objectives? Was it worth doing? If we do it again, what do we need to change?

Evaluations are often also referred to by the methods used, such as quantitative and qualitative methods:

- *Quantitative evaluation* is more statistical, involving the collection of 'hard' data like facts and figures through surveys and questionnaires, analysis of results, retention rates, applications, etc.

- *Qualitative evaluation* will rely more on words than figures, and use methods like interviewing, reflection and discussion to piece together a picture of what is going on.

Rowntree (1992) discusses a range of methods of collecting data for the purposes of evaluation, including review of programme documentation, review of relevant literature and case studies, review of records and statistics, review of assessment results, observations, conversations, interviews, discussion groups, questionnaires, diaries or learning logs, and learners' action plans. Morgan (1997) similarly argues for an approach to evaluation that is pluralistic, with the use of mixed methodologies and a critically reflective interpretation of data to highlight tensions and ambiguity that are not revealed in simple survey methods. As practitioners, we are informally collecting 'data' all the time to evaluate our practice – comments and anecdotes from learners and colleagues, as well as our own observations and reflections. These all contribute towards a sense of 'what's happening and how can I make it better'.

It is not intended to delve too deeply into evaluation here, as there are many good resources available to open and distance educators. As we discussed earlier, your efforts in evaluating assessment tasks will usually go hand in hand with broader evaluative activities regarding the subject and programme as a whole. Some useful and thought-provoking suggestions include:

1. Mary Thorpe's 1988 book, *Evaluating Open and Distance Learning*. This is a very practical book with a strong practitioner focus, which steps through the issues and processes of evaluation, including sample case studies.
2. Derek Rowntree's 1992 work, *Exploring Open and Distance Learning*. Chapter 7 contains a broad overview of open and distance evaluation, including issues, purposes and methods.
3. Alistair Morgan's 1990 chapter, 'Whatever happened to the silent scientific revolution? Research, theory and practice in distance education' in *Research in Distance Education 1*, and his subsequent 1997 chapter, 'Still seeking the silent revolution? Research, theory and practice in open and distance education', in *Research in Distance Education 4*. Morgan argues for a more critical approach to evaluation of open learning programmes, including the politics and cultures of organizations and their impact upon evaluation and change.

Conclusion

We hope that this part of the book has prompted many ideas to enrich your assessment practice. As discussed in the introduction, we have sought to avoid replication of material from other books on assessment, although in many instances it has been necessary to broadly summarize the major issues and debates in the field. Where possible, we've referred you on to the wealth of literature about assessment in conventional education, which will provide more detailed coverage of issues and processes.

Yet we're aware that if you are new to assessment, you may still require support in activities such as devising and communicating assessment tasks, and marking and grading students' work. These are, after all, relatively complex and sensitive tasks. Don't forget the wealth of experience that resides with colleagues in your department or institution. You could consider negotiating a mentorship with an experienced colleague with whom you have a rapport. Your mentor could act as a sounding board for your assessment plans and ideas, and also support your developing skills as a marker with some double blind marking and discussions about grading, standards, interpretation of criteria, and so forth. Many teachers have acquired these abilities through years of trial and error, but others rarely draw upon their expertise. It is an appropriate acknowledgement of your mentor's expertise and a wonderful opportunity for you to gain confidence and experience in a 'safe' setting.

PART C
Case studies

Introduction

In this final section we present a collection of short case studies that illustrate assessment from many angles. Our overall aim is to provide a series of easy to read stories about how assessment is managed in a broad range of contexts. Our primary concern has been to present a broad sample of innovative, contemporary practice, although these case studies are by no means the 'last word' in assessment. Indeed, there are both strengths and weaknesses identified in most cases, and contributors were at pains to stress that they considered their assessment activities to be 'work in progress'. We encourage you to dip into this selection and browse the contents of these case studies over and over again, while also considering how they may be applied to your own situation and student groups.

Some of the case studies describe whole programmes of study and the assessment strategies that have been developed to support them. Others describe subject-based (or unit-based) assessments, while some describe only a portion of a much larger assessment task. We have given a brief indication of the relative weighting of each example within its own context.

In order to also provide a useful resource for assessment practitioners we have structured the case study examples to make explicit the relationship of assessment to curriculum design and workplace or organizational contexts. While there are only a couple of examples from the industry sector included here, it is clear from the case study table (Table C.1) that many academics are now encouraging and supporting students to ground their responses to assessment tasks in authentic practices with immediate relevance to themselves.

Gathering the case studies

The cases were gathered between March 1998 and April 1999 by a number of means. Visits to several Australian and New Zealand universities provided some good leads initially, and e-mail requests to four discussion lists (DEOS-L, WWWDEV, ITFORUM and ISL-mailbase) yielded the majority of overseas examples. The list of contributing countries includes the UK, the Netherlands, South Africa, New Zealand, Canada and Australia.

Although examples were sought from the USA, none were finally forthcoming that represented good open and distance practice as we have conceptualized it in this book. Assessment in open and distance education in the USA still seems to rely heavily on essays and examinations. Where innovations are evident, it is usually in the use of online technologies to provide quizzes, e-mail submission of assignments or as a supplement to classroom activities.

The emerging use of online technologies for teaching and assessment was an added factor in our hunt for cases. We started with the aim of finding innovations in teaching, learning and assessment in open and distance education that were not solely dependent on online technologies for their success. Several examples showcase creative and innovative uses of older technologies such as audio, video, teleconferences and television programmes.

The possibilities for blurring the distinctions between modes of study through the use of computer mediated means has impacted upon our selection. Therefore, approximately half of the case studies show a purposeful use of computer mediated communications and learning activities in dual-mode delivery, and in this way our collection reflects the emerging use of online technologies in face-to-face as well as distance teaching.

No doubt there are many other (and better) examples of the assessment practices to be found in the open and distance education field. Please feel free to contact us if you have assessment innovations that would be appropriate to showcase in future editions of this book.

Organization of case studies

For our organizing structure, we have chosen to use the eight categories of learning outcomes used by Nightingale *et al* (1996) in their collection of case studies, *Assessing Learning in Universities*:

1. Thinking critically and making judgements.
2. Solving problems and developing plans.
3. Performing procedures and demonstrating techniques.
4. Managing and developing oneself.
5. Accessing and managing information.
6. Demonstrating knowledge and understanding.
7. Designing, creating, performing.
8. Communicating.

This structure was chosen in preference to the more usual 'assessment methods' categorization of case studies as it highlights the close connection between assessment, learning and the development of generic, transferable skills and abilities. Although Nightingale *et al* (1996) were illustrating on-campus assessment procedures, the same set of outcomes seemed to comprehensively take account of most if not all possible areas for learning by open and distance mode. Table C.1 summarizes the case studies and features.

We hope these case studies will prompt considerable reflection on the kinds of abilities you wish to engender in your learners, and some innovative ways of achieving your assessment goals, as well as those of your learners.

Table C.1 *Summary features of case studies*

No.	Title of case study	Discipline area	Attend/ support	Online	Sector based	Postgrad
1.1	Think-aloud protocols	Library Education			•	
1.2	Discussion among learners	Social Science		•	•	
1.3	Diary to the teacher	Education		•	•	•
1.4	Analytical thinking	Religious Studies				
2.1	Collaborative decision making and clinical problem solving	Nursing		•	•	
2.2	Creative problem solving and constructive autonomy	Business			•	•
2.3	Integrated planning project	Geography	2 day		•	
2.4	Developing consulting skills	Business		•	•	•
3.1	Developing expertise in neonatal resuscitation	Nursing			•	•
3.2	Dissecting rats and providing evidence	Biology			•	
3.3	Developing competences in writing research proposals	Business	1 day	•		
4.1	Contract for personal change	Rural management	3 teleconfs			
4.2	Participation in open learning	Education	1 teleconf	•	•	
4.3	Becoming an OZKidsConnect volunteer	Library Education		•	•	•
4.4	Whole-of-course portfolio	Education		•		•
5.1	Delivering a scientific research paper to an audience of peers	Natural Resource Science	3 day			
5.2	Sharing development and discussion of case study method	Public Health		•	•	•
5.3	Presenting an exhibit at an arts conference	Teacher Education	2 day		•	•

No.	Title of case study	Discipline area	Attend/ support	Online	Sector based	Postgrad
5.4	Writing a proposal, researching and reporting findings	Anthropology			•	
6.1	Testing knowledge using online multiple choice quizzes	Economics		•		
6.2	Reasoning and logic	Philosophy		•		
6.3	Simultaneous off- and on-campus multiple choice tests	Business and Law		•		
6.4	Mathematics self-assessment on CD ROM	Mathematics				
7.1	Designing online training	Professional Development		•	•	
7.2	Video report of artistic development in ceramics	Visual Arts	Interview			•
7.3	Conference and Web site for a science community	Agriculture	1 day	•		
7.4	Creating and appreciating photographic expression	Visual Arts				
8.1	Oral communication and audiotape interview	Agriculture	1 day opt			
8.2	Computer conferencing	Education		•		•
8.3	International debate	Business		•		
8.4	Online collaboration	Psychology		•		•

1. Thinking critically and making judgements

The ability to think critically is a central goal of university education and our capacity to develop this ability through traditional distance education has been relatively straightforward. Through essays, reports and journals students have been able to demonstrate their ability to plan, research, develop and communicate a sustained and supported argument or belief. However, with the creative use of media including the rapid communication of networked computers, the higher order skills of reflection, analysis and critique can be supported more effectively through interaction and dialogue.

The four case studies in this selection each illustrate the incremental process of personal and professional development. Although only two of the cases (1.2 and 1.3) use e-mail to support the learning process, the other two are also concerned with students' learning processes, though in contrasting ways. The first case study describes a unit designed to challenge students from the start and to document their own development process. The second case provides a community of learners with opportunities for critical dialogue and discussion on assigned topics. The third illustrates a developmental conversation with a teacher and the fourth develops thinking skills through intensive feedback from the teacher.

Norris and Ennis (cited in Nightingale *et al*, 1996) identify four elements of critical thinking:

1. reasonable thinking, which relies on sound evidence and leads generally to the best conclusions or judgements;
2. reflective thinking, which reflects on the reasonableness of one's own and others' arguments;
3. focused thinking, which is purposeful and consciously directed towards an end goal;
4. decision orientation, which is about making judgements based on the weight of evidence.

They also point to certain important dispositions present in effective critical thinking, such as a commitment to open-mindedness, and a willingness to be well informed, to actively seek divergent views, and to remain open to a range of possible outcomes.

Issues in regard to development of critical thinking include the question of discipline-specific applications. Is critical thinking necessarily discipline-specific? Can, for example, a school teacher or theologian, librarian or adult educator all question their practice in the same way? Do people of different backgrounds demonstrate critical thinking in the same way? Is it culturally influenced? Have we framed our assessment task to inadvertently make judgements and test ideologies rather than critical thinking?

1.1 THINK-ALOUD PROTOCOLS

Case study from Education (postgraduate)

James Henri, Charles Sturt University, Australia

The following case study is an edited version of the written materials James Henri provided, together with additional comments he made after seeing the first draft and subsequent e-mail exchanges.

The focus of assessment in this unit is on the process of self-assessment through reflection. The technique of think-aloud-protocols used in this example requires postgraduate education students to talk about their thinking. If students can explain their decisions as they are writing and editing their work, then their journey is revealed to the assessor. This metacognitive activity is valued for its honesty and depth of reflection. Think-aloud-protocols are also used in qualitative research to collect on-the-spot responses from participants (Lockwood, 1997).

Context

Students are practising teachers (class or teacher librarians) and study by distance education. Electronic supports such as listserv and forum are an integral component of the subject.

The subject ETL401 Teacher Librarianship is a compulsory subject in Master of Education (Teacher Librarianship)/Master of Applied Science (Teacher Librarianship). The broad aim of the subject is to provide:

- an overview of the role of the teacher librarian;
- detailed coverage of the curricular role of the teacher librarian with special attention given to the pursuit of information literacy.

Abilities being assessed

The emphasis of the assessment in this example is for postgraduate students to enhance their teaching practice by immersion in a metacognitive environment. The focus of assessment in this unit is on personal understanding through self-reflection. The relative weighting of tasks – 70 per cent on process and 30 per cent on product – reflects this. The assumption is that students concentrate on those tasks that are rewarded by the assessment grade. By rewarding the reflective process, it is expected that students will place a high value on how they are learning. Since teacher librarians have a central role in sculpting an information-literate school community, it is essential that they go beyond knowing about information literacy to personal understanding of the process.

Audiotapes of students' think-aloud critiques of their own written product, the 3,000-word essay, form a pivotal and highly experimental component of the assessment.

Assessment task

Assignment 1

Not graded. Due in week five of the session. Students provide an initial profile of themselves (detailed questionnaire) together with a self-efficacy measure (22 information literacy strategies in a 'can-do' style checklist and confidence rating 1–10).

Assignment 2

Forms 100 per cent of grade. Due in the penultimate week of the session.

Part A (Product). Essay, minimum 3,000 words (30 per cent) – a negotiated topic that allows discussion of central issues in teacher librarianship and includes research of literature, interaction with colleagues, other professionals, other students and staff, and students' own experience.

The stimulus for this essay is a scholarly paper that is included in the students' study materials. The question that prompts the essay topic is dense and requires the student to form a focus from a general area. Focus formulation is regarded as a critical skill within the information literacy rubric.

Part B (Process). Evidence of learning, variable in length (70 per cent) – this part of assessment consists of five components:

1. The 'can-do' checklist (submitted for Assignment 1 and revisited for Assignment 2).
2. A diary of actions, decisions and procedures undertaken with respect to the product up to writing of the final draft. Students are encouraged to note feelings, confidence and attitudes about tasks and progress, and not to self-censor. A listserv and forum are available for students with network access.
3. Drafts of the paper (noting draft number) are to be submitted for final presentation.
4. An audiotape recording of students' thoughts in the process of constructing the final draft, eg reasons for rejection or inclusion of information, decisions to use quotations or write in own words, structure of argument, thoughts on quality, satisfaction.
5. A completed research continuum based on how much actual working time each stage of the process (outlined below) has taken.

Continuum: A————————————————————————Z

Point A represents the point at which students read the assessment task and point Z represents the point at which students submit the task.

Students are asked to place on the continuum any or all of the following elements that have occurred while undertaking the research task. Add or omit elements as appropriate:

- Planning.
- Collecting information.
- Deciding which information to use.
- Organizing the information.
- Starting to write first draft.
- Starting to write final draft.
- Others (please specify).

Finally, students are asked to note on a scale of 1 (low) to 10 (high) their level of concern/confusion/stress along the continuum.

Marking

In this qualitative approach to assessment, the assessor is looking at the big picture, taking the whole assessment experience into account and not just adding up scores on individual pieces. One looks for evidence of learning, of the 'ah ha' experience, of willingness to ponder and reflect. Evidence of authentic writing is also sought.

The process of assessment is individual – a journey revealed rather than simply the arrival at a destination. Students who are able to relate their three learning domains (actions/thoughts/feelings) will do better than students who are unable to go beyond their actions.

Both the quality and quantity of diary entries are considered. A student who has made few entries is considered to have not seen the value in the process. Students who make the link between their learning and their working environment demonstrate that they are learning and are prepared to test their theory in practice. For example some students have set think-aloud-protocols as assignments with their own students. Others have begun to use diaries and shown the value of this by reading their own entries out to their student groups.

Strengths

Product

Students are able to mould the question and to form their own focus. The question is authentic and therefore cut-and-paste answers are impossible. In addition, the question requires the students to draw links between theory and their own experience and current practice. They are given the entire session to produce the task. This means that the product can be expected to be of a high quality and each student is able to negotiate an appropriate balance between study, work and living.

Process

Product-based assessment in a distance environment is dangerous. It is impossible to know what the student has learnt or in fact whether the student has undertaken the assessment task or whether someone else may have produced the work.

The combination of qualitative tools that are used place the focus on the learner rather than on the product of learning. The assessment task assesses learning, not just learning outcomes. The tools promote critical reflection and self-evaluation in both cognitive and affective domains.

The use of a diary provides continuity for students and is a good way to ensure the authenticity of students' submissions. The tools (other than the think-aloud-protocol) enable the students to understand information literacy through personal experience. In fact, each student is required to plot his or her individual information-processing model. The think-aloud-protocol is employed to force students to reflect upon their own personal mental model. This in part creates student awareness of the importance of a metacognitive environment.

The range of tools provide alternatives for the full range of learning styles and multiple intelligences. Experience has shown that students do learn through these techniques. Students become more experimental in their own teaching environments and are much more understanding of their students' journeys. Not surprisingly their essays are better for it. Many papers have been of publishable standard.

Challenges

Some students who have spent their lives in a product-dominated assessment environment find the emphasis on process rather daunting. This is especially true for those who do not maintain personal diaries.

Most students found the think-aloud-protocols a challenge and some see the process as an intrusion into their private worlds. However, there is overwhelming agreement from students that the tool achieves its purpose. Some students argue that a single assessment task prevents formative feedback. This limitation can be addressed by asking students to submit diary entries every few weeks.

The major challenge is the assessment workload, which is very heavy for the marker. This is especially true for the think-aloud-protocols. (It should be noted, however, that they provide a stimulating alternative to drive-time music.) At least one student has claimed that the allocation of 70 per cent to process is a con – that the assessor must pass or fail students on the basis of the 30 per cent essay. This is not the case, although assessing qualitative assessment tasks is difficult for the novice marker. In this context, debates about criterion referencing versus peer referencing are also interesting. Evidence of learning, and signs that the student has gained a personal understanding of key concepts is critical; however, this evidence is very idiosyncratic and certainly not absolute.

1.2 DISCUSSION AMONG LEARNERS

Case study from Social and Workplace Development (postgraduate)

Lee Dunn, Southern Cross University, Australia

The following case study is an edited version of the written materials Lee Dunn provided, together with additional comments she made after seeing the first draft.

Reflection on practice and reflective discussion are not only fundamental skills in most practice-based tertiary programmes, but are also effective strategies for supporting deep approaches to learning. With the benefit of computer mediated communication, reflective group discussion can now be an integral component of off-campus study and can readily enhance workplace-based projects and independent learning.

The following example illustrates methods employed to support development of critical thinking in an online programme for the vocational education context. To enrich the process of critical thinking, a series of postings to a discussion list of student peers is required. These contributions are graded according to predetermined criteria.

Context

This programme offers a postgraduate qualification for teachers and trainers working as vocational education and training (VET) practitioners with adult and adolescent students or trainees. It is expected that students are concurrently in a vocational education or training role and therefore the degree is taken part-time and in distance mode.

The unit, Teaching for Diversity, requires students to apply theories of learning to their own VET workplace by designing and implementing vocational education or training methods that are inclusive of groups of students who have a variety of learning needs.

Students may choose to be assessed by contributing to an Internet discussion that involves a number of original contributions at set times during the semester as well as comments on the contributions of at least one other student who has also contributed to the Internet group discussion.

Abilities being assessed

The Internet option provides students with the opportunity to reflect upon the application of theory to practice. They are encouraged to maintain their focus on the unit's learning objectives as they make their own contributions and examine the views of their co-learners in the group discussions. Set readings are supplemented by relevant Internet resources.

Abilities being assessed include learners' capacity to:

- analyse the diversity of VET clients, their training goals, cultural backgrounds and perceptions of the learning process;
- incorporate an understanding of their legal rights, responsibilities and obligations into their interactions with VET clients;
- design and implement a broad range of relevant inclusive methods into VET programmes.

Assessment tasks

Each of the two assignments for the unit is designed to allow for the development of critical thinking as students discuss set readings and the activities that they and their co-learners undertake in their VET workplaces.

Each assignment is in three parts, each part taking place over the course of a particular week. The Internet discussion is asynchronous to enable students to contribute at any time during the particular week, and also to allow time for study and reflection on their own work and that of co-learners.

Assignment 1

This assignment addresses learning objectives 1 and 2. Students first identify their place of work and its context, then conduct a survey to identify and analyse the range of student or trainee diversity and their own rights and responsibilities towards students and trainees.

The final part of the assignment is a synthesis of their findings from readings and the workplace survey. They also respond to their co-learners' contributions to the discussions at each stage of the assignment.

Assignment 2

This assignment addresses learning objective 3 and the Internet option is again in three parts. In the first part students write a critical appraisal of their current training methods in the light of their reading. In the second part of the assignment they provide a rationale for their redesign approach. In part three, having piloted their new training methods, students post a contribution to the discussion list evaluating the effectiveness of their practical application of inclusive methods. Once again they discuss co-learners' postings as an integral part of the assignment.

Marking

The assessment criteria implicit in each of the learning objectives are discussed and clarified online early in the semester. Students receive grades for their overall contribution to discussion in each three-part assignment based on how well the learning objectives were met.

Strengths and limitations

Strengths

These include a high level of motivation among those who take the Internet assessment option. Students valued the opportunity to submit their assignments in smaller parts and learnt through having access to the views and experiences of their peers. Each assignment is both summative and formative, with the formative aspects being evident as the reflective discussions developed at each stage of the assessment process. Students appeared to gain insight through their interaction with their peers and by considering how their co-learners approached the application of theory to practice.

A particular strength of this form of assessment is that through the ongoing discussion, students can demonstrate the development of critical thinking, which, in this case, is an important skill incorporating 'understanding', 'analysis' and forming a rationale for 'design' of learning methods.

Limitations

These include the workload for academics. Students generally seem to demand a higher level of response from lecturers when studying online and in this case their postings are being assessed, so anxiety and the demand for immediate feedback has increased. Students find it hard to keep to the word limits for the individual parts of each assignment, and their comments on each other's postings to the discussion list, while relevant to the learning objectives, add to the marking workload.

Students raised another possible limitation, querying the reliability of results as this unit is also taken by students who study at a distance and send assignments by mail without the kind of feedback gained by the 'Internet students'. However, assessment was similar and aligned to the learning objectives for both groups, and it did not seem that the 'Internet group' gained higher grades than the 'distant group'.

1.3 DIARY TO THE TEACHER

Case study from Education (postgraduate)

John Garner, University of New England, Australia

The following case study is an edited version of the written materials John Garner provided, together with additional comments he made after seeing the first draft.

For qualifying teachers, the process of learning to teach involves the development of several skills. One core skill is that of critical reflection – the ability to reflect and critique one's own classroom experiences, decisions and actions. Students in this unit develop these higher skills of reflection on theory and practice, along with techniques for classroom teaching. They are challenged to actively adapt their style to suit different pupils and different circumstances.

In this example the identification and development of a student's own style of teaching is developed through an interactive conversation with the teacher based on a journal of reflection and critique. Teachers of this unit support students in a one-to-one process of identifying their own theories in action and those theories that have immediate implications for their practice. The reflective process is conducted in a computer mediated conversation through repeated submissions of students' journals. A range of theoretical frameworks is explored as deemed necessary by students and the dialogue requires reference to literature and theory.

Context

The unit, Introduction to Learning and Teaching, is a core unit in the Graduate Diploma in Education and provides a knowledge base of generic teaching and learning skills. It also seeks to support the higher order skill of critical reflection.

The reflective practice framework underpinning this unit is based upon three principal areas of knowledge – pedagogical knowledge, knowledge of learners, and pedagogical content knowledge. These areas as defined by Shulman (1987) represent an analytical approach to examining the practices of teaching. Since the teacher–student dialogue is in a reflective and analytical style, students are also engaged at a metacognitive level.

Abilities being assessed

At the completion of this unit students should be able to:

- articulate the relationships between learning experiences and learning outcomes;
- formulate rationales for desirable learning outcomes, ie justify sets of learning objectives in terms of a 'philosophy of teaching';
- integrate new knowledge into existing schema;
- design learning experiences based on knowledge constructed through the integration of new knowledge into existing schema.

An explanation is given on how to take an active approach to learning by interrogating and interacting with the material in the series of 10 resource booklets provided.

Assessment tasks

Students are required to keep a 'reflective journal' in which they write:

- a record of their understanding of, and response to, the text material provided;
- a statement of the implications for practice of the outcomes of the previous step;
- any other comments, ideas, critiques, that they feel help them to develop a personal perspective on the teaching/learning process.

This journal is submitted on five occasions after pre-set amounts of unit material have been covered. Submission may be either by post or e-mail. Response to the content is best seen as the development of a conversation between reader and writer, ie marker comment endeavours to correct any instances of gross misunderstanding of the text material, but the main purpose of the comment is to help students develop their own understandings and philosophies. Encouragement is the principal function of the response rather than correction.

Marking

The programme of self-development that students undertake in this unit of study has led to the adoption of an ungraded assessment approach. The unit is ungraded in the sense that journals are deemed to either satisfy requirements or to fail to do so.

The criteria for satisfying requirements are that the student entered seriously into the process of developing a 'philosophy of teaching' and made the required number of journal submissions.

Strengths and limitations

Strengths

The main strength of the assessment procedure is that it explicitly denies that there is a correct view and that the student's task is to discover and express that view. Since journal comment is in the nature of a discussion – not an evaluation – a majority of students come to see themselves as makers rather than takers of meaning. Many students comment that this is one of very few university units in which they feel free to develop their own opinions in a supportive climate.

Limitations

The main weakness is that the feedback practices are extremely time-consuming since the 'development of conversations' requires a high level of involvement with the content of the student writing.

1.4 ANALYTICAL THINKING

Case study from Religious Studies

Peter Donovan, Massey University, New Zealand

The following case study is an edited version of the written materials Peter Donovan provided, together with additional comments he made after seeing the first draft.

Much of the rhetoric of higher education and its philosophy assume students have an understanding of the skills required in the practices of critical thinking and analysis of data. However, few courses devote time to specifically address the mastery of these skills and rather assume the practice of learning itself will inform students of such higher order skills.

This example demonstrates that in order to master the precise skills of analytical thinking, students can be given focused feedback on their efforts. Here students are given three minor practice writing tasks using a reflective approach. Early and comprehensive feedback is provided with an emphasis on formative support via the rapid turnaround of written work.

Context

The Religious Studies Programme, in the School of History, Philosophy and Politics, offers a major within the BA degree. Students are introduced to world religions, and topics studied include Hinduism, Buddhism and Pacific Primal religions, Judaism, Christianity and Islam.

These topics are particularly popular with students entering tertiary studies for the first time through distance learning. Teaching and assessment strategies are chosen that assist in developing early confidence with analytical and interpretative methods.

Abilities being assessed

At the completion of this unit students should be able to demonstrate:

- early 'attack' on a written work project;
- close reading of a small piece of key text;

- analysis and interpretation under suggested types/categories;
- effective summarizing and expressing of results.

Assessment tasks

The assessment process comprises three short exercises (10 per cent each) and a final examination (70 per cent).

The first exercise is vital and will be the focus here. It falls due in the third week of study and requires no reading beyond a one-page extract from sacred scripture, myth, or a description of ritual chosen for its intrinsic interest.

A method of analysis and interpretation of the given extract, to be attempted in the first exercise, is explained as a skill to be acquired for continued use in the later exercises and the examination. For most this is a new procedure, unlike that used in essays or other research projects they may have done elsewhere.

Students thus have an early and manageable new task for which they are rewarded marks towards their total grade, and clear comments reinforcing good work and coaching for improvements. Individualized feedback on exercises is welcomed by students and has proved more effective than 'model answers' in raising performance levels throughout the course.

The exercises themselves may be done successfully in a variety of ways since there is no one 'right answer'. The main objective is to have basic analytical and interpretative methods adopted by students and used confidently across the range of topics they will encounter in their further study of religions.

Marking

Grades for exercises indicate achievement levels within the class and show individual progress through the three exercises. In order to provide some norm for multiple markers, a 'key points' sheet is used and a copy returned with the students' own exercises. Marks from exercises accumulate towards a 30 per cent share of the overall grade.

Strengths and limitations

Strengths

A major strength is the early 'bonding' of students to the course. (Research has shown higher retention levels in courses with early assessment and feedback.)

Generous feedback provided by markers provides individual tuition, which is especially valuable given the wide range of abilities and backgrounds of distance learners. The skills taught and assessed in the first exercise are basic academic tools, improved in the further written work, and readily adapted for use in other courses.

Limitations

The goal of providing generous feedback on exercises fits uneasily with an (otherwise admirable) institutional policy of ensuring rapid turnover in the marking of written work. Assessment done thoroughly under strict time constraints is labour-intensive and demanding.

Students also find the exercises labour-intensive, even though there is little wider reading involved. They have to learn a new skill and apply it at the same time. There have been requests for a higher proportion of assessment marks to be given for exercises, with a corresponding reduction in the examination. This has been re-sisted so far, as it is believed the present balance between ongoing assessment and final examination best reflects the course content as a whole.

2. Solving problems and developing plans

The success and future careers of many contemporary learners will rest on their abilities in planning and problem solving within their discipline area. Problems can be divided as follows:

- *Defined problems* – all the information needed to solve the problem is available and known to the student. Algorithms (step-by-step procedures) are available to guarantee arrival at the solution if correctly applied. These problems are more likely to be found in competence-based programmes.
- *'Ill-defined' problems* are more complex ('real-life') problems often without criteria for determining when the problem is solved or without all the information needed. There may be no one 'correct' solution. Heuristics (inductive reasoning from past experience of similar problems) is often used. This kind of complex problem solving is more appropriate for education in the professions.

We need to think through carefully what it means to be a problem solver in our own disciplines, ensure that students' abilities are supported by the teaching methods employed, and that this is all reflected in the way we assess. Steps often cited in problem solving (Hayes, cited in Nightingale *et al*, 1996) include:

1. diagnosing the problem;
2. explaining the problem;
3. devising a plan;
4. carrying out the plan;
5. evaluating the outcome;
6. consolidating learning.

Examples of useful marking criteria for ill-defined problem solving (Nightingale *et al*, 1996) include:

- identifies indicators that the problem exists;
- identifies further information needed to better understand the problem;
- demonstrates understanding of knowledge concepts underpinning the problem;
- uses knowledge to:
  - generate ideas;
  - pose alternative workable solutions or improvements to the problem;
- justifies choice of a plan of action (including moral and ethical dimensions);
- carries out the plan;
- evaluates the success or otherwise of the plan;
- evaluates the problem solving strategy used;
- reflects on own learning.

The four case studies in this chapter each illustrate the features of collaboration in or about workplace contexts. The use of real-life problem scenarios in all four cases has been approached in quite different ways. The first requires nurse learners to work collaboratively to solve the nursing problems presented. The other three examples require learners to be located in the workplace providing either advice or a solution of the identified problem.

As we see, problem solving needs to be located firmly in a disciplinary context, and assessors should be aware of the novice–expert continuum in their own field (eg Benner, 1984) in order to clearly identify the standard of problem solving expected. The power of real-life scenarios is considerable and can be enhanced by the processes of metacognition, whereby students are encouraged to be aware of their own thinking as they tackle problems.

2.1 COLLABORATIVE DECISION MAKING AND CLINICAL PROBLEM SOLVING

Case study from Nursing

Mary Oliver, University of Southern Queensland, Australia

The following case study is an edited version of the written materials Mary Oliver provided, together with additional comments she made after seeing the first draft.

Traditionally, nurses have been disenfranchised within their profession. As student nurses in distance education, they have experienced isolation and lacked skills in networking. To some, studying nursing online would seem an impossibility. This example shows that making nursing decisions and solving problems through peer discussion and collaborative case review using computer mediated communication is not only possible, but also highly effective in supporting learning.

'Trends and Issues in Nursing' is conducted entirely as an online classroom with guest lecturers joining in discussion and introducing the case studies. The case studies form the focus each week as students consider nursing with respect to the key domains of law, ethics and practice. Collaborative problem solving is the basis for each of the three assessments. This is an empowering activity because for much of the time students learn from each other and see the value in sharing information. Tutors take on the role of facilitator and learners set the pace for their own learning.

Due to the large number of students who take this unit, discussion groups usually contain approximately 25–30 students in each group. The emphasis is on developing lifelong skills and to this end students are rewarded in many ways for their collaboration. Collaboration is also essential for a successful partnership with other healthcare workers upon entering the workforce.

Context

This is a core unit in the Professional Issues strand of the Bachelor of Nursing curriculum and students enrol in this unit during the final semester of their course. The healthcare environment has become increasingly complex, evidenced by expanded technology, decreased length of hospital stay, increased patient acuity and reimbursement practices. Correspondingly, the nurse's role is expanding proportionately and with it the complexities of decision making concerning patients' health outcomes. This unit is about decision making, concerning legal, ethical and practice issues governing nursing.

The emphasis in this unit is on learning (as opposed to teaching) and the focus is on coaching students in solving clinical problems through the use of authentic case studies with complex problems. The rationale for this approach is that nursing graduates who enter the workforce are not finished products – although they are able to take on a caseload of six or more patients they are unable to anticipate patient problems with multiple foci. Nurse-learners gain such knowledge from situated learning and experience. The authentic case studies in legal, ethical and practice areas in nursing can be used to successfully bridge the gap between theory and practice for novices.

Abilities being assessed

Abilities being assessed in this unit are:

- critically reading, writing and evaluating peer performance;
- clinical problem solving and developing action plans;
- accessing and managing information;
- collaboration.

Assessment tasks

There are three major pieces of assessment – one for each module: law, ethics and practice. The final assessment task for each of the three modules requires the learners to submit a 1,000-word critical reflection report based on the context of the case study, their research and group opinions in problem solving, using the collaborative problem-based framework.

Authentic case studies are used to present hypothetical clinical problems. Students are required to prioritize the care of the individual and family by setting realistic goals. This begins from week one of the semester when students articulate their first perceptions of the problem/s in the case study. They submit their conjectures to their allocated discussion group and these activities continue on a weekly basis throughout the study period.

Students are required to research the topic as well as the peer reflections posted to the discussion group. They must make insightful comments on the postings and be in a position to begin reviewing their initial perceptions and continue to expand on them. With wider research and collaboration students are able to review the content under discussion, debate, and reach their own conclusions about how to solve the problems in the case studies presented.

Marking

In grading the students, searching databases and critically reviewing the literature are given weighting in each module (tied to the case study). Case studies are given weightings of 30 per cent for the legal assignment, 30 per cent for the ethics assignment and 40 per cent for the practice assignment (more for the practice module since nursing is fundamentally a practice-based discipline).

The body of knowledge that is generated through collaborative online discussion, debate and individual contribution to generating this body of knowledge is also assessed. Collaborative learning is the focus of this course and students are rewarded for their collaborative problem solving skills by earmarking 10.5 per cent of assignment weighting for each of the law, ethics and practice modules. The marks are given for evidence of developing collaborative problem solving skills in self and others.

The marking criteria are generic to the three modules and each week students make insightful comments to the peer reflections posted to the group discussion. As the weeks progress so do the students' collaborative problem solving skills because they learn to critically review the work submitted by their peers. This is evident in the body of knowledge that evolves over a period of four weeks, for each of the case studies.

An example of marking criteria for Assignment 1 is as follows:

- Preliminary reflection (Week 2: 5 per cent)
  Students to articulate their first perceptions of the problem in a computer-supported collaborative learning environment.
- Reflection (Week 3: 5 per cent)
  Review peer reflections, explain and justify your first perceptions of the problem in the computer-supported collaborative learning environment. Make insightful comments on peer reflections.
- Review (Week 4: 5 per cent)
  Review peer reflections and identify any new or related issues to the problem. Make insightful comments on peer reflections.
- Critical analysis (Week 5: 15 per cent)
  Students to present a critical analysis of the problem based on the following guidelines:
  - nature of the problem (eg definitions, assumptions, clarifications, etc);
  - issues that surround the problem (eg assumptions, clarifications, etc);
  - perceptions that people may have about the problem;
  - implications of these perceptions for nursing practice;
  - data and its sources that are relevant to the interpretation of the problem;
  - personal or group position on the problem.

Strengths and limitations

Strengths
Students find the course provides them with skills in peer evaluation and confidence in appraising others' work. They are able to clearly see the calibre of assignments that attract a higher grading, and in their opinion the grading of assignments is fair.

They feel empowered to pursue collaborative activities with peers and believe that it helps them to cope better with the occupational demands on entering the workforce. They also learn to consider time management, which is vital to clinical practice. Action plans assist learners in developing documentation skills that are also vital for professional practice.

In students' opinion, this type of learning is fun and they wish they had been exposed to such learning strategies earlier in the course. Students enjoy the comradeship that evolves over the 16 weeks of the semester. Other than this, they have often only worked in small groups.

Limitations
Negative issues that were encountered in the teaching of this unit included difficulties with technology. Relying on e-mail for discussion, though having its limitations, was in the end the most equitable approach.

2.2 CREATIVE PROBLEM SOLVING AND CONSTRUCTIVE AUTONOMY

Case study from Business (postgraduate)

Jane Henry, Open University, UK

The following case study is an edited version of the written materials Jane Henry provided, together with additional comments she made after seeing the first draft.

Problem solving in the management context can bring together the areas of creativity and leadership. The Open University Business School MBA programme includes a subject called 'Creative Management'.

This subject is designed to enhance the capacity of managers to identify challenges present within their own organization and respond creatively to problems or opportunities. Central to the course is the idea of 'constructive autonomy' – the sense that personal values, responsibilities and initiatives can be channelled to benefit wider community goals. Through the idea of constructive autonomy in the workplace, this example shows the development of students during their real-life learning encounters.

The real-life aspect of the course is promoted as being of immediate professional benefit to students at a personal, team or organizational level of development. The course provides opportunities to analyse one's own management style or that of an organization, apply creativity techniques to a problem or situation, to explore creative strategies in the students' chosen organization, to take some steps towards applying these creative strategies and to reflect on outcomes.

Context

This postgraduate course is structured in four 'blocks', each involving approximately 40–50 hours' work. Block 2 includes a four-day residential school (offered in several UK locations) where practical work in problem solving is carried out in teams or as solo techniques.

Students are provided with study guides and readers, as well as audio and video cassettes, television and radio broadcasts/cassettes, software tools and tutorial support. A Web site further supports the students' activities and provides supplementary resources.

During the course, students are encouraged to develop networking as a deliberate skill in order to discuss, reflect and share information or resources. Students are further reminded that this kind of professional networking by phone, fax and e-mail may be continued beyond the duration of the course.

Assessment tasks

There are three assignments for the course and a final exam but we will restrict ourselves here to the three applied assignments. The first requires an analysis of the students' own or their organization's styles of management. The second assignment asks students to apply creativity techniques to a problem or opportunity. For the final assignment, students must explore creative strategies in an organization they know and take some steps towards implementation.

For students who have good access to an organizational context, it is possible to link their assignments and thus produce a more integrated approach to creative problem solving. Strict confidentiality must be observed by students since the real-life cases that form the basis of assessment must not breach organizational security or privacy agreements.

Assignment 1 – situation and style analysis

Through the application of principles and tools introduced in Block 1, students are asked to present an analysis of the strengths and weaknesses of their own style, particularly as it relates to creative management.

An analysis is also required of the students' organization's climate, focusing on management style and values that predominate in their own work-related area. A discussion is to be provided on how this impacts upon the possibilities for creative management in that situation.

Thirdly, students identify an area for development regarding creative management and propose a project or activities to explore, either briefly in this assignment or to follow up in more depth through subsequent assignments.

Assignment 2 – techniques for creative problem solving

Students pick a problem of interest that is amenable to a creative problem-solving approach. Students then select and apply a technique (or phase thereof) under workplace conditions to the identified and appropriate concerns. They observe and record the outcomes and note reactions of colleagues. Students must further find ways to communicate with and explore how to use professional or collegial networks for enriching the problem-solving process.

Assignment 3 – creative strategy in an organization

Students are asked to select a subset of approaches from Blocks 3 and 4 that could be usefully adapted to their organization. They must include in their report:

- the context of the issue and the reasons why the chosen approach will meet the organization's current or future needs;
- an explanation of how each approach will be applied and reasons for these strategies;
- some steps taken to implement these creative strategies; and
- reflections on the outcomes of their workplace-based attempts.

Marking

Students are encouraged to present additional information with each assessment item, though this remains optional. Such details could include their perceptions on the weight balance of components of the assignment question, a self-appraisal with comments and notes on links to earlier assignments, or details of the negotiated agreement between themselves and the tutor.

The overall marking principles that apply to each assignment include:

1. *Depth of treatment and skill in working with the approaches taught.* The outcome of creativity approaches can never be guaranteed, so marks are given for clarity of problem definition and skill in working with the approaches rather than for the quality of outcome. It is expected that discussion will cover both successful and unsuccessful aspects.
2. *Explicit evidence of careful and thoughtful study of the Block.* Use and reference to course materials in an integrated and appropriate way throughout written work.
3. *Good presentation and clear thinking.* This includes good written style and layout, including good use of diagrams, references, well-reasoned argument, presentation of valid evidence, demonstration of an ability to see other points of view and appropriateness for the target audience.
4. *Evidence of constructive autonomy.* This includes showing initiative, a willingness to take creative risks, a general independence of judgement, capacity to experiment and to learn by reflecting on students' own experience or that of others, an ability to appreciate and take account of stakeholders' perspectives and a constructively critical approach to ideas generally.

Students are also referred to the study materials for further directions supporting clear argument and constructive critique.

Strengths and limitations

Students do not consider these three assignments easy, but they are valued as interesting, relevant and useful to their personal and working lives. The course has remained the most popular elective in the OU MBA for the last eight years and is rated very highly indeed. The majority of students generally rate the residential school associated with the second mini-project as better than other equivalent MBA residential schools.

Creative Management is now taken by over 1,000 people worldwide per year. Successive evaluations suggest students especially value modules 1 and 2. Students appreciate the following features because they give them the chance to do something useful, relevant and interesting:

- beginning from an analysis of yourself and the management situations;
- moving to a project that entails working with others;
- adapting material to your circumstances;
- planning strategy;
- starting to implement.

This type of assignment is so open-ended that it does not need much updating each year.

Over the years the proportion of students finding it difficult to get colleagues together for a decent amount of time for the second mini-project has increased due to the increasing work pressure people seem to be under. We are contemplating allowing some of this work to be done at residential school and encouraging an element of Internet search for students who find it hard to get this time. The first and third mini-projects have retained their appeal more or less unaltered.

2.3 INTEGRATED PLANNING PROJECT

Case study from Geography

Angus Witherby, University of New England, Australia

The following case study is basically in the words of Angus Witherby with only a few editorial changes.

This example fluently describes another case of situated learning. This time students undertake fieldwork as the basis of their project report and reflective presentation. Note also the criterion referenced marking scheme.

Context

Urban and regional planning is taught at the University of New England (UNE) by both internal and distance education. The unit is GeoPlan 250, Transport and Land Use, a core unit in the Bachelor of Urban and Regional Planning and is typically taken in the second academic year of study. The pedagogical approach is problem-based learning. The unit is designed to provide a learning environment where the use of external print-based teaching materials, internal face-to-face teaching, and use of the Internet and a field school combine with the assessment regime to create an integrated learning environment.

Support for the unit is provided not only through the print-based and Web-based teaching materials, but also through the operation of peer assisted study sessions (PASS).

Students undertaking the unit come from a range of backgrounds, including second-year undergraduates who have come to university straight from school, through to mature-age professionals in the final phases of their career. An important part of the learning environment is the interaction between students of different backgrounds, ages and abilities.

Abilities being assessed

The unit has the combined aim of delivering an understanding of the sub-discipline of transport planning, while also developing competences to students consistent with the eight formal competences of UNE graduates:

- knowledge of the discipline;
- communications skills;
- a global perspective;
- information literacy;
- lifelong learning;
- problem solving;
- social responsibility; and
- teamwork.

In addition to these general competences, the unit seeks to develop skills in problem identification, working to a time-frame, logistical organization and professionalism. In general terms, the learning objectives of the unit relate to developing skills in researching local area transport issues, evaluating the literature and analysing the problems within their context so as to develop realistic, practical solutions capable of implementation. In addition, students are expected to gain an appreciation of the role of local area transport planning, traffic management and engineering within the economic, financial, social and political contexts that influence policy and practice. Finally, students develop an awareness of the history and geography of transport and the related theoretical underpinnings of current practice.

Specific professional skills objectives include displaying a professional attitude towards meeting deadlines, planning and managing time. In addition, students are expected to demonstrate competence in the management of complex projects including interpersonal communication and management skills. Finally, students will produce reports that exhibit a high level of written communications skills and an attention to detail in line with the expectations of the planning profession.

Assessment tasks

Assessment operates in a variety of ways. In terms of assignment work, the main assignment is the preparation of a client brief and consultant response. This piece of work focuses specifically on problem definition and the development of an appropriate methodological response. This assignment is expected to be placed in the context of the theoretical literature. The second major piece of assessable work is the fieldwork component. Students either undertake this at the field school in groups, or as an individual project. The aim of this second piece of work is to provide students with the opportunity to put into practice the conceptual and developmental skills achieved through the first assessable piece of work.

For internal students, peer assessed tutorial sessions are conducted. These are moderated by academic staff, but the operation of the tutorial programme and its assessment lies largely in student hands. The tutorial sessions have the aim of first, demonstrating communications skills, secondly, developing small group facilitation skills, and thirdly, developing a variety of presentation skills. Presentation of tutorials is backed by the submission of a formal written paper to further develop students' understanding of the difference in presentation style between spoken text and written communications.

The unit also has an examination. This is based on the tutorial questions, which are made available at the beginning of the semester to all students. Students are informed that all the tutorial questions will appear, in some form, on the examination paper. The focus of the examination is not, however, on the reproduction of standardized answers to the tutorial questions. Instead, the emphasis is on students demonstrating their conceptual understanding of the issues raised by the questions (and indeed of the questions in combination) based on the level of information that they have had access to during the course of the unit.

Marking

The primary method of assessment of work is grading within the various grade bands. A mark is then used to indicate where in the band the work lies. It is explained to students that a mark of 7.5 out of 10 is not 'just a little bit better' than a mark of 7.4 out of 10. Instead, one may represent work that has certain general characteristics, but performs poorly within that framework while the other may represent work with less satisfactory general characteristics, but which has been well carried through.

Results are used as a deliberate tool to shape students' trajectory through the unit. In particular, extensive use has, at times, been made of the mark of 4.9 out of 10. This mark has been particularly effective in encouraging students to address major shortcomings in their work, while still acknowledging that significant effort has been put in.

Strengths and limitations

Strengths

The major strength of the assessment framework is the progressive development of skills commencing with the development of problem definition and methodological response from a desk-based exercise through to an actual project. The assessment regime is designed to reinforce the importance of a strong intersection between theory and praxis.

Peer appraisal operates at both the field school and through the tutorials (in the case of the on-campus students). Peer appraisal has particular advantages in developing skills in self-reflective practice, which are important in the personal and professional development of people seeking a professional career.

Limitations

The major limitations of the assessment regime are, first, the relatively time-consuming nature of assessment of individual project work (noting that group work at the field school is quite time-efficient to assess) together with the lack of opportunity to provide effective feedback from the examination.

2.4 DEVELOPING CONSULTING SKILLS

Case study from Business (postgraduate)

Aad Vijverberg and Kathleen Schlusmans, Open University of the Netherlands

The following case study is an edited version of the written materials Kathleen Schlusmans and Jos Rikers provided, together with additional comments they made after seeing the first draft.

This example illustrates various levels and types of communications that are necessary to succeed in problem solving as a consultant within an organizational environment. In this subject, students study at a distance from the university and interact with their academic 'coach' via e-mail and the Internet. Attendance at the university is only required at the final assessment meeting and even this can be avoided with the use of itinerant examiners.

The focus for the consulting project is selected from among the problems identified by students with respect to their own organizations or outside networks. Over a six-month period students are required to interact in teams of four and to assist the client by providing advice on and solving or managing a particular problem. Although the team's presence and intervention may provide support to the organizational client, the problem is always owned by the client and managerial responsibility for decisions and their consequences remains with the client.

Context

In September 1997, the Faculty of Business Administration at the Open University of the Netherlands implemented a new consulting course to be delivered in an electronic environment as part of its MBA programme. The course is called 'Practicum Strategy and Organization' and aims to develop consulting skills on strategy and organizational issues.

During the whole of the consulting process, the 10-step assignment is undertaken by teams of four students, each having their own 'coach'. An electronic logbook becomes the monitoring and principal communication instrument for the six-month duration of the subject. Coaches have several roles:

- to oversee and at times facilitate the consultancy process;
- to provide feedback when students fill in each of the 10 progress reports;
- to play an important role in the final assessment.

The consulting process is modelled on the action learning cycle having three phases:

(a) orientation;
(b) action planning; and
(c) implementation.

The underlying philosophy adopted in this course is that consulting is informed by both experience and theory. Therefore, the teaching staff in this course select from the problems that are brought in by students to ensure the existence of a body of literature in all the areas selected.

In the practical sense, student teams of consultants are encouraged to get 'things done without being in charge'. Student teams are also charged with the independence of providing a consultancy free from bias. The team must be in a position to make an unbiased assessment of any situation, tell the truth and recommend frankly and objectively what the client organization needs to do without having any second thoughts on how this might affect their own interests.

Consultancy is a temporary service and takes place over a fixed period. Within that period a serious contribution to solving the problem must be delivered by the team. This contribution is assessed by the client, the students in the team, the guide and the examiner. After this period, the team has completed its assignment and will leave the organization.

Abilities being assessed

The abilities being assessed are:

- demonstrated insight into the basic principles of management consulting;
- competence in basic management consulting skills;
- the ability to carry out a management consulting project in a real company (in a group, within given time restrictions).

Assessment tasks

The main purpose of the consulting assignment is the solving of a strategy or organizational problem. This problem solving can't be separated from the organization's purposes and objectives that the management of the organization pursues. The problem solving has to add value to the client organization, and this value should be a tangible and measurable contribution to achieving the client's main purposes. The task of the consulting team is described as professional assistance in identifying, diagnosing and solving problems concerning various areas and aspects of the management and business.

The term 'problem' is used to describe a situation where there is a difference or discrepancy between what is actually happening or will be happening and what should or might be happening. A problem can only be described in relative terms, as a difference between two situations, and someone has to be concerned about this difference and aim to overcome it, or to reduce it. The client is mostly the problem-owner.

A current situation can be compared to one that existed in the past, or compared to some standard (benchmark) and this comparison reveals that the current situation is not satisfactory. Consulting, whose purpose is confined to corrective measures aiming to restore a past situation or attain a standard already met by other organizations, may produce significant and relevant benefits.

But targets in terms of consulting aims can/must be formulated at a higher level because ultimately an organization must anticipate future developments and identify and seize opportunities in that future environment. This enhances the process of becoming a learning organization. The team's role in that learning process is very subtle. The purpose is to empower the client by bringing new competence into the organization and helping managers and staff to learn from their own and the team's experience. This approach to problem solving means that the consulting team deals with 'other people's problems'.

A correct definition of the problem to be resolved and the purpose to be achieved by the consulting project is critical. The team doesn't have to accept the client's perception of the problem at face value: the problem may be wrongly defined and the team will be caught in a trap. Either the team will work on a wrong problem, or the problem may not justify the team's intervention and the costs incurred. The teams have to make their own independent assessment of the problem by interviewing other persons concerned in the organization.

The problem to be solved is always placed in a larger context. This implies that the team always has to ask and clarify a number of questions about:

- the purposes of the client organization and its key constituents;
- the focus and the significance of the proposed assignment; and
- the immediate and ultimate benefits to be obtained by the client if the current problem is resolved.

Marking

After each of the 10 steps in action learning consultancy, students fill in a progress report (using the electronic logbook). Logbooks are available through the subject-related Web site and it is hoped development will soon be complete of a database system for storing student input, making it searchable and accessible.

Coaches provide formative feedback and the whole process is assessed mainly by the coach, but the outcome of the project is also evaluated by the manager in the organization and by the examiner.

Part of the assessment procedure is a questionnaire to be completed by students. In this questionnaire, students assess each other's contribution as well as their own. The final assessment is undertaken at a meeting with the coach, the examiner, the group of students and the manager of the client organization.

Strengths and limitations

Action research, action learning and constructivism

Methodologically, consultants learn a lot from researchers and vice versa. Action research is on the borders of research and consulting. It aims simultaneously to solve a meaningful practical problem and to yield new knowledge about the social system under study. Action research involves changing that which is being investigated. Conventional research does not.

Action learning as in this example is also akin to constructivist approaches to learning. The features of constructivism in this example include the way students are encouraged to build their understanding and to make decisions on the basis of information obtained. Through the use of the 10-step consultancy approach, the client organization is also empowered to learn from the experience of managers, staff and students involved in the projects. The students' contribution to the client organization is thus not a simulation but has the elements of a real solution to the identified problem, in the style of action research.

Arrangements with client organizations and remote students

This assessment practice relies on institutional arrangements with workplace-based partners. A strong organizational infrastructure is required to support applied projects such as this. Without such off-campus arrangements, administrative arrangements could easily become unwieldy and prohibitive.

As the assessment task is based around teamwork within an organization, students need to be in proximity to each other and the client organization. This makes the scheme suited more to an off-campus course in a metropolitan area rather than for a regional or international cohort of students.

3. Performing procedures and demonstrating techniques

3.1 Developing expertise in neonatal resuscitation
3.2 Dissecting rats and providing evidence
3.3 Developing competences in writing research proposals

This chapter includes tasks that require performance to a predetermined standard of competence. The procedures or techniques to be carried out are specified, and usually a benchmark is set by which competence is judged. Assessments may be graded or ungraded, such as pass/fail awards, depending on whether the required performance standards have been reached. Abilities assessed using these methods include using equipment, following detailed procedures and protocols, and applying theory to practice. Nightingale *et al* (1996) point to three components of successful performance of procedures: prior knowledge; psychomotor skills (such as dexterity and hand-eye co-ordination); and appropriate attitudinal factors such as care and concern.

Teaching and assessing procedures and techniques at a distance has often been difficult, unless residential schools or face-to-face sessions are organized for the purpose. Videos are often employed as a means of both teaching skills and assessing student performance at a distance, although in some instances this can be cumbersome for students and unreliable from the assessor's point of view. Workplace mentoring and assessment schemes have gained considerable popularity in recent times – the learners appoint an appropriately skilled mentor/assessor with whom they practise procedures and techniques in their workplace (or lifelike setting) until they have achieved the standards specified by the educational institution. In open learning contexts, these assessments should be criterion referenced. In addition, there should be opportunities available for learners to repeat performances until the desired level of mastery is achieved.

The case studies in this section represent a broad range of abilities, from basic biology dissection skills to complex neonatal resuscitation knowledge and techniques. The final case study in this section, the development of competence in writing research proposals, is of a slightly different kind, as competence is ultimately judged by the final outcome rather than the procedure undertaken, although significant formative feedback is provided on the process. These case studies exhibit some of the familiar tensions of open and distance assessment, including that of certification vs promotion of learning, and the respective significance placed on formative vs summative assessment. Distance is usually overcome in interesting and innovative ways.

3.1 DEVELOPING EXPERTISE IN NEONATAL RESUSCITATION

Case study from Nursing (postgraduate)

Judy Jamieson, Newborn Emergency Transport Service (NETS) Victoria, Australia

The following case study was compiled from the written materials provided by Southern Cross University and Judy Jamieson, NETS Education Manager, together with additional comments made by Judy after seeing the first draft.

Postgraduate nursing studies commonly include a range of areas for theoretical and practical professional development. Speciality clinical nursing areas taught by open and distance education include programmes tailored for remote area nurses such as the following example from Australia, which supports training at a distance in neonatal emergency management.

Learning the skills to save the lives of newborns requires specialist training – observation, guidance, practice and reflection on practice. Midwives in speciality wards of metropolitan or teaching hospitals gain greater access to the practices of resuscitation and initial nursing management of the neonate than midwives working in remote areas, who have little specialist staff back-up.

In the case of antenatal and neonatal nursing, knowledge of and skills in procedures during the small window of opportunity in emergency situations can make a critical difference. Upskilling remote-area nurses in resuscitation practices for emergency care, and initial management of the neonate until transfer to a specialist facility, is thus considered learning that is vital to supporting an essential emergency service.

Reliance is placed on a mentorship model of teaching and learning. Hypothetical case scenarios also help to place these exercises in context.

Context

Clinical Teaching Associates (CTAs) – specialist nurses or nurse educators who are accredited by the university and the industry partner, NETS Education – carry out the work-based clinical assessment in this programme. Depending on the context (level of hospital, location in relation to a major teaching hospital, access to accredited assessors, etc) there is scope in this CTA role to also act as a mentor and supervisor, especially in the neonatal special care context.

Learners enrolled in this unit work through print-based educational materials and practise skills with their mentor while working in their normal routine on the hospital ward. Assessment can sometimes be carried out in actual emergency situations. Students who cannot find real opportunities via which to be assessed, can use a manikin as a substitute neonate for demonstration of resuscitation skills and knowledge.

Established procedures are listed in skillsheets, practised with CTAs and checked off by the assessor (who may or may not be the mentor). Reflective case study analysis and synthesis of relevant up-to-date literature form the written components of assessment, which are submitted to the university for marking and grading.

Students study for either professional development or accreditation into the Newborn Emergency Care strand of the Master of Health Science programme, Southern Cross University, Australia.

Abilities being assessed

- Clinical observation and identification of 'at risk' factors.
- Application of knowledge in workplace-based practice.
- Demonstration of resuscitation skills.
- Making judgements regarding transfer of 'at risk' newborns.
- Demonstration of neonatal care and maintenance procedures.
- Understanding of physical examination procedures, assessment techniques and emergency retrieval requirements.

Assessment tasks

There are three assessment items in this unit – two essays and the demonstrated mastery of clinical practice skills in the nurse's workplace. The successful completion of two essays requires the development of understanding and presentation of an argument based upon nursing decisions to be made in a choice of emergency scenarios.

The four compulsory clinical skill sets that must be assessed as satisfactory for students to pass are – bag and mask ventilation, external cardiac massage, use of manual radiant heaters, and operating a manual incubator. Eleven additional skill sets are also taught through this unit with the help of clinical mentors in the workplace. These additional skills are not assessed but are used to provide a comprehensive study package and continuity in the mentorship relationship.

The range of skills to be learnt cover a knowledge of both equipment and procedures in all aspects of neonatal emergency management. Skillsheets provide students with detailed guidance from three perspectives – rationale, description of the activity, and performance standard. The clinical competence assessment form, which is used to determine the satisfactory achievement of mastery, is included as Appendix C.

Marking

The competence of students is assessed according to a clinical assessment scale that rates students along five defined levels of competence – 'dependent', 'marginal', 'assisted', 'supervised' and 'independent'. A list of 15 clinical skills is provided on a checklist against which each skillsheet is measured and rated by the CTA according to the level of competence shown by the student (see Appendix C).

Three attempts at the clinical assessment tasks are permitted in order to satisfy the requirements of mastery. The student must achieve a score of 3 or more for each criterion to be considered competent in performing the clinical skill. The four compulsory clinical skills must be completed satisfactorily for the student to pass this unit.

A summary of the student's strengths and weaknesses is also requested from the mentor in the clinical context to supplement the assessment documentation, along with the learner's comments.

Strengths and limitations

This assessment is based on criterion referenced definitions for rating scales by Bondy (1983) and Benner (1984). It is also seated in the workplace context and the outcomes are linked directly to learning objectives. On both counts it can be called authentic assessment – real-life situations add value to the learning experience as students can relate theoretical knowledge and specific clinical skills more readily to their own experience. Students find the assessment relevant and worthwhile.

This model can run into difficulty in finding real-life situations in which students can demonstrate their level of competence. However, the use of manikins and hypothetical case scenarios overcomes this problem to an extent. The assessment relies on CTAs gaining accreditation from Southern Cross and NETS Education to qualify as assessors, although this has not been a major problem to date.

The clinical skills assessments are time-consuming for the CTAs to complete, particularly as midwives are multiskilling across all areas of care and few CTAs are able to have specific time allocated in their working shift to undertake these assessments.

The student must have achieved competence in all of the compulsory clinical skills to qualify for a pass in the unit. These skills are not graded. Marks are derived from assessment of two written assignments that are graded.

3.2 DISSECTING RATS AND PROVIDING EVIDENCE

Case study from Biology

Peter Freeman, Jenny Mosse and Wendy Wright, Monash University, Australia

The following case study has been edited from the written materials Peter Freeman provided, together with additional comments he made after seeing the first draft.

In the absence of mentors and demonstrators, the performance of procedures, skills and techniques can be learnt through guided exploration or reflective trial-and-error experience. Learning is reinforced by written reflection on experiences and observations.

Beginning students of biology need only have access to a few speciality resources and a home kitchen to be introduced to the skills of dissection and to explore anatomy and physiology in a real-world application. Monash University supplies the kits, complete with preserved rat specimens and the students make arrangements for the use of a microscope in their own local area. Evidence of practical activities completed by students is required through drawings or photos.

Context

The School of Applied Sciences delivers a Bachelor of Science programme via on-campus and distance education (DE) modes with a range of major and minor streams including laboratory-based science subjects.

The two first-year Biology subjects (ASC1626 Cell Biology and ASC1637 Biology of Mammalian Systems) have no compulsory attendance requirements. In both these subjects, laboratory kits are forwarded to DE students. All experiments can be safely completed at home. Some experiments require access to a microscope, which can usually be obtained from a local secondary school. Letters of introduction included in the subject materials facilitate this access. The experiments are essentially identical to the exercises conducted with on-campus students, with only minor modifications to suit equipment and materials being used at home.

One experiment in the ASC1637 Biology of Mammalian Systems subject is the dissection of a rat. This experiment was developed by Dr Peter Mosse and has been delivered in distance mode since 1990.

Abilities being assessed

Abilities we are assessing are:

- recognition of the major anatomical features of the mammalian body, with particular emphasis on cardiovascular, digestive and urinogenital systems;
- accurate recording of observations;
- linkage of observations to theoretical concepts;
- production of a scientific report.

Assessment tasks

A. Recognition of the major anatomical features of the mammalian body

Students are given the option of attending the Gippsland campus to complete this experiment. Many students are unable to choose this option, so the 'full' laboratory kit includes all materials and instruments required to complete the dissection exercise. This includes a formalin-preserved, double-injected rat in a sealed bag, a set of dissecting tools, and a dissection guide. The laboratory notes for the exercise take the student through the dissection, with the dissection guide providing an aid for recognition of structures observed by the student.

B. Recording of observations

At several stages during the dissection, the students are directed to record their observations by drawing (or photographing) and labelling the structures they observe, and noting any measurements made.

C. Linkage of observations to theoretical concepts

Questions within the notes prompt students to make links back to the theory components of the course, and to extend that theory by considering possible reasons why differences exist between the rat and humans.

D. Production of a scientific report

One of the objectives of this subject is to develop skills in scientific report-writing. Inclusion of detailed report-writing guidelines in the subject material and prompt and informative feedback on submitted work achieve this. The rat dissection report is the second of five submitted by students, so constructive feedback on this report is essential.

Marking

The five laboratory reports contribute 30 per cent to the final grade in the subject. Reports are weighted according to the complexity of the practical undertaken. The rat dissection is one of the larger exercises and is weighted accordingly. Marks are allocated for clarity of presentation, structure of the information and the content of the answers to the questions posed within the laboratory notes. Report-writing guidelines provided to the students include the marking criteria.

Strengths and limitations

Strengths

Strengths of the rat dissection include the development of outcomes that are linked directly to learning objectives. Students regularly comment on the enhancement of understanding of both the anatomy and the related physiology of the systems examined during the rat dissection. Students find the dissection exercise relevant and worthwhile.

Limitations

These include the moral objections of some students to the use of animal tissues for experimentation, and the safety issue of possible exposure of students (especially those who may be pregnant) to formaldehyde from the preserved rat. In addition, Customs Regulations prevent despatch of the preserved rat to DE students outside Australia. These issues can be addressed by the development of a human surface anatomy exercise as an alternative to the rat dissection. The dissection exercise may be enhanced by the use of appropriate multimedia (CD ROM and/or WWW) support materials, such as the E-Rat simulation currently being developed in the Department of Biological Sciences. Teaching staff must ensure that rapid turnaround of submitted laboratory reports is given a high priority.

Use of results

The marks are derived from the graded laboratory reports. The remaining 70 per cent of marks for the subject come from a mid-semester test and an end-of-semester examination. This subject is a core subject within the biotechnology stream of the BSc degree, and an elective in other streams.

3.3 DEVELOPING COMPETENCES IN WRITING RESEARCH PROPOSALS

Case study from Business

Kathleen Schlusmans, Gerard van den Boom and Huibert de Man, Open University of the Netherlands

The following text is taken from a paper presented by Kathleen Schlusmans, Gerard van den Boom and Huibert de Man, together with additional comments made by Kathleen Schlusmans after seeing the first draft.

The following example of a competence-based approach to developing research proposals is interesting for its tension between preserving openness in learning while structuring tutor-paced activities with students using computer mediated communications technology. Formative feedback has been maximized in this example through the use of peer review and feedback. Students report their wish to also have more individual feedback from tutors.

Context

Students in the faculty of Business Administration have to carry out a final research project at the end of their studies. They often experience considerable difficulty in writing research proposals, especially when it comes to defining the research problem and designing the research plan.

Since 1994 the faculty of Business Administration has been organizing one-day in-house workshops for students about to start their final project. The students' research proposals are presented and discussed in these workshops. While a good step in the right direction, these workshops provide students with little scope for reflection and revision and offer insufficient opportunity to react to one another's work.

In October 1997 the Dutch Open University acquired a stable Internet infrastructure and it was decided to set up a virtual workshop with a duration of two months in which the students were guided step-by-step in drafting their research proposals. The underlying assumption was that this approach would provide more opportunity for collaborative learning and more time to reflect on the research proposals without taking much more tutorial time.

A pilot workshop on the Internet took place during October and November 1997. This workshop is part of a wider attempt to redesign the Business Administration curriculum at the Dutch Open University along the principles of competence-based learning.

A World Wide Web site was developed for the final project, which comprised all the general information about the final project, the project manual, a database of resources and the virtual workshop itself. One general and four specific newsgroups were used in addition to the Web site.

Abilities being assessed

In this 'virtual' workshop, students learn to write a research proposal:

- selecting a (relevant, interesting) research topic;
- defining the research problem;
- selecting a relevant research method;
- carrying out preliminary research to clarify the problem and the methods used.

Assessment tasks

The virtual workshop

The virtual workshop consists of eight assignments, which are published one-by-one on the Web site on a weekly basis. The students carry out the assignments and post their work in one of the workshop newsgroups. The assignments are:

1. Introduction
2. Critical review
3. Revised review
4. Problem analysis
5. Problem definition
6. Research design
7. Research plan
   (One-day seminar)
8. Revised proposal

The students start with an icebreaker and are allocated to specific newsgroups according to their special subjects, such as marketing or logistics. Each specific newsgroup has its own tutor. The students start with a critical review of an imaginary research proposal. In the second assignment they do this informally, off the cuff. In the third assignment they revise their reviews, using a list of formal criteria deduced from a text on business research which is provided as part of the assignment.

From this assignment onwards the students are divided into pairs. In the four next assignments the students design their own research proposals step by step using specific guidelines and instructional texts which are provided. Each week the students post part of their proposals in the newsgroups. Their partner's task is to give feedback, using the criteria mentioned above. When the proposals reach their final stage, a residential one-day seminar is organized in which the students present their work to their own group and receive individual feedback from all participants. The final assignment requires students to revise the complete proposals based on the feedback they get at the seminar.

The manual and the resources

The manual outlining formal requirements for the final project is sent to students; it is also available on the Internet. A database of relevant resources for setting up business research projects is developed and published on the Web site.

Tutoring and logistics

In order to keep the tutor time down, it was decided to limit the contributions of the tutors in the Internet part of the workshop. Tutors are now only required to summarize the contributions of the different students and to reflect on the most important problems that occur. The individual feedback is postponed until the residential seminar.

The workshop keeps to an extremely tight schedule with strict deadlines, which is very unusual in Open University courses. Thus it is absolutely necessary for one of the staff members to act as a logistics controller. He or she publishes the assignments on the dates allocated and contacts students and tutors who do not meet the deadlines. The logistics controller also provides a helpdesk service for technical and general problems.

Marking

The final research plan is assessed by the tutor, with improvements in the research plan in the whole course taken into account. The criteria used are clarity of problem definition, relevance of methods, clear planning and deadlines.

Strengths and limitations

Students

A large number of students had technical Internet problems at the beginning of the workshop, yet all but one of them completed assignments 1–7 and attended the seminar. Only a few also completed the final assignment. After the seminar most of them considered the workshop finished. The whole workshop including the seminar took the students about 50 hours of study.

All the students completed a questionnaire and most of them were satisfied with the way the workshop was set up. Although they found the schedule rather tight, they appreciated the fact that so much got done in such a short time. The students reacted positively to being able to look at other students' contributions and the pair work was thought of as very stimulating and effective. More than half the students found their partners' feedback very useful and some of them even said that they learnt as much by giving feedback as by receiving it. However, the tutors' contributions in the newsgroups were rated rather negatively. Students expected personal feedback and felt cheated when they only got remote messages.

The students were extremely satisfied with the residential seminar. They appreciated being able to put faces to names and they finally got the individual feedback from the tutors they had been seeking.

The manual and the resources on the Internet were hardly used at all. The students relied on the printed version of the manual. Most students reported that they appreciated having the resources available but that they did not have enough time to consult them in the workshop. Nevertheless, they thought that in the next phase of the final project, access to these resources could be most useful.

The assessment method is still under discussion. The criteria have to be validated and there is discussion about the issue that students can have learnt a lot without actually at the end producing an excellent research proposal.

Tutors

Four tutors were involved in the workshop. Three of them experienced considerable difficulties working with the Internet. The tutoring time varied from 60 to 100 hours per tutor, including getting to know the Internet software and reading all the contributions of the students.

The tutors were positive about the direct communication and the high level of involvement of the students. Some tutors also appreciated having access to the reactions and feedback of other tutors. The tutors were less satisfied with their own role and involvement. They felt they needed clearer instructions on what was expected of them.

As far as the research proposals of the students were concerned, three tutors indicated that the quality was higher than following previous workshops and that students were more aware of the criteria used to evaluate research proposals. One tutor remarked that some contributions were of a standard only usually achieved after several months of individual coaching.

Developers

The workshop was developed by one faculty member and two educational technologists. The development of the Web site took only a couple of weeks, much less than a regular Open University course. Using Web pages and newsgroups makes it possible to develop materials quickly with a high degree of flexibility and adaptability.

Suggestions for improvement

All participants agreed that more time needed to be spent at the beginning of the workshop on solving technical problems and on training students and tutors in using the Internet. Moreover, the working schedule had to be a little less tight, especially for those assignments in which students are required both to work on their own proposals and to give each other feedback. Furthermore, students indicated that individual feedback from the tutor on the Internet would provide significant added value to the workshop.

In the first run of the workshop the technical and logistical problems were rather underestimated. Moreover, students and tutors alike needed a great deal of help in getting used to working with the Internet. Although the students complained about the tightness of the deadlines, they were most enthusiastic about the overall approach. The quality of the proposals they wrote was highly rated by the tutors.

The workshop has now been improved based on the experience gained with the first. The approach used in the workshop will be extended to other Business Administration courses and activities.

4. Managing and developing oneself

This chapter contains a spectrum of assessment case studies aimed at helping students to take responsibility for their own learning and development. Although self-directed or autonomous learning is often cited as a central aim of open and distance education, in practice it often takes a back seat, due to the prominence of teaching texts and accompanying packages of resources, which tend to have the reverse effect on learning. Additionally, concerns are commonly raised by teachers about the open-endedness of these kinds of assessments and consequent difficulties of reliable marking. The additional time demands of individualized learning are also raised as an issue, along with the range of skills that learners need to have for them to undertake highly self-directed tasks adequately. Certainly self-directed learning needs considerable thought and planning, and yet this ability is perhaps the single most important quality of any graduating learner. Nightingale *et al* (1996) identify a number of abilities that are encompassed within this broad heading, including:

- planning and managing one's own learning;
- evaluating one's own learning;
- understanding and managing one's own feelings and being sensitive to the feelings of others;

- making ethical judgements;
- working collaboratively.

To varying degrees, these case studies demonstrate many of these elements, although in different ways, given factors such as the discipline area, the level of study, the point learners are at in their studies, and learners' own personal and professional needs. Assessment methods include portfolios, learning contracts, dialogue and journals.

4.1 CONTRACT FOR PERSONAL CHANGE

Case study from Rural Management

Barbara Johnson, Orange Agricultural College, University of Sydney, Australia

The following case study has been edited from the written materials Barbara Johnson provided, together with additional comments made by Barbara after seeing the first draft.

In the post-secondary environment, the ability to identify one's own learning needs, to decide how to address those needs and then to actuate these decisions, is considered the basis of self-development. This example of managing and developing oneself shows a well-established and supportively structured process. The assessment of learning is the 'icing on the cake' for these students when they report getting so much out of the personal development exercise itself.

By use of teleconferencing to facilitate groups of six to eight members, staff guide these management learning groups (MLGs) to support group members in the development of a learning contract and in peer reviews of final reports. Approval must be given to a proposed personal change project and this is determined according to the scope and depth of the literature identified.

Context

Managerial Development I and II are core units in the third year of the Bachelor of Management course within the School of Rural Management. Offered over consecutive semesters, the units focus on facilitating students in developing management and leadership abilities. Areas covered include self- and group management, gender and ethics as management issues, and leadership within the context of complexity and change.

As their major assessment, students undertake learning contracts, which address learning goals specifically relevant to them. Largely self-directed, the students work on their chosen goal within the supportive context of an MLG of six to eight students. A lecturer guides the process. Students 'meet' via teleconference three times a semester and review each other's final submission.

There is a strong emphasis on process and on developing self-directed learning skills within an experiential framework.

Abilities being assessed

At the completion of the unit students should be able to:

- identify learning needs and goals;
- review and reflect on literature/information sources;
- develop learning strategies;
- implement strategies, analyse and evaluate learning outcomes;
- reflect on individual learning approaches;
- provide constructive feedback to peers.

Assessment tasks

All parts of the learning contract task are explained in some detail in the unit information, with trigger questions to help students work through each stage. This is reinforced by an audiotape of the process. There is a strong emphasis on the links between theory and practice, and on lifelong learning: students are not expected to necessarily 'complete' their goal by the end of semester.

Identifying learning needs and goals

Students skim the learning material and prepare a learning contract proposal that states their learning goal, why they want to focus on it, and what they will present as evidence of achievement. This proposal is sent to the lecturer and each member of the MLG. A teleconference is held by the third week of the semester where proposals are discussed and any changes identified, such as making the goal more manageable within the time available. Contract proposals are not graded, but need to be approved by the MLG and the lecturer.

Reviewing literature, reflecting, and developing learning strategies

Students complete a Section 1 report, which consists of:

- a review of some of the literature on their goal;
- their reflections on the literature and its implications for their goal;
- an assessment of themselves/their group/organization depending on the goal's focus; and
- a methodology that details strategies that they will follow to work towards their goal.

This is completed by the fifth week of the semester, and students then work on their strategies over an eight-week period.

This Section 1 report is submitted as a draft, and is not graded. However, the learning strategies need to be approved by the lecturer. Students receive detailed feedback on their draft, and they revise it as required for submission with the final graded report.

The main reason for the draft report is to help students develop skills in undertaking a literature review and develop learning strategies within a supportive environment. These processes are new and daunting for many students.

Implementing strategies, analysing outcomes and reflecting on learning

Students implement their strategies, modifying them if needed within an action learning approach. They are encouraged to keep a learning diary over the implementation period. A teleconference is held mid-semester that enables students to hear how others are progressing, swap ideas and generally provide support and encouragement for each other. Students are also encouraged to phone each other and the lecturer at other times if needed.

After approximately eight weeks, students prepare their final contract report, which includes Section 1 (revised as required), and Section 2, which consists of their learning in action (results), analysis and evaluation, and a reflection on their learning approach. This report is graded.

Each student peer reviews the reports of two other members of the MLG. This peer review is given orally at a final teleconference, and hard copies sent to each reviewee and the lecturer. This review is not graded, but is a unit requirement.

Marking

Students are given a qualitative grade on the final contract report, across HD, D, C, P or F. A written explanation of the grades, based on Ballantyne and Packer (1995) and Biggs (1992) is given to students at the beginning of the semester. Guidelines for the final report include trigger questions for each section to help students think through their learning outcomes and prepare a comprehensive report. These trigger questions are quite central in helping students to develop skills in, for example, describing outcomes, reflection, analysis and evaluation.

Strengths and limitations

A formal evaluation carried out in 1995 shows an overwhelmingly positive response from distance education students.

Learning contracts

Although learning contracts were new to most students, the large majority enjoyed working on a learning goal that had direct relevance for them. They believed that the processes used had helped them understand their own learning, and would help them manage their learning in the future. Some specific comments include:

pushed me to learn about myself;
helped me learn how to put theory into practice;
gave structure to the learning process and made learning relevant to me;
enabled me to work in my own community.

Learning contracts can create problems for students, at least initially. Most reported feeling very anxious when they first received the learning materials. Only one student said that the learning contract was not worthwhile, but gave no details. Comments on how learning contracts could be improved include:

would like to see examples of reports (now included);
hard to grasp the new learning concept;
would like more grounding in self-directed learning skills (this is being addressed).

Management learning groups

Although a small percentage of students felt uncomfortable discussing their learning with others, the large majority felt MLGs were an essential part of their learning. They also believed that they learnt much more about the area of management and leadership through reviewing the reports of their peers. Comments include:

good to share ideas and sort out problems;
support helped combat the isolation of distance;
good to get to know other students;
it was the force that kept me going;
developed skills in constructive criticism;
initial defensiveness led to openness.

MLGs can be quite daunting for some students. Usually this unease recedes as they get to know each other, the lecturer and the process better. Comments on how to improve them include:

facilitate more communication between members;
occasional technical hitches (eg poor phone line) marred the process.

The first of these problems is being addressed as Web sites for discussion are now being set up to expand the interaction available for MLGs and lecturers. However, meeting via teleconference will remain an essential part of these units.

Informal feedback from students since 1995 mirrors the above findings. Both students and staff working in the units comment on the powerful nature of the learning, and on the way students develop a process to guide their future learning. Staff using these processes find that although workload increases to some extent, the learning processes followed and the outcomes for students are well worth the effort. A major increase in students' confidence in the process and their learning effectiveness is noticed as they progress from Managerial Development I to Managerial Development II.

The lecturer developed these processes, adapted initially in 1990 using material from RMIT University. They have been honed over the years through observations and reflections, and feedback from students and other staff with shared responsibility for the units.

4.2 PARTICIPATION IN OPEN LEARNING

Case study from Education

Roy Lundin, Queensland University of Technology

The following case study is from the written materials Roy Lundin provided.

This unit, Open Learning and Flexible Delivery, deals with the concepts and research relating to open and distance learning as well as flexible and workplace delivery, using a range of information technologies and telecommunications. The unit is designed to experience open learning and flexible delivery both from the learner's and the developer's points of view.

Context

The unit is at undergraduate level and is supported by two teleconferences and one optional face-to-face session on campus. Internet connection is a prerequisite, as the use of online facilities is an integral part of the learning experience in this subject, being both subject matter and process. Students are typically adult or workplace educators, delving into the issues of open and distance learning for the first time.

Open learning and flexible delivery are dynamically changing and rapidly developing areas. While we can all quite freely explore the Internet and find discussion groups of general interest, this unit requires a serious engagement with students' local community as well as an online community of their choice within the general area of open and distance education. The onus on students is to:

- observe and participate in their local community with regards to open learning;
- discover the rules of online discussion;
- take an active part by contributing to debate or discussion; and
- reflect upon their experiences as well as the usefulness of open learning practices for their own teaching and learning.

The application of lessons learnt to students' own teaching and learning environment arises from managing their interpersonal and online contributions and behaviour among a virtual or actual community of scholars.

Abilities being assessed

Upon completion of the unit students are expected to have developed:

- an understanding of the concepts, principles and practices of open learning, open access, distance learning, flexible delivery and 'just-in-time' learning;
- a basic familiarity with and skills in the operation of communications and information technologies for flexible delivery;
- an introductory understanding and acquisition of skills in educational design, strategies and techniques in the use of flexible delivery options;
- an awareness of the future trends and developments in open learning.

Assessment task

There are three assessment items.

1. An open learning incident (1,500–2,000 words, 40 per cent)

Students are asked to investigate an open learning incident within their own local or professional community. Students provide an analysis of how technology supports interaction, the problems and benefits. Observation and data collection are required as well as reference to the principles presented in study materials. Essays must include a description of the open learning incident and a brief description of the context, the technologies used, discussion of their purpose, suitability and practicality issues.

2. Online learning communities (1,400 words, 20 per cent)

This assignment is based upon student participation in online events throughout the semester. Debates and discussions are held online as well as students being encouraged to join suitable online communities for experience and applied reflection. The initial submission is to comment on the students' participation in an online event, their impressions, feelings, others' reactions, how dialogue flowed, accompanied by printouts of their contribution to the discussion.

The second submission is in two parts – two short reviews of online communities. Students describe the purpose, content and value of two online communities they experienced. Details of subscription to list or archive are required.

The third submission requires students to discuss the potential of online communications for adult education and training in the workplace.

3. Designing an open learning programme using interactive telecommunications technologies (2,000 words, 40 per cent)

Students are required to design a small number of training sessions for an open learning context that utilizes at least one communications technology.

Marking

Students are graded on specific criteria for each of the assignments, which include:

- completeness of the description of the open learning incident and technologies used;
- critical evaluation of the suitability of technologies for the context and curriculum;
- clarity of the statement of position on an issue related to open learning;
- contribution to online dialogue and discussion, promoting interaction with other students;
- evaluation of an Internet resource or online community for open learning specialists;
- curriculum planning skills;
- planning of open learning implementation;
- justification for the use of technologies within an open learning programme.

Strengths and limitations

Strengths

Since the use of telecommunications facilities is an integral part of the learning experiences in this unit – being both the subject matter and process – students must take a metacognitive approach to their learning. The integrated nature of assessment, based on experience, reflection and literature, ensures the achievement of higher order outcomes including critical reflection and communication with professional peers. Experiential and situated learning in this case also ensure that students apply their knowledge as it develops.

Limitations

A limitation of the assessment structure of this unit occasionally arises when students, despite their best efforts, are unable to access or handle the technologies required. On the other hand, the tendency in this unit had been for students to carry out more activities than are assessable. This can be seen as both a strength and a limitation (where an over-involvement with one unit may jeopardize progress in other units of study).

4.3 BECOMING AN OZKIDSCONNECT VOLUNTEER

Case study from Education (postgraduate)

Lyn Hay, Charles Sturt University, Australia

The following case study has been compiled and edited from the written materials Lyn Hay provided.

OZKidsConnect is the Australian arm of the US-based KidsConnect question-answering, help and referral service for K–12 students on the Internet. OZKidsConnect is an electronic referral service designed to:

- help students learn to navigate the Internet;
- increase the national (and international) profile of teacher librarians;
- provide high quality information services in response to student needs;
- help teacher librarians fulfil their role as information skills teachers.

KidsConnect is operated in partnership with the Information Institute of Syracuse, Syracuse University. Through e-mail or via Web-based request (www.ala.org/ ICONN/AskKC.html) students contact the KidsConnect service and receive a message from a volunteer library media specialist with assistance within two school days. The role of a volunteer is outlined at (www.ala.org/ICONN/kcvolunteer.html).

Context

Information Environment is a core subject in the Master of Education (Teacher Librarianship) programme. This postgraduate degree is vocationally oriented and students are required to have a four-year undergraduate degree in education. Students do not necessarily have to be currently working as a teacher librarian in a primary or secondary school, and the majority of students are practising classroom teachers.

The Information Environment subject introduces students to the global information environment and focuses on how the teacher librarian facilitates access to a range of information sources and services for school community members. The nature of reference work is explored in detail, with particular emphasis placed on the design and implementation of search strategies when using manual and electronic sources and services. Digital reference services are presented as an emerging and important part of information service provision in schools using the Internet as an information source.

Students completing this subject are required to have a reliable and regularly accessible e-mail account and access to a WWW browser (eg Netscape, Internet Explorer) either at home or at work. Students are expected to interact with peers and academic staff via a subject listserv and e-mail. Subject materials are sent to all students in the form of a hard copy mail package, which includes subject outline, study guide and readings. The study guide contains many URLs for WWW resources, and is also available via the CSU Online Web site, allowing students to follow the embedded hyperlinks while working through each topic. Students are also provided with trial access (for the duration of this subject) to a number of commercial information services such as MacquarieNet, Electric Library and EBSCOhost's World Magazine Bank.

Abilities being assessed

At the end of this subject students should be able to:

- assess the appropriateness of a variety of information agencies, services and sources in providing information for school library users, and access these as required;
- describe the role of the teacher librarian in effectively managing the school as a total information resource, including print, non-print, electronic and human resources;
- identify the information needs of the school community and provide information services to best meet these needs from a range of existing information networks (local, national and international);
- effectively develop information literacy skills and access and provide appropriate and timely service to the K–12 Internet community of learners;
- understand the processes involved in creating new information networks.

The assessment items for this subject have been designed with these outcomes in mind.

The following example is given to students as one of the options they may choose for assessment in Information Environment. If this option is selected, access to e-mail and the Internet is naturally a prerequisite.

Assessment task

This option consists of three parts:

1. OZKidsConnect training.
2. AskKC requests.
3. Evaluation report.

Part 1: OZKidsConnect training

Students must satisfactorily complete the KidsConnect one-week online training programme co-ordinated by Syracuse University during a specified fortnightly period. This training consists of reading through the KidsConnect Web-based instructional material, practice questions, and one-to-one training with individual feedback for each volunteer.

Students need to allocate approximately one half hour each day throughout the training week to complete readings and activities. They are expected to keep a portfolio (in hard copy) of all e-mail correspondence with the KidsConnect trainer during the training week and submit it as Appendix 1 to their report.

Part 2: AskKC requests

Students are expected to complete at least two genuine AskKC requests from school students. These are allocated after students complete Part 1: OZKidsConnect training. A hard copy of two AskKC requests and the reply/answer as an OZKidsConnect volunteer is also submitted.

Part 3: Evaluation report (1,000 words maximum)

Students must complete an evaluative report of the OZKidsConnect programme based on their experiences as an OZKidsConnect volunteer. The report should include:

- an evaluation of completion of the KidsConnect training programme, including problems and difficulties encountered, and the skills acquired/refined during the training;
- a short evaluation of two AskKC requests and the students' replies, including how effectively they responded to each request and what aspects of the search process or reply they would, on reflection, change/improve;
- a short statement on (what students consider to be) the value of the OZKidsConnect service in supporting the information needs of the Internet school users.

Marking

Students complete a total of three assessment tasks in this unit. The value of these items is 45 per cent and the approximate word limit is 2,000.

Part 1: OZKidsConnect training

Students automatically receive 15/45 marks for satisfactorily completing the training course. Students are required to complete at least two practice questions (some students are required to complete a third question if the trainer feels the student needs more practice) before completing the requests in Part 2. Satisfactory completion of the training is therefore determined by the lecturer in consultation with a Syracuse University volunteer trainer and evidence provided in the portfolio of e-mail correspondence.

Part 2: AskKC requests

Students are allocated a mark out of 15 for completion of the two genuine AskKC questions in Part 2 of the assessment task. This grade is allocated by the lecturer based on criteria relating to learners' abilities to:

- prepare a response to student inquiry;
- adequately research the question and refer sources;
- conclude and send the message.

Part 3: Evaluation report

Students receive a mark out of 15 for their evaluative report. Students are expected to critically evaluate the effectiveness of the training programme and reflect on how 'satisfactorily' they answered the two genuine AskKC requests. Students are also required to identify the information and technology skills they developed during completion of this assessment item and how they relate to their role as an information specialist in a school. Finally, students are asked to comment on the value of

OZKidsConnect as a question answering and referral service for K–12 students using the Internet.

Overall marks are allocated for clarity of presentation, adherence to the assessment guidelines, and evidence of synthesis, analysis and evaluation in compiling the report.

Strengths and limitations

Strengths

This assessment item's particular strength is that it contributes to the achievement of each of the first eight expected student outcomes for this unit. Students are also exposed to the online training of a 'real' digital reference service, which is far more practical than completing a series of 'dummy' reference exercises developed by the lecturer. Students become part of a professional 'learning team', are provided with step-by-step instructions with a variety of examples on which to 'model' their answers, and are given individual and immediate feedback as they compile each reply to their practice questions. This process contributes to students' understanding of the mechanics of 'best practice' in training modules.

The portfolio of e-mail correspondence and completion of an evaluative report is designed to encourage students to become reflective practitioners, the intention being that students gain a personal understanding of the concepts underpinning the Information Environment unit. This reflects the lecturer's approach to curriculum design and teaching in general, which is principally inquiry and resource-based within a constructivist domain. For MEd (Teacher Librarianship) students to become effective teacher librarians and meet the information and learning needs of teachers and students, they must understand what it is involved in becoming an independent learner within an increasingly complex information environment.

Students have found this assignment an extremely valuable 'hands-on' approach to understanding the potential of digital reference services in meeting the information needs of their school community members. Over a six-week period, students who consider themselves 'novice' Internet users, feel more confident and proficient in diagnosing learners' information needs, developing effective search strategies and manipulating WWW subject directories and search engines.

Limitations

Some limitations exist with this assessment task. First, co-ordination of this assessment involves an information service external to the university's infrastructure. Success of such collaboration is dependent upon the personality and goodwill of the KidsConnect co-ordinator and the lecturer of this unit. In 1999, it was agreed that students completing this assessment task would complete a third compulsory practice question in the form of an FAQ (Frequently Asked Question). This was negotiated on the lecturer's behalf to ensure that the KidsConnect service received some long-term benefit from this student training (while some students may nominate to become permanent volunteers, many did not).

Other limitations include dependence upon the reliability of students' Internet connections and the ability of the KC trainer to turnaround student feedback in a timely fashion (time zone differences could potentially cause problems with a 48-hour turnaround time). It is also the lecturer's role to act as a conduit between the KC trainer and the students, and meet the needs of both parties when struggling with technology problems or a delay in turnaround. However, the quality of students' work and appropriateness of this assessment task in consolidating much of the theory, practice and expected outcomes of this subject, far outweigh the potential problems or limitations.

4.4 WHOLE-OF-COURSE PORTFOLIO

Case study from Education (postgraduate)

Lorraine Stefani, University of Strathclyde, UK

The following information has been edited from materials provided by Lorraine Stefani.

This example describes an assessment approach pertaining to a whole programme of study. The same assessment ethos and format are used across several subject areas, with the concept of a whole-of-course portfolio being developed by students during their progress through the course.

The ethos underpinning the accredited programme in Advanced Academic Studies is to provide a framework for self-directed professional development for academics. The course aims to promote the concept of reflection on theory and practice contextualized to different disciplinary needs and encompassing different learning styles and processes.

The course is designed essentially to accommodate distance and self-directed learning. There is timetabled formal contact time for each module that does not exceed 20 hours. This contact can take different formats. While it is possible to encourage course participants to attend module-related workshops, for the many participants who cannot attend, any course materials are sent out either using conventional internal or external mailing arrangements or by use of the WWW. Also there is a strong emphasis on peer collaboration within the course so every effort is made to encourage the development of a community of scholars engaged in peer learning. Much of this is carried out using e-mail communication, bulletin boards or electronic chat rooms.

As an example of managing and developing oneself at postgraduate level, this assessment strategy illustrates an integrated approach.

Context

There is increasing public and political interest in quality assurance in higher education, which is reflected in a perceived need for preparation and continuing professional development for academic staff. This perceived need was given further credence by the recommendations of the Dearing Report (1997) that academic staff should seek accreditation pathways for their academic practice and subsequent membership of the proposed Institute of Learning and Teaching. The postgraduate Certificate/Diploma Course in Advanced Academic Studies is the University of Strathclyde's response to these recommendations and requirements. This modular course is open to all academic and related staff members who have some direct responsibility for teaching and assessment. The course is also available, at a cost, to any member of academic or related staff from outside the University of Strathclyde.

The Certificate level of the course involves participants completing a compulsory module in Personal Development Planning, a compulsory double module in Teaching, Learning and Assessment and an optional module chosen from an extensive range of modules which include Academic Writing, Web-based Teaching and Learning, and Academic Management. To complete the Diploma participants are required to choose three optional modules from the range on offer and to complete one final Integrating module.

Participants will present their portfolio to the external examiner and if they have successfully completed the course to Certificate level they will be able to apply for membership of the Institute of Teaching and Learning.

Abilities being assessed

Throughout the programme, participants are encouraged to build up a portfolio of assignments and other evidence of good academic practice. Progression through the course should enable participants to become more effective practitioners through theoretically informed reflection and research on their own teaching and related activities. Participants have the opportunity to reflect on their own work in relation to teaching and learning as an integral part of the assessment and evaluation of their own progress through this course.

Assessment tasks

Assessment within the programme is intended to provide evidence that appropriate academic standards have been achieved. Course modules are subject to two kinds of assessment criteria:

1. general criteria that apply to all modules;
2. criteria that are specific to the processes, outcomes and content of each individual module.

The assessment tasks consist mainly of assignments; these require an appropriate balance of understanding of principles and grasp of relevant knowledge. Other assessment tasks may take the form of presentations, reflective reports and specific projects as agreed and negotiated with module tutors.

General criteria

The general criteria for assessment, which are clearly articulated for participants within the Course Handbook, include participants displaying:

- evidence of professional development;
- an ability to learn independently;
- a critical grasp of concepts and principles related to the module through appropriate use of language, analysis of situations, response to problems and choice of research methodology;
- an ability to locate, comprehend and critically analyse relevant information from the published literature;
- proper ethical standards of behaviour (crucial in dealing with confidential data).

Module-specific criteria

Each module associated with the course has clearly stated module-specific assessment criteria.

To illustrate this it is best to take a module example, Web-based Teaching. This module involves the design and creation of a Web-based course with integrated on-line assessment. This is intended to equip participants with the necessary skills to use the WWW for teaching. During a series of case studies participants explore the practical and pedagogical issues of using new technology to enhance more traditional teaching methods. For satisfactory completion of this module participants must undertake the programme of work and publish an original course on the WWW. Participants must include for assessment:

- a written report outlining the aims, objectives and pedagogical design of the course to be submitted in both paper and electronic formats;
- an educational Web site comprising a minimum of 10 Web pages with text, graphics, hyper links and e-mail contact. The design of these Web pages is included in the assessment;
- an electronic assessment that must be integrated into this Web site, comprising free text entry and computer marked questions with appropriate inbuilt feedback.

Marking

All assignments are assessed on a two-point scale – satisfactory or unsatisfactory – with participants having the opportunity to resubmit an assignment just once. If the assessment is deemed unsatisfactory for a second time, the participants may be asked to re-register for the module.

Definitions of 'satisfactory' and 'unsatisfactory' are provided for students with respect to each stage (ie 1–4) of the assessment process, and include the need to link the design and critique of Web sites to current literature and to demonstrate original thinking.

Strengths and limitations

Comments from lecturer: the main weaknesses in the assessment criteria are in how to define 'unsatisfactory' in terms of relating the pedagogical design of a course to current literature. This is not clear-cut and contains an element of subjectivity. Another perceived limitation is the participants' access to the WWW. Some participants may have limited access, though Web and e-mail access is a requirement for registration on the module.

The main strength of the assessment is that it will be online and will eventually be openly accessed. This means that the assessment material will remain within the ownership of the participants and can be used for teaching and learning.

In addition, the integrated structure of the portfolio style of assessment allows a great deal of self-directedness in students' approach to learning – a feature most appropriate at postgraduate level.

5. Accessing and managing information

5.1 Delivering a scientific research paper to an audience of peers
5.2 Sharing development and discussion of case study method
5.3 Presenting an exhibit at an arts conference
5.4 Writing a proposal, researching and reporting findings

In this so-called 'information age', accessing and managing information in learners' discipline areas is an ability that continues to develop throughout learners' professional lives. The foundations of these abilities should be laid during undergraduate years, where assessments will focus upon their development with incremental degrees of difficulty. Some disciplines, such as law, have highly specialized sources of information and data, which may require a specific approach and a step-by-step teaching method. Others may be approached more generally, where skills in the use of bibliographic software are developed in concert with skills in purposeful reading, critical thinking and the management and presentation of information – the case studies in this section belong to the latter category. These case studies have been selected for their particular strength in building and refining skills of looking for data or information, retrieving it, and then using that information meaningfully in their disciplinary settings. They also demonstrate an innovative array of responses to issues of distance, and the collaborative, social aspects of learning.

5.1 DELIVERING A SCIENTIFIC RESEARCH PAPER TO AN AUDIENCE OF PEERS

Case study from Natural Resource Science

Andrew Boulton and Graeme Moss, University of New England, Australia

The following case study is an edited version of written materials Andrew Boulton provided, together with additional comments he made after seeing the first draft.

This example describes the process of accessing and managing information in an authentic and situated context. Students experience the process of making an application for research funding, carrying out the proposal (on a shoestring budget) and presenting the report of findings to a review panel of peers.

Context

The B.Nat.Res. is the oldest degree in natural resource management in Australia and has been offered since 1973. In external mode, the degree is popular with staff from government agencies who seek exposure to the latest technology and information in a range of field and analytical techniques in ecosystem management and can apply these skills to their present job. The unit, Resource Survey and Habitat Evaluation (RSHE), has proved especially useful because it integrates field survey methods with data analysis. Previously, these topics were treated separately ('ecology' vs 'mathematics') confounding the learning approaches. Teaching practices in the school now focus on integrating 'real-life' scenarios with skills such as proposal preparation, peer review, community consultation, budget management and report preparation for a range of audiences (lay to professional).

The RSHE unit is an elective in the B.Nat.Res. degree. One aspect of the assessment is the preparation of a research proposal following Australian Research Council (ARC) guidelines, with a limited 'budget'. The students submit this for peer assessment, and are themselves part of a panel to review other applications. Based on the peers' and teachers' comments, the research outlined in the proposal is carried out, the data analysed, and the results presented verbally and in a written report.

Abilities being assessed

Abilities being assessed are:

- solving problems using a conventional scientific method;
- preparing a research proposal that concisely describes the approach;

- conducting field surveys or experiments, using quantitative and qualitative techniques, analysing, managing and presenting scientific data for verbal and written presentations (including correct representation of statistical significance);
- written and verbal communication for a range of audiences (peers and professionals for the proposal, a lay audience for the report summary, professional audience for the report).

Assessment tasks

A. Solving problems and preparing a research proposal
Students choose their own topic and prepare a research proposal according to ARC guidelines. They are assessed using the same criteria provided to professional referees for ARC grants (available on the Internet). They must use the conventional scientific method (ie framing a testable hypothesis, identifying alternative hypotheses, and outlining an approach that would unambiguously address the specific hypothesis) and present this within the limited space available on the electronic submission form that is issued to students.

B. Conducting research
Although field skills can be described in a proposal, their *technical* competence can only be developed through experience. During a 'hands-on' residential school, over half the time is devoted to field training. The management and presentation of data are the skills that students find most difficult to master, partly due to a 'fear of mathematics' and limited numeracy. Appropriate survey and experimental design (including replication and randomization) must be evident. The correct choice of statistical approaches and data presentation methods are assessed in oral and written forms.

C. Written and verbal communication
The assessment task requires the submission of a 2,500-word proposal for review by peers and the teachers (25 per cent of marks, with peer review worth 5 per cent). The 10-minute seminar on the results (5 per cent) is marked by peers and teachers simultaneously, and the final 4,000-word project report (25 per cent) is handed in for assessment by the teachers only. This task is worth a total of 60 per cent of the overall grade. The timelines are:

- the proposal – five weeks;
- peer review – one afternoon;
- turnaround for teachers' assessment and comments – three days;
- project executed during the three-week mid-semester break; and
- the report due eight weeks after peer review.

Marking

Students receive marks for all of the three assessment tasks. For the proposal, students are given a detailed marking proforma (broken down by sections), which is also used by the teachers in the final assessment. Marks are allocated mainly for clarity of hypothesis, elegance of design and execution, and succinctness. For the seminar, a proforma is also used, assessing clarity of speech and visual aids as well as correct data presentation. The report is marked using all of the above criteria. In all cases, 5 per cent of the total mark per assessment task per day is deducted for late work.

Strengths and limitations

Strengths

The main strength perceived by students is the task's direct workplace relevance, dealing with a series of skills that are seldom covered in other units (ie proposal preparation and assessment). The *logic* of the research process – the sequence of question formulation, hypothesis generation, testing and analysis, communication of outcomes – is evident because the process takes place chronologically, with practical experience at each step. The peer involvement in each other's projects is especially popular and leads to collaboration in some cases. Students learn much from assessing others' proposals, and recognize the personal investment in this process. Outcomes from the student's personal development in research skills are linked directly to learning outcomes, allowing students to identify their own strengths and weaknesses in this process. Students and assessors report that they find the assessment programme relevant and worthwhile.

Limitations

Limitations/problems include the necessity to turn around the research proposals for each student within three days, yet identify flaws in research design and 'red herrings' introduced by the peer reviews. Some students take criticism poorly, particularly from peers (this may be a cultural issue) whereas other students feel uncomfortable about giving face-to-face commentary to their peers when they identify a serious flaw in a proposal. In the weeks following the return of the proposal to the students, there is much intensive face-to-face teaching for which we budget time, recognizing that this may be some of our most effective teaching in this unit!

5.2 SHARING DEVELOPMENT AND DISCUSSION OF CASE STUDY METHOD

Case study from Public Health (postgraduate)

Ross Bailie, Flinders University, Northern Territory Clinical School and Menzies School of Health Research, Northern Territory University/University of Sydney, Australia

The following case study is an edited version of written materials Ross Bailie provided, to-gether with additional comments he made after seeing the first draft.

This example of case study method illustrates the principles of accessing and managing information in a social ethnographic context. The case study matter to be studied for this unit is restricted to the field of public health. It is not ex-pected that students will achieve the scale and rigour of a research project, but rather a critical reflection on a public health-related matter that has happened in the past and has reached some sort of logical end point for the purpose of the case study.

Students are expected to draw on the knowledge and skills of other units in the Master of Public Health, and on their work and other relevant experience, to conduct a critical review of a public health-related matter of their choice. The matter should ideally have been part of their own work experience, and one for which they can gain access to relevant information.

Context

The unit, Case Studies in Public Health, is run over one semester (18 weeks). Each student is required to identify, in consultation with the unit co-ordinator, a specific matter for the case study. The focus for the case study should be on policy develop-ment or policy implementation in relation to this matter. Students are expected to conduct a critical review of a policy development/implementation process by draw-ing on documentary evidence and interviews to develop a case study.

The matter for the case study, the background to the matter, and a proposed ap-proach to the case study are to be the subject of a presentation by each student dur-ing the teaching residential. This is a work in progress presentation during which other students and staff contribute to the development of the case study by suggest-ing alternative approaches, further direction and sources of information. Students and staff are from a diverse range of backgrounds, mostly working in the health field, including doctors, nurses, physiotherapists, teachers, project officers, health educators, administrators, etc.

Although students are required to develop their own case study and are graded for their own work, they are encouraged to do this in collaboration or consultation with other students in the cohort. They are also encouraged to work with other col-leagues who have knowledge of the subject of the case study, including at least one person to be identified as a 'tutor'. This tutor can be nominated by the student and the appointment is approved by the unit co-ordinator.

Abilities being assessed

The overall objective of the unit is to further develop the range of skills students have acquired to date, and to learn to integrate these skills in developing a critical analysis of a matter relevant to their own work environment, specifically focusing on policy development/implementation. The unit also aims to encourage students to:

- apply the principles of public health through critical reflection on management and outcomes of policy process;
- effectively communicate their analysis.

On completion of this unit students are expected to develop competence in:

- critical analysis of problems and interventions within a specific setting through the clear definition of problems and the appropriate gathering and analysis of data;
- making a presentation of their work, responding to questions, and engaging in constructive discussion of their own work and the work of their colleagues;
- report writing.

Assessment task

All students are required to develop their own case study. This may be done in consultation with other students as well as one person selected by the student and formally identified as a 'tutor'. Acknowledgement of collaboration is mandatory but the individual student must clearly have a leading role and marks are allocated on an individual basis. Students are encouraged to have ongoing discussions regarding the direction of the case study with the unit co-ordinator. An initial teleconference supports the development of case study proposals.

Oral presentations at the residential tutorial are allocated 10 minutes with an additional 10 minutes for discussion. This requires students to be prepared to respond to questions and to engage in constructive discussion of their own work and the work of their colleagues.

Following submission of the written report, a final teleconference is held where students present their individual case studies. Approximately five minutes per speaker are allocated with additional time for brief questions and comments.

Marking

Eighty per cent of the grade is allocated to the written report of case study (maximum 3,000 words). Reports are assessed on:

- clarity of introduction and initial overview of the case study – its aims, objectives and purpose;
- clarity of description and appropriate use of methods for gathering and analysing data and information;
- demonstration of knowledge and understanding of locally important issues;
- demonstration of knowledge and understanding of the broader context (regional/national/international) of the matter;
- appropriate discussion of the findings of the case study, and appropriateness of conclusions drawn;

- compliance with requirements for presenting a report for publication, including referencing;
- clarity of expression, accuracy of grammar and spelling.

Twenty per cent of the grade is allocated to presentation. Presentations are assessed on:

- clear definition of the subject of the case study;
- demonstration of knowledge and understanding relevant to the subject;
- ability to hold the interest of listeners and use of audio-visual aids;
- ability to keep to the 10-minute time limit for the presentation;
- response to challenges and questions from the audience;
- strength of justifications demonstrated through discussion and presentation.

Strengths and limitations

Strengths

This unit requires students to identify and critically assess a real policy development/implementation matter within their own work context. This means the unit is practical and relevant, since students:

- focus on their own work environment;
- apply concepts to real-world issues;
- bring their own unique issue forward for discussion and group reflection;
- develop shared understandings;
- provide a supportive peer learning environment.

Limitations

Limitations include the need to have small class groups and thus a high teacher to student ratio. Some students may have difficulty identifying suitable policy issues from their own work environment.

5.3 PRESENTING AN EXHIBIT AT AN ARTS CONFERENCE

Case study from Art Education (postgraduate)

Robert Harris, Charles Sturt University, Australia

The following case study is an edited version of written materials Robert Harris provided, together with additional comments he made after seeing the first draft.

It is a core skill in the field of art education to be able to assess one's own work and the work of others. Peer assessment is a useful method of supporting such skills development. In addition, peer assessment gives these education students the experience of another assessment technique, thus enhancing the scope of their own teaching practices. In particular, this example illustrates how students access information and resources from their regional community and present their exhibits to a live audience. While at the two-day end-of-semester conference on an art education theme, students also access and manage a very social and interactive range of information sources.

Context

Within the School of Education, the Graduate Diploma of Education (Secondary) provides the opportunity for students to choose to study art education, or a range of other specialist teaching areas at postgraduate level through on-campus or distance education modes. The subject, Curriculum Studies 2: Art, taken in the students' final semester, is the second and final curriculum study in the course. Content and assessment strategies are planned to develop broadly-based knowledge and attitudes about education.

The course is vocationally oriented, preparing students for employment in private and public education systems in all Australian states. Students are drawn from a wide geographic area within Australia, with some studying from overseas.

Abilities being assessed

Students are assessed on their ability to:

- develop, implement, assess and evaluate art programmes for secondary schools;
- exhibit confidence in developing and presenting original material to a group of peers through written, verbal and visual presentation;
- identify and utilize a diverse range of local and regional resources in the development and implementation of educational programmes.

Assessment tasks

Assessment is progressive and cumulative. The first two assignments cover aspects of syllabus and programme planning, which allows for application to the students' personal interests and needs.

The third assignment, nick-named 'VACATION' (Visual Arts Conference Action) is at the end of the semester and requires students to attend and participate in the conference presentations and assessment of their peers together with students studying by full-time, on-campus mode (a total of 20–30 students).

A diverse range of presentation ideas is made possible through the open nature of the assignment topic. Students' decisions are based on researching and documenting regional resources that could be beneficial to the implementation of a visual arts programme for secondary schools, for example artists/craftspeople, facilities such as art galleries, empty shops, open spaces, walls, communications media and so on. Full-time students are required to present a slightly different topic, so enhancing the diversity of this shared conference experience.

Students develop conference papers to focus on their region. They travel from many areas of Australia to Wagga Wagga in the Riverina district of southeastern New South Wales to attend the two-day conference. A resources file is also brought to the conference by all students so they may share the contents with the other students.

All students are sent a conference registration form in which they provide details of their specific presentation topic together with a brief summary. These topics are printed in the conference agenda. This procedure aids pre-planning by the students and allows balanced planning of the conference timetable. They are encouraged to support the presentation with multimedia.

A timetable of half-hour time slots for presentations is structured to allow for adequate breaks and socializing over the two-day period. A summary of each paper is prepared by the presenting student and distributed to all other students prior to the presentation. This assists the students in planning as well as providing all participants with examples of many different ideas that they might apply to their own situations when teaching.

Peer assessment sheets are prepared and distributed to guide students in the assessment criteria of the assignments. Students complete an assessment sheet for each presentation, and are encouraged to write further comments on each sheet. All sheets are submitted at the end of the two-day conference, so allowing students to re-evaluate earlier presented papers. Being aware of this model prior to the conference helps in their planning to meet the requirements of the conference paper. It also gives them experience in another form of assessment, which they can apply to assessment tasks in their future teaching positions. While comparative assessment plays a minor role, criterion-based assessment is the major focus.

For the opening of the conference people such as the head of school, course co-ordinator and a representative from the Department of Education and Training are invited to briefly address these final year students. At the conclusion of the conference, summary remarks are made by the subject co-ordinator, all assessment sheets are collected, and final assessment is completed within the next week and distributed to students with relevant evaluative comments.

Social aspects of learning

Students may choose inexpensive accommodation where a number of them stay together. Information is supplied to them on venues and costs. Others may choose to be hosted by on-campus students in the same course. Both of these options give visiting and local students the opportunity to informally share ideas about the course and teaching in general as well as providing a venue for relaxed socializing.

Students are invited for supper to the unit co-ordinator's home on the first night after settling into their accommodation. This allows for some face-to-face meetings and for students to feel more relaxed together prior to the conference presentations. A conference dinner is planned for the second night at an inexpensive venue in the city. An entertaining speaker is invited to give an informal and light-hearted after-dinner address. The on-campus coffee shop and student union are approached to gain concessions for morning and afternoon teas.

Strengths

For students

This model brings students together for a focused period of time to experience the advantages of a 'get together', interactive learning and socializing with people, many of whom have not previously met.

It gives students an opportunity to do an assessment task that is not just theory driven, but emanates from their identification of a facility, need or situation in their own region, the consideration of which has very practical foundations and outcomes. The openness of the assignment topic and the mode of presentation allow for a range of very diverse topics and ideas to be shared with all participants. Peer evaluation provides a general commonality of assessment that can modify and support the thoughts of the academic assessor, often providing some fresh insights.

The whole experience gives students a model of the procedures involved in submitting presentations at conferences of professional organizations related to art and education. Students feel cared about and develop identity with the university and its staff through the welcoming addresses at the conference and the dinner. They feel more part of a profession.

For markers and the university

As the last assessment item in the subject it is easier, after being involved with the conference presentations and having the modifying peer evaluation sheets, to provide a shorter return time to students for the final assessment and grading of the subject. Local media can raise the profile of different types of learning at universities by covering the conference.

Limitations

Some students experience some difficulties for geographic reasons, which affect the costs and time expended on travel. Some students gain exemption from attendance for these and other personal reasons. In these cases the assignment is still done, and summaries shared, but only written/visual work is submitted.

The two-day period is barely long enough to comfortably fit in the required number of half-hour presentations. It may be necessary to reduce the amount of time allocated to presentations or increase the duration of the conference.

Students have commented that it would be better to meet earlier in the course for this type of activity. There can be organizational difficulties involving the co-operation of other academic staff with regard to timetabling and room usage during the two-day conference period. The end of semester is a busy time… but what time isn't? The conference is worth every minute of the time spent in organization.

5.4 WRITING A PROPOSAL, RESEARCHING AND REPORTING FINDINGS

Case study from Anthropology

Linda Driedger, Athabasca University, Canada

The following case study is an edited version of written materials Linda Driedger provided, together with additional comments she made after seeing the first draft.

This example describes an assessment scheme that is employed across a complete Bachelor's programme. The structure of the assessment scheme is highly appropriate for students planning to continue on to the postgraduate level, being designed for students to identify their own learning needs and to carry out independent study.

The particular unit referred to in this example is one of the independent study units that students elect from the Anthropology major of the Bachelor of Arts degree. It illustrates a range of learning outcomes but has been included here principally as an example of managing and accessing information, since the assessment requirements are based on these student-centred principles rather than on set questions on content or knowledge.

Context

The Bachelor of Arts is a four-year distance programme of study that includes major streams. One of the streams is the programme in anthropology, intended to be an introduction to the four major areas within anthropology:

- physical anthropology;
- archaeology;
- linguistic anthropology; and
- social-cultural anthropology.

Graduating students are expected to have a basic education in all four. Within the anthropology programme majors, the student can enrol in a series of courses that are individual studies in special topics, regional studies, and method and theory in anthropology.

In these units students are required to develop a proposal, conduct research in a particular regional or theoretical area, and write a major paper based on this research. They conduct interviews with members of the community and subject experts, and they use library and Internet resources available to them.

Abilities being assessed

Abilities being assessed are:

- development of own proposals;
- accessing, assessing and managing information;
- development of written communication.

Assessment tasks

Development of research proposals

Stage I. Students are required to have some concept of what they would like to research independently before they are allowed to register. Students meet this requirement by agreeing a verbal contract with the academic co-ordinator.

Stage II. Once registered in the unit, students complete their first assignment. This is a written assignment in which the student defines and analyses the topic, generates a thesis statement that will guide research, and compiles the list of sources of data. These elements of the proposal are used as the basis of a formal report. The topic should be challenging and appropriate, and there should be research materials and sources available. This forms the basis of the formal evaluation scheme, and it is worth 15 per cent of the overall mark.

Accessing, assessing and managing information

As part of the first assignment students are required to provide a list of their sources and data in an annotated format. This illustrates their ability to access and manage the information they need for their next assignment, which is to develop a formal outline of their essay or report. The annotated format of this particular assignment also requires students to assess the materials they are using.

Development of written communication

Students are required to complete a formal outline in preparation for their essay or report, which consists of 25 per cent of the overall mark, and development of the essay or report, which is worth 60 per cent of the mark.

Marking

Students receive marks for all three assignment tasks. The first stage of the proposal, in which the students must complete the verbal contract as a prerequisite to registration, is not marked. The graded components of assessment are based on the written work. Marks are allocated on the basis of coherence, organization, clarity, voice and presentation. These independent study projects are conducted over a period of six to nine months.

Strengths and limitations

Strengths

These include the validity, development of outcomes that link directly to the learning outcomes, and development of outcomes that link directly to the individual learning goals. In the process of study students learn how to conduct interviews and to access and evaluate community and library resources as research tools. Students respond well to working on drafts of papers, and they particularly enjoy working on their own projects.

Students find assessment in this unit useful for the continued development of their project skills in respect to the programme as a whole and in preparation for postgraduate study.

Limitations

Limitations/problems include the necessity to be available to waive prerequisites and direct students in the first stages of their project. Initial selection of a topic is often far too broad, and the ability to focus the topic from the beginning of the process is very important. Initial discussions can be key in this regard.

6. Demonstrating knowledge and understanding

Assessing content knowledge and understanding has been a traditional activity in higher education and one which, we have argued, has been overused in the context of open and distance learning (ODL). The principal method of assessment of these abilities has been the invigilated examination, which has tended to promote reproductive learning and turns its back on the rich learning contexts and holistic, authentic assessment opportunities available to open and distance learners. Moreover, as Boud (1990) notes, successful performance in examinations does not necessarily correlate with a coherent grasp of the very concepts that were supposed to have been tested. Examinations have also commonly been criticized for their failure to provide formative feedback to learners. Yet objective testing has an important place in many discipline areas of ODL, and is most sensibly employed as only one of a series of assessment strategies across a programme as a whole.

Although computer-based objective testing is no substitute for assessing higher order skills such as critical, analytical and reflective thinking, it can be employed thoughtfully to support learners come to grips with bodies of knowledge and difficult concepts, and to employ basic problem-solving skills. The case studies selected here demonstrate tests, quizzes and other objective tests that have a highly formative function, in contrast to the use of terminal examination for summative purposes only. With the judicious use of computer mediation, learners have the benefit of rapid turnaround of assessment results with supporting information on their progress in achieving objectives.

6.1 TESTING KNOWLEDGE USING ONLINE MULTIPLE CHOICE QUIZZES

Case study from Continuing Education in Economics

Peter Sephton, University of New Brunswick, Canada

The following case study is an edited version of written materials Peter Sephton provided, together with additional comments he made after seeing the first draft.

Learning economics can be an accretive activity, where new blocks of knowledge are built upon foundations of understanding. It is therefore appropriate that quizzes and tests are used in both formative and summative assessment contexts for measuring student learning in this example.

Context

'Introduction to Microeconomics' is an online continuing education unit and part of the degree in Adult Education. To complete this open access learning programme, students can enrol in a number of online electives and put different emphasis in different areas where they wish to earn credit points. The online multiple choice questions (MCQs) included in this unit allow students to practise their knowledge and understanding towards a series of mastery tests.

The course is based on 20 chapters from the set textbook. Online lecture notes provide students with material identical to that delivered in on-campus lectures.

Abilities being assessed

Specific learning objectives are found in each module of study but overall, students are required to demonstrate knowledge and understanding of:

- demand and supply;
- pricing;
- market structure;
- government intervention.

Assessment tasks

Students in this unit are assessed using multiple choice testing. The unit is built around a textbook, with text chapters acting as 'modules'. Students work through the module at their own speed (with six months to finish each unit) and take five tests (worth 10 per cent of the final grade) and one final exam worth 50 per cent of the final grade.

At the end of each module students can take a practice quiz to check their understanding of the material. After several modules they are given tests (initially after the first five introductory modules, then every three modules or so). Students can take the practice MCQs as many times as they like but only get one attempt at the actual test covering that module. There's little overlap in most cases between the tutorial questions and the real test questions.

The testbanks contain about twice as many questions as are in a test, with questions randomly drawn from the entire testbank. Answers are randomized too in the sense that even if two students sitting side by side write the same test and by chance get the same question, the correct answer will most likely be placed differently (one may be the 'a' response, for another it may be the 'd' response).

Students practise these tests under the same conditions as the real tests. They are timed, and questions are drawn from a tutorial question bank that may have, at most, 5 per cent overlap with the real testbanks. Many students have said they wait to get 75 per cent or more consistently on the tutorials before they attempt a real test, and it is suggested to each student in their introductory mailing that this is a good approach to learning the materials.

With regards to the five time-limited tests and one time-limited final examination, students have about 70 minutes to complete 50 questions from the time they start the test (each should only take about 50 minutes but 70 minutes have been allocated to allow for server and modem response time), and 210 minutes to finish 100 questions in the final exam (which should take much less than three hours).

On-campus students are evaluated differently (assignments take the place of several tests) but there are mid-term and final exams (with similar weighting schemes).

Marking

Each of the five tests is worth 10 per cent of the final unit grade, with the final examination carrying a weight of 50 per cent.

The short quiz at the end of every chapter consists of 10 MCQs. Results are used for formative purposes only and do not count towards the final grade. These practice questions provide an opportunity to reveal the correct response and students get immediate feedback, which helps to target areas in which they should focus their study.

All test results are automatically graded and returned immediately to students. The university runs a letter grading system, so the final component is to translate the numerical grade into a letter grade using the same system used for 'traditional students'.

Strengths and limitations

Students have the opportunity to go to a conferencing topic for each learning objective in each chapter of the material, and they can send e-mails as often as they like. Many questions are sent to the academic co-ordinator, some showing greater depth of understanding than others, and students have found they like the one-to-one response they are able to achieve in comparison to being in large classes and the impersonality they have felt in other courses.

Throughout the study materials there are links to Internet sites related to the unit content. Given the variety of platforms students have, multimedia components of the units have been kept to a minimum, in order to make them as accessible as possible. However, in Economics, heavy use is made of figures and diagrams, so there are a large number of visual items for students to comprehend. On-screen graphics break up the text and help students understand and demonstrate verbal arguments.

All tests and the final examination are automatically graded and returned, so feedback on the test is immediate. Students comment that they really like the automatic feedback.

6.2 REASONING AND LOGIC

Case study from Philosophy

Aubrey Townsend, Monash University, Australia

The following case study is an edited version of written materials Aubrey Townsend provided, together with additional comments he made after seeing the first draft.

It is the assessment strategy rather than the learning outcomes that has resulted in this example appearing in this chapter on demonstrating knowledge and understanding. We have chosen to use this example to illustrate the development and demonstration of logic and reasoning skills; however, it could equally have applications for assessment of critical thinking and making judgements. It is also a good example of mastery learning, where students have the opportunity to set their own targets in relation to the standard achieved.

Context

The principal objective of a philosophy course is to make students think about important issues that are deeply embedded in our views about the world and our place in it. Philosophy should draw out the fundamental presuppositions of our thought and allow us to examine them. That is what this unit, Reason and Moral Choice, challenges students to do. The foundations of moral thought are examined and students are encouraged to approach the unit with an open mind.

Because argument and critical evaluation of reasoning are fundamental in philosophy, the unit also includes an elementary logic course that aims to sharpen the 'tools' or 'intellectual muscles' students need to use. The aim is not only for students to examine their own views, but also to do this in a rigorous and disciplined way. A training in basic logic is therefore seen as being as important to philosophy as mathematics is for a scientist.

Abilities being assessed

Students from a whole host of study programmes and with a range of aspirations who want to be able to understand philosophical problems when they face them, and ultimately get answers to them, will require at least a basic training in philosophy. This philosophy unit, which focuses on reasoning and logic, is fundamentally concerned to develop open-mindedness together with the various skills of critical appraisal. Those who possess these virtues are well placed to gain a better understanding of both themselves and their culture.

Assessment tasks and marking

The most important feature of this subject is the method of assessment – in fact it is much more than a method of assessment, since it shapes the whole course and students' approaches to study.

There are six assessment tasks (ATs) and a final exam. One AT (number 5) is an essay; the others involve various short-answer questions. They are designed to take students through the syllabus, encouraging them to think about the key issues. They are also designed to develop skills in argument and writing that are needed for philosophy. Students must complete each AT to a satisfactory level before moving on to the next. Students can retry any task and the exam if the earlier attempt was unsuccessful. A retry will be an alternative version of the task.

Most ATs have two parts. The first, comprising very short questions, tests whether students have a satisfactory grasp of the basic work. Students must achieve mastery in this part; that is, they must answer 75–80 per cent of the questions successfully. The second part has longer and more searching questions and students' score on the ATs depends on this part, with the pass level set at 50 per cent. The one exception to this pattern is AT5, which is an essay.

Students have some say in determining what constitutes a satisfactory level, since they are invited to nominate the standard, ie pass, credit or distinction, that they want to achieve. Students could for example nominate credit as the standard to maintain and retry any tasks until they reach this standard. It is their choice, though they need not decide till AT2 has been completed.

Although the nominated standard may be reached in each AT, the students' final grade may be higher than the minimum level they set themselves. The following components are included in deciding the student's final grade for the unit: the essay (20 per cent), the best four ATs (40 per cent) and the exam (40 per cent). Students are allowed to miss one AT in the series (not the essay); they either don't do it or accept an unsatisfactory mark and move on.

The exam is used as a verifier and, to pass the subject, students have to gain a mark in the exam that is consistent with the scores obtained in the series of ATs. As with ATs, if students fail the exam they can try again until the cut-off date when results must be collated. So as to have a flexible arrangement for scheduling the final exam, it is proposed that students make their own arrangements for the day, place and time with someone approved by the university, for example being supervised by a librarian at the local library, a teacher at the school, a member of the church or similar institution. This person will certify the identity of the student.

Strengths and limitations

Strengths
An essential feature of this approach is that there should be very rapid feedback on the assessment tasks. With the benefit of e-mail, ATs are usually returned within three working days of receipt, though the essay may take a little longer. Although there are due dates given as guidelines, students are encouraged to organize their study schedule to suit their own pace. The final due date is not negotiable and extensions cannot be granted at the end of the semester.

Limitations
Limitations include the need for multiple versions of the ATs and/or exam where students wish to retry at different times. To accommodate a flexible pace for students' progress through the ATs and to sustain the rapid turnaround to all students, there needs to be a tutor on duty at all times to receive, mark and despatch the ATs within the three-day timeframe.

6.3 SIMULTANEOUS OFF- AND ON-CAMPUS MULTIPLE CHOICE TESTS

Case study from Business and Law

Wes Obst and Helen Scarborough, Deakin University, Australia

The following case study is an edited version of written and published materials provided by Wes Obst and Helen Scarborough, together with additional comments they made after seeing the first draft.

This example illustrates the use of online multiple choice testing, which has the potential to be used to align assessment for courses that have both on- and off-campus enrolments. The computer mediated approach makes it possible for all students in these courses to log onto the test at the same time and, having demonstrated their knowledge and understanding through multiple choice questions, be able to receive their grade immediately the testing period has elapsed.

Context

This case study reports on the conduct of computer managed multiple choice tests (MCTs) for the purpose of assessment in two commerce courses, Income Taxation Law and Practice, and Managerial Economics, which are offered by the Faculty of Business and Law at Deakin University. The two courses have distinct student bodies. Income Tax Law and Practice is a second-year subject within the Bachelor of Commerce, which is offered in both on-campus and distance education modes, and Managerial Economics is offered as a distance education course in the Master of Business Administration.

Abilities being assessed

This component assesses the demonstration of knowledge and understanding. Multiple choice assessment is used in both courses to provide efficient and effective feedback to students, to enable them to identify areas of deficiency in their knowledge, and to gain an appreciation of the key issues underlying the content of their course.

Assessment tasks

The online MCTs were devised by teaching staff and uploaded to the electronic delivery system by support staff. The test delivery software was developed by the university's educational development branch in consultation with academic staff.

To undertake the test students are required to log into the university's World Wide Web site during a 12-hour specified time period. After entering, their login and password are presented with the MCT (student names and identification numbers are used for login identification). All test instructions, including methods of obtaining results and feedback, are included in the online system. Information for access to the online test is provided to distance students through the university's computer conferencing facility, and to on-campus students in classes. Access to the programs is made via either a local area network or remote modems enabling both on-campus and distance students to participate.

The interactive interface of the software enables students to select the most appropriate answer for each question by clicking on the selected answer. Students are also able to scroll backwards and forwards through the questions in order to change their responses. When the students are satisfied with their responses they submit the test by selecting the appropriate option. Once the 'submit' option has been selected the student is not able to access the test again.

Following the end of the testing period students can again log into the test site and obtain their individual result and an analysis of the class results. The feedback provided by the online system enables the students to review each question and to obtain an explanation of why their answer is correct or not. Where a student has given an incorrect answer guidance is provided as to the concepts that need to be revised.

For staff, the programme generates a report that includes the individual student's name, number and result and also an analysis of the performance of the class for each individual question. These results are available electronically so that they can be downloaded into grade calculation software.

Marking

The multiple choice format enables testing of complex problem-solving skills and technical knowledge, and provides a means of rapid feedback for correction (formative) and assessment (summative).

A relatively low level of grading is attached to this component of the total assessment (10 per cent of total grade), enabling students to recover from a poor performance.

Strengths and limitations

An evaluation of these two online MCTs was conducted by the Deakin Centre for Academic Development (Holt, 1997). The discussion here is based on the findings of this formal evaluation and the perceptions of academic staff of the assessment process.

Strengths

Accurate and efficient feedback is very important to students as it enables them to gauge their progress in the unit. The online testing system provides rapid feedback, which enables students to correct misconceptions and deficiencies in knowledge before their rate of progress in the unit is impaired. Analysis of the student survey indicated that most students found this rapid feedback was valuable in determining their progress.

Online testing also reduces the assessment and administrative load for academic staff thereby enabling the provision of more regular feedback to students. Consequently, this system of online testing encourages constant revision and regular study patterns and facilitates self-paced learning.

Students report that access through the Internet provides a reliable and efficient platform that delivers the software effectively to all users, regardless of whether it is Macintosh or Windows based. Students also report that the test delivery software is easy to use and requires no training, and that the online testing approach provides a convenient and easy to use method of obtaining feedback on progress in the unit. One student said:

The technological advances made with the ... le cheating on ...
Internet are to be congratulated. Being a re... ble ... user ...
was still a little wary approaching the termina. ... the ... y ... clear in...
tions and preparation given were comprehensive, a... d the ... its of ... li-
ate assessment transparent.

Limitations

As with all assessment the issue of cheating needs to be considered. In both units this assessment task was limited to 10 per cent of final assessment, as there was no means of preventing collaboration or of ensuring that the individual student actually completed the test. It was emphasized to students that the online test was designed as a learning tool and the responsibility to gain maximum advantage from the process was placed on the student.

Although in this case the technological problems were very minor, the success of this assessment process still hinges on the reliability of the technology at the time the test is being conducted. Hence the technology, while being a strength also presents potential difficulties.

6.4 MATHEMATICS SELF-ASSESSMENT ON CD ROM

Case study from Continuing Education

Janet Taylor, University of Southern Queensland, Australia

The following case study is an edited version of written materials and the CD ROM provided by Janet Taylor, together with additional comments she made after seeing the first draft. Further information is available at http://www.usq.edu.au/users/taylorja/Selftest.htm

Many students have forgotten their school mathematics by the time they commence university study. Mathematics Refreshment for Engineering, Science and Technology is a support programme on CD ROM for external students who have little or outdated prior knowledge in mathematics (in this case algebra and calculus). This CD ROM provides a way for enrolling students to find out how much they have forgotten and how to catch up.

Developed initially from a government grant, it is the first in a series of self-assessment CD ROMs being developed at USQ. Students aiming to enter, or having recently entered a degree in engineering, science or technology, can complete this short programme and are advised that it should be achieved within the first four weeks of the semester to be of most support to their other studies.

Context

Mature-age students entering engineering studies come from a range of backgrounds and experiences and can encounter difficulties in the area of mathematics. Mathematics Refreshment for Engineering, Science and Technology is a support programme on CD ROM for external students enrolled in mathematics (Algebra and Calculus 1) for engineering science and technology studies. This CD ROM allows students to assess for themselves their level of mathematics proficiency and provides them with modules of mathematics so they can refresh.

The project was a joint initiative of three sections of the university (Office of Preparatory and Continuing Studies, Faculty of Engineering and Surveying and Distance Education Centre) involving staff Janet Taylor, David Ross, Michael Morgan, Glen Postle and David Grant. The project was funded by the Committee for Advancement of University Teaching in 1995 and USQ.

Programme description

Students are asked to complete a written diagnostic test, including all their working. Using Self Test (Taylor, 1998), a specially designed component of the CD ROM, students are also to mark the test and be provided with a study plan to refresh their mathematics, indicating which topics they have not mastered. These topics are provided on the CD ROM along with mastery tests using Self Test so that they can assess their mastery of each topic. The programme is given to students as soon as they enrol and they are expected to complete it by the first four weeks of the semester. Students are also provided with access to tutors over this period and academic counselling if they encounter problems. The programme is described in detail in Taylor and Morgan (1996) and is demonstrated at http://www.usq.edu.au/users/taylorja/Selftest.htm

Abilities being supported

The CD ROM aims to:

- provide refreshment in particular topics deemed essential for success in Algebra and Calculus 1;
- develop students' self-confidence with basic mathematical knowledge and skills;
- develop students' ability to be autonomous learners;
- provide a support network in mathematics in the initial weeks of studying Algebra and Calculus 1.

Assessment tasks

The CD ROM provides students with an initial skills test upon enrolment and mastery tests associated with each module of work. The self-assessment model used here is different from other models and was designed so that novice students:

- when presented with a problem, were encouraged to write out their solution in detail, including graphs and diagrams;
- would have a way of deciding if their solution matched a model solution;
- would have a number of alternative model solutions available to them if appropriate;
- would be credited, if necessary, when they got only part of a question correct;
- would have a summary at the end of each self-assessment session detailing which topics they still had to master.

The key to the production of a final diagnosis for students is the inclusion of a set of vital points for each question. They are necessary to guide a student through a solution, indicating which parts of a solution are essential and are linked to topics. Ticking a vital point indicates mastery has been achieved for that point.

Strengths and limitations

The package (Taylor, 1998):

- is very user-friendly;
- is easily delivered to distance students, giving them instant feedback on assessment questions;
- allows students to mark questions as well as an expert tutor;
- recognizes that students answer questions in different ways;
- credits students with getting parts of a question correct;
- produces an individualized study plan;
- allows students to easily assess their own strengths and weaknesses in mathematics.

The self-assessment of gaps and competences is based on a self-paced mastery model. Students demonstrate to themselves the level of knowledge and understanding upon enrolment and are given suggested study plans according to the scores they obtain. This self-assessment strategy is designed to support students in identifying their own learning needs effectively enough to access additional support when needed.

The package is not cross-platform and can only be used with PCs.

7. Designing, creating, performing

This chapter encompasses a range of abilities that synthesize to create a product or a performance. Many of the case studies in this section draw together elements of aesthetics, creativity, analysis of theory, design skills, problem solving, technical disciplinary skills, and performance or communication of results. As the level of synthesis is high, formative feedback is an essential element in all cases.

Another challenge of these assessments is the subjective nature of judgements regarding the quality of the product or performance. Much thought has been invested in the criteria by which judgements are ultimately made and the method of grading that most appropriately communicates students' achievements. Not surprisingly, peer and self-assessment have an important formative and summative role to play, not only to develop these important skills in learners, but also to relieve the pressure from teachers as the sole arbiter of students' achievements when aesthetics are a prominent component of the outcome.

These case studies also demonstrate a range of creative ways in which to overcome distance. These abilities are not easy to develop and assess at a distance, but teachers in these instances have made full use of learners' own environments to create and support rich, holistic assessments, offering learners a high level of choice and autonomy in their learning. Potential weaknesses in terms of lack of face-to-face contact are converted into strengths through the promotion of networks between students, as well as their broader professional communities. Disciplines represented here include education, art, science and photography, each with a notably different balance to be struck between questions of technique, understanding, practical skills and creativity.

7.1 DESIGNING ONLINE TRAINING

Case study from Training and Development (Open learning)

Robin Mason, The Open University, UK

The following case study was compiled from written materials and Web site information from Robin Mason, together with additional comments she made after seeing the first draft.

Designing Training for the Internet was prepared for training departments interested in developing online training for their organization. Its overall purpose is to help staff acquire the necessary skills to design learning modules for delivery over the Internet to technical and supervisory personnel. With the flexibility of enrolment provided and its focus on the Internet as a medium for distance learning, this unit can be applied to tertiary, industry and corporate settings. This skills-based design unit very much practices what it teaches.

Context

This unit is an 80-hour self-paced professional development course based on four stages of practical work (modules). It is delivered entirely online and includes narrative commentary, hypertext links, tutor supported discussion and templates for student use.

The unit works on a rolling intake – students start and finish the course at their own convenience. A threaded Web-based bulletin board is used where students can raise issues, interact with other students on the course, and read the comments of tutors and other students who took the course previously.

The unit is designed so that students have practical work to do at the end of each of the four major modules; this work is progressively building up, so that at the end the student has completed a piece of Web teaching material. This material forms the basis of students' own workplace-based activities since they are encouraged to base this practical work on the institutional commitments they already have. In other words, this work is an authentic activity with an immediate application.

The unit is written in an engaging style that involves the readers/students and helps them to consider the issues as they work through the material. Students also consider the matter of appropriate learner support and tutorial services using computer mediated communication.

Some self-assessment questions are included with suggested answers both to stimulate the student to apply the course material and also to show what can be done in Web-based assessment. A file area has been set up, open to all students, where the completed work is sent and viewed by all. This allows students to get ideas and inspiration from the work of other students.

Tutors provide direct, individual and specific feedback by e-mail to each student on the work he or she submits. An assessment questionnaire is linked to the course and asks students to provide feedback for the subsequent rewrite of the unit.

Abilities being assessed

On completion of this unit students should be able to:

- produce Web pages in simple Hypertext Markup Language (HTML) according to principles of good design;
- evaluate online training courses according to educational and human-computer interaction criteria;
- assess the best means of online delivery of conventional print-based distance learning material;
- design and manage remote tutorial interaction using a range of computer mediated communication media;
- prepare and deliver online training modules to meet a training need for a particular target group and topic in their own organization.

Assessment tasks

Since the study materials are delivered entirely online, there is an acknowledgement that learners will choose their own pathways through the topics. However, a recommended pathway is provided, both as a list and a flowchart. If students follow the recommended pathway they are required to complete a stage of their practical online design assignment at the end of each of the four modules.

Practical instructions are given, additional resource links are provided and templates are set up for students to begin their creative development activities.

The stages of the assessment project are:

1. Create a front page of own Web site and a page of external links of personal interest.
2. Support interaction over the Internet from the perspective of learners, self and other trainers, technology and communications.
3. Create a model course.
4. Create a study guide and a tutor's guide.

Marking

There are no grades given for this study unit, so there is no assessment involved. Tutors appraise the student project work on the basis of professional experience. An ungraded 'Certificate of completion' is awarded upon demonstrated output of all four stages. Some informal peer review is encouraged in this unit, but it is not a formal requirement.

Strengths and limitations

Strengths

The professional development nature of this unit makes it very accessible, versatile and flexible. It is self-paced, asynchronous and online, and can therefore successfully reach its target audience of trainers anywhere, anytime.

Through the use of such a student-centred and resource-based design, this unit successfully demonstrates what it teaches. It illustrates both flexibility of student time as well as utilization of institutional resources. Tutors support individual learners, thus avoiding the need for group facilitation or collaboration – which is difficult to support alongside the flexibility of enrolment.

Limitations

The delivery of this unit ultimately relies on robust connectivity. Students must be prepared for technical frustrations during their study and learn to use the medium strategically – downloading to hard drive, printing or reading on screen as preferred.

The assessment activities are completely task-based and little sense of online community develops among students. Some informal peer review is encouraged in this unit but, without a sense of community, little discussion is directed to the group. Most comments are directed to the tutor. This is not always considered a limitation.

7.2 VIDEO REPORT OF ARTISTIC DEVELOPMENT IN CERAMICS

Case study from Art and Design (postgraduate)

Owen Rye, Monash University, Australia

The following case study was compiled from written and published materials provided by Owen Rye and Robyn Benson, together with additional comments they made after seeing the first draft.

Although it is agreed that the teaching of visual arts is ideally carried out in face-to-face contexts, this example shows that it is possible to provide a valuable learning experience for postgraduate students by distance education. When the supervisor is not able to see students' artwork at first hand, giving feedback and guiding students in the development of the conceptual and technical aspects of their work present special challenges. In this example, postgraduate ceramics students prepare a video report on the development of their artwork and receive a response by telephone from their supervisor. Care is taken to clearly articulate the negotiated criteria for assessing the innovative and creative aspects of the studio component of work.

Context

The Graduate Diploma in Visual Arts is a one-year postgraduate qualification primarily aimed at professional artists and teachers (especially tertiary) working in the studio arts. The qualification has a vocational emphasis towards professional practice although it also enriches the experience of teachers in the tertiary sector.

Since 1985 the Graduate Diploma has been offered both on-campus and externally (part-time). Here we will consider the external option in ceramics where students complete a studio component in their own location and submit a written paper. Upon enrolment they are issued with:

- a course guide book;
- a video camera with manufacturer's instructions and standard accessories;
- an introductory video of about 25 minutes (showing introductions from other new students, their work prior to enrolment and their proposals);
- a video handbook (which describes procedures for video report development and submission).

Abilities being assessed

The abilities to be assessed are:

- completion of monthly video reports of work in progress;
- kiln building and firing;
- planning of work, including drawings and preliminary tests of materials;
- discussion and critical analysis of one's own work with visual reference to it;
- written report of work and analysis of personal progress.

Also included in the video reports are elements that show:

- exhibitions seen by students;
- students' studios and equipment;
- visual details of kiln building and firing, and problems requiring discussion;
- full three-dimensional views of students' work (eg rotating on a turntable), including close-ups of details for discussion.

Assessment tasks

Students elect their course of study for the year via two proposals, one for new studio work and one for a paper. These initial proposals establish the criteria for each of the final assessments. In the studio component, the final assessment consists of a presentation of both developmental and final artwork showing the progression by which students have reached their current highest level of achievement.

For the written component, students submit at least two written reports per semester at a time of their choice rather than at a due date. Students send regular drafts of the paper to their supervisor through the course. All being well the paper is 'satisfactory' by the end of the course. This continuous assessment and feedback is delivered via monthly e-mail and fax until final submission is accepted.

Visual communication is mainly by means of video reports prepared by students. Supervisors and students are able to enter into dialogue by e-mail and phone, focusing on the video reports submitted. These video reports are copied onto a master and returned to students to avoid delaying the filming of progress of students' work.

Deadlines are established for each student individually with a degree of 'for all concerned'. There is a definite advantage in not receiving everything all at once from the markers' perspective, and students do other things with their lives than study, so their work schedule is best when flexible.

Marking

Written component

The continuous assessment of progress is not graded but is seen as a process of critical dialogue between student and supervisor. Throughout the course this is initiated by student progress reports in their studio component, or via drafts of their paper and followed up by supervisor contact. A separate grade is not awarded for the paper; the supervisor (as a member of the assessment panel) advises the panel that the paper is 'satisfactory'. If the paper was not satisfactory arrangements would have to be in place for it to be completed after the studio assessment, but this has only happened once. Normally, the frequent sending in of drafts over the course assures that the paper is satisfactory.

The 'informal' standard used to judge 'satisfactory' is: 'With modifications for suitability, is this paper worth publishing in one of the professional ceramics journals?' Note that sometimes the papers are modified (usually shortened) and published. The final paper is assessed by the student's supervisor. Copies of the paper are available for other members of the panel to check this advice if desired.

Studio component

The basic criterion is the 'Studio proposal' prepared by the student at the beginning of the course (and modified somewhat as the work progresses over the two years). The basic question asked in assessment is: 'To what extent has the student fulfilled the studio project proposed by themselves?' In practice the assessment is also based on the regular 'art assessment' criteria such as the 'reach' of the work (is it normal humdrum work or is it ambitious?), and the quality of the artwork (as compared with general standards in this course and relevant others).

A panel of at least three and up to five assessors performs the final assessment; at least one of the assessors is external. The grade is determined in practice by allocating a 'temporary' grade as each student is assessed. At the end of all assessments these grades are reviewed upwards or downwards in the context of all the students being assessed in the year, of former assessments in previous years, and knowledge of standards in comparable courses in other institutions. Grades are given as a percentage (which has a pass to high distinction range equivalent).

Only one numerical grading is made after the final assessment (percentage grading plus HD/D/Cr/P/F grade).

Strengths

Formative feedback

Both e-mail and fax allow a rapid turnaround time, which is important to effective feedback. In relation to the paper this continuous assessment and feedback process means that the final draft when submitted is almost invariably sound and of high quality.

Video reports

Despite the ease with which still and moving visual material can now be communicated via the Internet, video is still the preferred medium for visual communication. Advantages summarized by Benson and Rye (1996) include not only the capacity to see student work in a near three-dimensional perspective, but to evaluate 'unconscious' messages such as the students' confidence or lack of it during their dialogue, their capacity for organizing and presenting ideas, and even environmental factors that may, with or without their awareness, influence their work. The technology of Internet communications hinders this aspect of communication.

Another very important use of video is the capability of distributing to all students excerpts of interest from individual reports. For example, this allows a student to video an exhibition in Queensland that can then be circulated for viewing by students in other states.

Additional benefits

The establishment of a network among the external students is seen as a very high priority in this course.

The skills acquired in video-making are useful after the course to students making submissions to galleries and conferences and are regarded as a valuable part of their professional expertise.

Both supervisors and students involved in this course found an improvement in students' analytical skills resulting from video reporting, compared with previous methods of reporting by distant students (Benson and Rye, 1996).

Limitations

Representation rather than real

The biggest deficiency in the video reporting process was considered to be the effect of the medium on the audience. A real object of art has a very different effect on a viewer than a video or another kind of representation of it.

Slow to exchange videos by mail

The main difficulty of the video report medium is the reliance on postal turnaround times for submission and feedback. This lack of immediacy is seen to be a transient problem until videophones and desktop videoconferencing become readily available.

7.3 CONFERENCE AND WEB SITE FOR A SCIENCE COMMUNITY

Case study from Agricultural Science

Glyn Rimmington, University of Melbourne, Australia

The following case study is an edited version of written materials provided by Glyn Rimmington, together with additional comments he made after seeing the first draft.

This case study was found to be an exemplar of all eight learning outcomes, a remarkable design for integrated, situated and authentic teaching and learning. It has been included here as an example of designing, creating and performing since indeed it demonstrates these achievements by students, along with a great deal more.

Although taught as an on-campus subject, there are no attendance requirements other than a live presentation at the symposium. This occurs in week 9 or 10 of a 12-week semester, so there is a reflection phase for learning after the symposium. Students carry out all organizational and academic arrangements by e-mail and threaded online discussions. In principle, if students were able to travel to attend the symposium, this could be taught internationally and the event would thus be open to a stimulating mix of cultural and interdisciplinary exchange. Alternatively, international students could contribute using video conferencing or audiographics (Web and telephone).

Context

Science and Communication is a core first-level subject taught in both on-campus and flexible asynchronous modes as part of the Bachelor of Agricultural Science course at the Institute of Land and Food Resources. Graduates of the B.Ag.Sc. course are prepared for a variety of career outcomes with components such as biological, soil, animal and plant sciences, sociology and economics. An understanding of the special role of communication within scholarly work (such as peer-reviewed publications) and between research and industry is essential for all graduates, as is the ability to work in teams. Science and Communication lays the foundations for this important area. Students of other courses are also attracted to the subject, including Forestry, Horticulture, Commerce, Law, Science, Nursing, Arts and Engineering.

The focus of the subject is a one-day, scholarly symposium, held in week 10 of a 12-week semester. Students develop a Web page in the first two weeks of the semester. This forms the basis for communication about organizing and hosting the symposium. Teams are formed and arrangements begin via e-mail to find a theme, invite keynote speakers, develop a programme and all the necessary administrivia. In 1997 teams were self-selected. In 1998 they were imposed. In 1999, they will be formed using team-role behaviour profiling.

Students also conduct a literature review and write an abstract and a full paper on the theme of the symposium. They prepare a multimedia-assisted presentation and act as peer reviewers of other students' papers. At the symposium, they deliver their own presentation and review the presentations of others.

A Web site is developed in support of the live symposium event. The programme is published, registrations are taken, abstracts are published and peer reviewed and finally the proceedings are published – all online.

A reflection phase is the final component of assessment. This requires students to submit a self-evaluation of the value of their contribution to their community of peers.

Abilities being assessed

Abilities we are trying to assess are:

- developing and carrying out plans;*
- working in teams, group communication;
- written and verbal communication;
- design of conference and Web site;
- oral and multimedia presentation skills;
- critical thinking and reflection.

*In 1998, students developed their respective team's project plan as clients in a project planning consultancy with teams in a second-level unit.

Assessment tasks

Group folder

In specialist teams, the students prepare an online folder that comprises members' biographical data and roles, abstracts and bibliographies, peer review comments, plus minutes of meetings and the group's project plan. All the materials in the folder can be found on a combination of the team's home page and on the personal home pages of its members. (Abilities: 1, 2, 3; 20 per cent; group mark.)

Conference papers

Each student, working with up to two co-authors, prepares a 2,000-word paper. Other members peer review the papers to progressively refine them ready for the conference. These are linked to the home pages. (Abilities: 3, 4; 20 per cent; co-author mark.)

Conference presentations

Each student, working with up to two co-authors, prepares a 10-minute, multimedia-assisted presentation and delivers it at the symposium. Each presentation is assessed (with an instrument designed by the students) by two students and one staff member. (Abilities: 3, 4; 20 per cent; co-author mark.)

Self-assessment memorandum

Each student writes a two-page memorandum to the Head of Department setting out evidence for the mark (out of 20) they deserve for (i) improvements to other components on the basis of feedback, and (ii) contribution to organization of the symposium. (Abilities: 1, 2, 3, 4; 20 per cent; individual mark.)

Online essay

Students write an 'essay of the fortnight' on four out of a choice of eight essays, two topics per fortnight, of which the two best are marked. They receive extensive feedback and can re-submit an earlier essay. (Abilities: 3, 4; 20 per cent; co-author mark.)

Marking

Assessment is spread throughout the semester and extensive feedback is given, particularly for the early components so students have the opportunity to improve. Shortly after each deadline, marks are made available on the Web.

Each of these steps carries a weighting towards assessment and a matrix of assessment is applied. They are assessed as teams, as co-authors and as individuals. Assessment is by staff, peers and by self-assessment.

Strengths and limitations

Strengths

Strengths include gaining multiple perspectives on the peer-review process and tangible outcomes that are evidence of teamwork, group communication, scholarly writing, Web site design and presentation with critical thinking. The students benefit from early, extensive feedback, which helps them to achieve a higher standard. Students' reflective insights in the final online essays indicate a deep understanding of communication in science derived from experiential learning.

The benefits of the live event are more than the sum of its parts. Not only is the symposium attended by keynote speakers with expertise in the chosen theme, but it also draws an audience of peers, family and friends on the day. Publication of symposium details on the Web site further disseminates information designed, developed and published by the students to a potentially unbounded audience.

Also integrated into the student assessment process is a great deal of formative evaluation information that has enabled a responsive approach to adapting the subject and further improving it, semester by semester.

Limitations

The main limitations of this assessment approach were, prior to 1998, the logistics of manual preparation of online resources such as e-mail addresses and Web publishing areas, and the work required to provide quality, timely feedback. Both of these problems have been solved through the use of automated links with the student administration system and the development of a rapid, online marking system, with immediate e-mail feedback to individual students, respectively. Another limitation, or difficulty, has been the staff development required and the initial scepticism of students. The solution to these has simply been provision of leadership.

7.4 CREATING AND APPRECIATING PHOTOGRAPHIC EXPRESSION

Case study from Photography (Open learning)

Alex Syndikas, Royal Melbourne Institute of Technology (RMIT), Australia

The following case study was compiled from written materials Alex Syndikas provided, together with additional comments he made after seeing the first draft.

Photography taught by distance education presents a number of challenges. It might be a case of negotiating for support in the form of darkrooms and equipment provided by local schools or educational facilities wherever possible; or alternatively taking a more theoretical approach to photography and its elements of lighting, composition and production.

The following example has been chosen to treat the teaching of photography by distance education as an exercise in appreciation and critique. The central focus of this subject is the development of critical appreciation skills in photography and the resultant enhancement of students' photographic practice.

This subject is taught in conjunction with Open Learning Australia (OLA), which screens 13 half-hour television programmes to supplement the study materials. Students need not be enrolled in a degree to undertake the unit, but can receive credit into the BA at RMIT and other post-secondary facilities that are members of the OLA consortium.

Context

'Photography: An Introduction' is a unit for students who are not studying to be professional photographers. It is designed especially for people who have some application for photography in their own careers.

The unit considers the medium of photography first as a unique approach to human communication, secondly as an art form, and thirdly as a medium that requires the acquisition of a unique set of technical skills. Throughout the unit students are given specific photographic assignments designed to expand their own vision.

The television programmes that supplement the study resources include three Australian programmes and 10 from a US photographic series. Through practical demonstration, the programmes present key ideas of photographic theory and develop a theme. Three stages of work on each theme are suggested: research, exploration and personal development.

Students are required to take at least six 24-exposure rolls of film over the six-week practical period but are not required to develop and print their own photographs. For reasons of practicality, the assignment work in this unit is restricted to colour prints.

Abilities being assessed

At the completion of this unit, students should be able to:

- relate photography to an historical and a cultural perspective;
- identify the mechanisms of a camera and its accessories;
- understand and use the concepts of lighting;
- demonstrate basic photography skills and show an understanding of the communicative and artistic potential of the medium;
- discuss the relationship between content and form in photographs, as well as the relationship between one photograph and others;
- demonstrate familiarity with the historical development of photography.

Assessment tasks

The assessment tasks include:

- journal assignments (Projects 1–7);
- photographic portfolio assignments (A and B);

- a review of work completed (500 words in one hour under supervision).

Assignment 1, Journal Projects 1 and 2, draws on activities within the study guide. For Journal Project 1, Photography Around You, students choose a set of activities from a set list of options in the study guide. These activities are designed to begin to focus students' attention on the photographic medium, its purpose and impact, and personal reflections. The journal is submitted in three volumes, the first relating to Projects 1–2, the second relating to Projects 3–4 and the third to Projects 5–7.

At commencement of the six-week practical period that forms the basis of Assignment 2, students appoint a review panel of about four people from among family and friends. These people are asked to commit approximately half an hour per week over five weeks, to give their impressions of the student's work. The emphasis is on the impact of images upon an audience rather than technical skill in image production.

For Assignment 2, Portfolio A must be submitted. For this, students are required to submit a set of 12 prints from each of the four scenes from Project 3 and another set of 12 prints from Project 4, not mounted but clearly identified on the back.

Students must accompany the prints with a concise critique in their journal (Projects 3–4), indicating any technical problems they can see as well as any problems of composition they would want to address in remaking the images. Finally they are asked to identify the three images that they consider produce the greatest impact.

For Assignment 2 Portfolio B, students are required to submit a final portfolio consisting of the 20 prints they consider to be their best work since commencing the unit. Selection must be based on their own judgement, but also must take into account feedback provided by their review panel. Students must consider lighting, point of view and visual organization. Journal critique of Projects 5–7 is also required.

To meet the OLA's requirement that each unit must include at least one piece of invigilated assessment, this unit includes a review assignment that must be completed under supervised conditions.

Marking

The criteria given for marking Assignment 2 (Portfolio A) are:

- technical skill in using camera, film and the lighting combination chosen;
- artistic expression in the three images in each of the four subjects;
- judgement in assessing aspects of technique or artistic expression that could most benefit from improvement.

No criteria are supplied for Assignment 2 (Portfolio B). However, in order to pass, students must also submit Volume 2 of the journal, which includes no more than two to three pages' critique of images and review panel's comments for Projects 5, 6, and 7.

Strengths and limitations

Strengths

One of the primary strengths of this unit is the flexibility of enrolment. As with most OLA units, there are no entry prerequisites and students who enrol via OLA can gain accreditation towards a BA in several Australian institutions of higher education.

There is a clear overall alignment between the objectives of technical, artistic and communication nature with the assessment tasks. The integrated assessment tasks ensure authenticity of student submission. In this open learning subject an invigilated exam assures that a widely recognized basic academic standard is achieved.

Limitations

The inherent difficulties in assessing students' creative work at a distance have, in this case, resulted in the necessity for an invigilated component of assessment. Occasionally students also have difficulty in gaining access to effective members of a review panel.

8. Communicating

Although communication in either written or oral form is integral to almost any assessment task, this chapter contains case studies where the teacher is primarily concerned with the development and assessment of specific communications skills, whether written, oral or visual. Written communication skills have been traditionally assessed at a distance through essays, reports and journals, although the primary emphasis is usually upon the content rather than an explicit attempt to develop skills in written communication. Arguably, this is a significant oversight given the demands of disciplinary genres and vocabularies, not to mention methods of citation and the often confusing rules regarding plagiarism. Trial-and-error is the most common means for learners to gain proficiency in academic writing, and perhaps many of the conventions are not explained in any detail to learners because 'we, as experts, have so deeply internalized them that we do not even recognize them' (Nightingale *et al*, 1996).

Similarly, oral communication skills are usually assessed in combination with content of a presentation. Oral skills have been more difficult to assess at a distance, unless residential schools or audio and videotapes are employed for the purpose, with varying degrees of success.

The Internet has provided new ways of assessing communication skills at a distance, including debate, participation in discussions, negotiations and collaboration, and it has created new forms of disciplinary discourse. Communications in this medium provide us with new challenges, as they are neither the same as oral ex-

202

changes nor written communications. Rather, the Web medium creates new kinds of synchronous and asynchronous communications, with new linguistic conventions and an accompanying 'netiquette', which may shape disciplinary discourses in new ways. As these case studies attest, online communications provide a powerful new tool for learning and assessment.

8.1 ORAL COMMUNICATION AND AUDIOTAPE INTERVIEW

Case study from Agriculture

Tony Dunn, Charles Sturt University, Australia

The following case study is an edited version of the written materials provided by Tony Dunn, together with additional comments he made after seeing the first draft.

Assessment with an emphasis on such a transient thing as oral communication is a special challenge to support and administer at a distance. This example shows a higher order measure of interview skills through audiotape presentation and a weighting on contribution to group discussion or oral presentation. The overall assessment for this subject includes a large component of written work.

Context

First-year agriculture students (BAppSc Agric) do a subject called Introduction to Agricultural Systems (AGR120) by distance education. AGR120 is a 'systems' subject stressing an holistic approach to understanding agriculture on the farm scale. While it is not unusual for agriculture students to learn about a whole farm, a systems approach is less common. Furthermore, this subject uses a 'soft' systems approach that keeps people in the picture. Off-campus students must find a 'systems study farm' on which to do their studies.

Abilities being assessed

Abilities include:

- observation skills;
- communication and personal development;
- seminar presentation skills development;
- confidence building;

- understanding social processes;
- systems and holistic thinking and modelling.

Assessment tasks

Students must organize what is called a 'systems study farm'. They must find a co-operative farmer who is willing to support their learning, be interviewed and discuss issues arising during the semester, and whose farm can be used by the student to observe and collect data.

Assignment 1 – Audiotape report (farm description)

The first assignment is to describe the farm as a system and to make an audiotape interview with the farmer. To get good data students must get to know the farm and the people. The best assignments set the scene with the farm and the farmer – putting them at ease and asking questions that elicit useful data and gain the farmer's confidence.

In essence, this is a communication exercise in both face-to-face and distance media in that the student must set up and execute the interview in person, as well as produce a tape that conveys the information and feeling of the farm to a remote audience – the lecturer. In another sense this assignment is also a systems exercise because the student has to appreciate the whole farm and decide how to describe it to the listener via the interview.

There is a time limit on the tape of 10 minutes and students are asked to identify the tape and introduce the listener to the interview situation – including the participants. Ten minutes is difficult to achieve and good preparation shows through. It is also an ideal time for the listener to cope with, although well-structured stories often last 12 to 15 minutes. After this fatigue and boredom erode the mark rapidly.

Assignment 2 – Short issues talk

The second assignment is an oral presentation about a rural issue that moves the student to an industry focus and shows how the outside world impinges on the farm. This task is done either by an audiotape interview or as a short talk in front of a group of peers at a residential school.

To learn about issues in their industry students are required to 'discover' an issues topic (akin to current affairs) – a technical topic is not acceptable. It must involve people and be debatable, so that students develop the ability to observe and discuss complex problems. In a systems perspective this exercise enables students to see 'outside' the farm and to recognize 'environmental' forces that impinge on it.

For the off-campus students to put this on tape means that they need to do an interactive piece between two people, bearing in mind the marker as the audience. This makes it more interactive and interesting for the listener – especially if the interviewee has some background in the chosen topic. Students may also attend a residential school where they present their issues talk to a group of fellow students. Tape and talk times are five minutes. Talks are presented without visual aids.

Summary of assignments

1 (a). Audiotape interview with farmer (10 per cent).
1 (b). Written systems model report (10 per cent).
2. Issues in agriculture talk (10 per cent).
3. Residential school or audiotape discussion on 'Farm resources' (10 per cent). Students describe the farm resources and share views with other(s) in the group looking at common and unique features. Where attendance is impossible students send in the notes they would have used for the discussion and submit a five-minute audiotaped presentation.
4. 'Skills profile and field work record' (10 per cent). Students set their own practical farm skills learning tasks and tabulate what they learnt.
5. 'Monitoring and management report' (50 per cent).

Marking

The (70 per cent) written and (30 per cent) oral parts of the assessment are complementary in the way the student gathers and plans the presentation of information, but the presentations themselves are quiet different. Marking procedures vary accordingly. Discussion here considers the two oral parts of assessment – tape recordings and contribution to group discussion.

Marking tape recordings

There is an intellectual challenge in assembling a whole-farm view and converting this into a logical sequence of questions to convey by audiotape. These tapes are assessed by writing comments on content and process in two columns. By looking over these notes and reflecting on the mental picture left by the tape it is relatively easy to write an overall comment and determine a grade.

The assessment criteria implicit in each of the learning objectives are used to inform the marker, though marks are assigned in a purely qualitative way, ie a grade of PS, CR, DI, HD, FL, or GP (grade pending). Use is made of plus, nought and minus within each category to indicate high, medium and low.

Ten or 20 lines of summary comment on the cover sheet and specific comments on the text are written as feedback to students. Reference is made to how well or how closely students achieved the intended learning outcomes of the unit.

The audiotape medium has proven to be extremely reliable. It is virtually impossible to fake a tape. The realism of the task prevents any short cuts, and unprepared interviews clearly show up because they are too short or too confused to convey a word picture of the farm and farmer. Occasionally poor quality tapes are produced that are a dilemma where technical problems occur; however, most of these assignments usually also appear to be ill prepared.

Contributions to discussion at residential school

When students give oral presentations or partake in discussion sessions at the residential school, a standard proforma mark sheet is used. This has four categories each worth five marks, plus an area for comments. This is the only assignment that gets a numerical mark, and the sheets are returned together with oral feedback immediately after the talk.

Finally, all students in attendance assess one of their fellows for contribution to discussion and return these mark sheets for collation of final grade.

Strengths and limitations

Strengths

AGR120 adds the industry and people focus to what are essentially scientifically or technically dominated courses. Through the subject, students get the opportunity to interact with a farmer and learn from the experience. The assignments provide a structure to express this but whom they learn from, the particulars they learn and where they learn are up to them. On the other hand what students learn is constrained by the subject structure, in the study guides and readings, but there is little emphasis on right and wrong answers – more on substantiating and presenting the data and the experience. Assessment supports the development of oral and written communication skills in a most relevant and integrated way.

Limitations

The biggest limitation is that the subject used to run over a whole year – a farm year – and now it's only half a year and students have to imagine (and ask) what the first half was like. Students who live in the cities find it difficult to get enough farm experience and contact – but some is better than none. Students who already farm are encouraged to take their monitoring further and get wider experience, even on some other farm!

Perhaps some future networking by e-mail and the Internet can enhance communication processes between the communities of farmers and students, and provide another medium for submitting assignments in this subject.

8.2 COMPUTER CONFERENCING

Case study from Education

Nick Heap, The Open University, UK

The following case study is an edited version of the written materials provided by Nick Heap and Janet Macdonald, together with additional comments they made after seeing the first draft.

The use of computer-based technology is ideal for supporting collaboration, resource-based learning and for teaching at a distance to an international cohort of students. The rapid turnaround and structured anonymity in this example facilitate reflection in a safe and immediate environment. Students are required to link to the Internet for the acquisition of additional resources and for the purpose of conferencing with peers and tutors. The nature of the conferencing in this unit builds upon a number of higher order communication skills.

Context

IT and Society is a course that provides an innovative environment for resource-based learning in the context of distance learning, by giving students access to a personal library of academic articles on CD ROM and guidance to sites on the Internet, in addition to more traditional printed course materials. The students and tutors are all networked, and it is a requirement of the course that study support should be provided through computer conferencing.

Computer conferencing also offers the potential for frank and rapid feedback on the course and its assessment, and has facilitated the ongoing development of assessment in response to experience and evaluation. The course is assessed by six assignments, one of which is a compulsory double-weighted online collaborative project, and a final, closed book exam.

The attitudes of students to resource-based study and its assessment on this course has been the subject of a recent research project, 'Appropriate assessment for resource based learning', and some of the findings are summarized here.

Abilities being assessed

Students are assessed on their:

- computer conferencing skills;
- online collaborative skills;
- synoptic understanding of course issues;
- critical analysis;
- information handling skills;
- additional formative support, peer and self-assessment.

Assessment task

The following assignments require students to reflect on the process of their study in the new resource-based environment, while also covering the course content of relevance to each subject area.

Online conferencing assignment

This assignment is designed to coerce students into participating in their first experience of computer conferencing for collaborative work. Students are required to contribute to an online conference on a given topic over several weeks; to submit transcripts of five of their contributions, each supported by a message to illustrate interaction with fellow students; and finally to summarize the whole debate. In view of problems previously identified with online group management during the project, the assignment was modified in 1998 to include the production of a strategy for online collaborative working that might be of practical use for the forthcoming project.

Online collaborative project

Students are required to produce an informed critique of a fictional newspaper article describing a new IT application, based on an understanding of course issues and using the resources of the CD ROM database. The main part of the resulting report is an individual effort, and focuses on a particular course concept. The summary and conclusion are the result of co-operative endeavour, following group discussion in a computer conference.

Additional formative feedback

A computer conference supplements feedback in the form of model answers, marking schemes and a peer review activity. After assignment cut-off dates (ie the date by which the assignment has to be submitted to the tutor) conference participants are given the opportunity to see the marking schemes used by tutors. They are also presented with model answers, which are sometimes given to tutors with marking schemes as a way of defining the content required for shorter parts of the assignment. Finally, they are presented with a model essay and asked to 'mark' it using the tutor's marking scheme.

Building on experiences with the use of peer review and assessment for formative support in campus-based universities, it was decided to experiment with these ideas, using computer conferencing. The aim was to try to increase students' awareness of assessment requirements and to develop their abilities in self-judging their work. Students are required to strip identification from their assignment and send it as an attached file to the tutor. They in return receive another student's script. They are asked to grade the script and comment on it if they wish, then to grade their own work. The grades and comments are returned and re-routed to the originating student.

Marks or grades

Online conferencing assignment

Part 1 (50 per cent). Paper copies of five contributed messages to the group conference, supported by at least one other message demonstrating how the contribution has moved the discussion forward.

Part 2 (50 per cent). (A) (35 per cent) – a 400–500 word summary of the group's discussion. (B) (15 per cent) – a statement of the group's proposed strategy for collaborative working.

Online collaborative project

Group element	(total 30 per cent)
Report summary	10 per cent
Themes discussion in conference	10 per cent
Report conclusion	10 per cent
Individual element	(total 70 per cent)
General structure and coherence of argument	30 per cent
Use of supporting evidence and course materials	20 per cent
Contribution to group tasks and discussion in conference	20 per cent

Strengths and limitations

It appears that while online conferencing can potentially play an important role in supporting the resource-based approach in a distance context, the skills of conferencing need to be learnt, and practised in assessment, before students can be expected to benefit. Some additional findings from the research project are summarized here.

Graded contribution to discussion

While many students find the online conferencing assignment difficult because of the time required and the need to practise new skills, the fact that the assignment carries marks secures participation in the debate and influences the quality of contributions. In addition, the conferencing provides an important supportive role in giving the opportunity to share alternative perspectives to reading, and of course in providing moral support.

Collaboration for resource-based learning

Student feedback on the collaborative project indicates that this is by far the most significant assignment in terms of supporting and developing the skills needed for resource-based learning because it puts the approach into practice. The majority of students interviewed on its completion felt at home with the prospect of using a wide variety of sources to research a topic and this assignment had helped to emphasize and contextualize the main course principles.

Group dynamics online

The process of online collaboration, when working at its best, appears to support these activities. However, one of the commonest problems facing groups has been that of coping with the management of group dynamics in an online context. There are difficulties associated with non-participating group members, non-enforceable schedules and the delays inherent in using an asynchronous medium for communication. As a result of this finding, the conferencing assignment, described above, has been used to raise the profile of online group management with students.

Formative support in development of critical thinking skills

The additional formative support delivered through computer conferencing is well received, particularly in the initial stages of the course when students are 'finding their feet'. This could be a useful adjunct to tutor feedback, in future. The electronic peer review is a valuable exercise in improving self-judgement and seeing alternative approaches, although many find the exercise quite difficult to complete. The electronic network makes possible a rapid turnaround of scripts in addition to a guarantee of anonymity for those participating.

8.3 INTERNATIONAL DEBATE

Case study from Business

Ingrid Day, University of South Australia, Australia

The following case study is an edited version of the written materials and Web site information provided by Ingrid Day, together with additional comments she made after seeing the first draft.

Online communication can take many forms and debating is an ideal form of online activity. Asynchronous forms of chat allow preparation time before and during the debate, facilitate academic writing and can involve anyone, anytime thus introducing cultural perspectives to learning. This example features a formal online debate across three universities and two continents in the discipline area of communication and the media.

Context

Communication and the Media is a compulsory subject in the Bachelor of Business programme, which features an independent study component, carried out either in face-to-face small groups (on-campus students) through a series of print-based exercises (off-campus students), or via online study groups (available to both internal and external students). The endeavour is designed to offer all students increased study mode options, as well as to integrate two, often discrete, cohorts of students.

For students electing to participate in online exercises, assessment derives from individual and team-based work, carried out in online debates prepared throughout the semester and conducted over a period of two weeks at the end of the semester (prior to exam week, coinciding with the delivery of internal student oral presentations). The online debates are conducted between teams – deliberately institutionally integrated – comprising one student from each participating institution (in 1997 these were Governors State University, Chicago; University of South Australia;

and University of Technology, Sydney). The online debates offer opportunities for institutional, national/international, and intercultural collaboration and interaction.

Student preparation for the debates is carried out online, in secure designated sites within the subject Web site. The actual debate postings are accessible to all students and visitors to the Web site.

Abilities being assessed

On completion of this subject, students will be able to:

- understand and explain the importance of media in everyday life;
- critically analyse media texts;
- recognize and put into practice the different conventions involved in writing for academic, business and public communication purposes;
- carry out effective research;
- demonstrate understanding of how changes in communications technology are changing the nature and meaning of public communications;
- understand what is meant by 'globalization' and changes in international and intercultural communication.

Student abilities in these areas are determined by assessing their competences in developing persuasive arguments and in either defending or opposing debate topics such as:

'Print is alive and will survive.'
'The information society is characterized by social inequality and alienation.'
'The media dictate behaviour that should be valued and emulated by establishing, through omission or inclusion, those aspects of experiences considered important, and those considered unimportant.'

Assessment tasks

Activities

The study guide activities to be completed as a journal-in-progress throughout the weeks of the semester form one small component of assessment; they are valued at 10 per cent. Activities and questions are posed on a weekly basis and students report their experiences and reflections about media-related topics in a personal journal. It is handed in at the end of the semester when the exam and the debate are also due to occur.

Debate

The debate is also only valued at 10 per cent but helps students to become independent and interdependent learners. Students are formed into teams and given a debate topic in Week 7 in plenty of time to deal with the technicalities and the strategies for preparing a debate.

Preparation for the debates requires students to consult with each other via the designated team discussion site in order to decide who will assume responsibility for each speaking role (ie first, second and third) and to develop a coherent focus to their argument.

The debate is conducted according to standard debating conventions with three 'speakers' on each side. Students are asked to set aside their own feelings on the topic for a time and concentrate with the teams on developing a consistent and logical argument to support their case.

Speakers' direct their argument to the (virtual) chairperson rather than the audience directly. Each speaker posts 600–800 words in making his or her case or in summing up (third speaker). Students are expected to draw on and reference the readings and literature in the development of their argument.

The subject tutors act as chair and adjudicators. They sum up the debate and announce the result.

Written work

Eighty per cent of the marks for this unit are given for the formal written components and final exam.

Marking

Debate	10 per cent	Final two weeks of semester
Activities	10 per cent	Week 13
Assignment 1	20 per cent	Week 6
Assignment 2	30 per cent	Week 12
Exam	30 per cent	Exam weeks

Points are allocated to each speaker for content of argument, organization of material and method of presentation. The winning team is usually the one presenting the most convincing argument in the most entertaining and persuasive manner.

Teams are graded in two areas:

1. evidence of team interaction (via team discussion sites);
2. individual contribution (via debate postings).

The final grade for each student is the sum of the score for team interaction combined with individual aggregates. The method of assessment encourages individual commitment to team interests. Both Australian and US instructors frequently find that students exceed previous levels of work. Interestingly, there also appears to be a 'patriotic' dimension, ie a sense that individual efforts will reflect upon the academic reputation of the nation! The achievement levels can perhaps also be 'explained' by the wider visibility than is usual with written assignment work.

Criteria for marking relate to levels achieved in the areas listed under 'Abilities being assessed'. The 'winning' team receives no additional marks for being first; however, to be successful is intrinsically associated with achieving a high overall grade. It is considered important that the mark is not based entirely on debate 'performance', hence the inclusion of assessment for effective and consistent interaction throughout the semester.

Strengths and limitations

Strengths

Embedded in the team approach is the expectation that team members will share their research sources and findings. Indeed, the 'success' (in terms of grade achieved) of each team is ultimately seen by the instructors to relate directly to the level of collegial interaction that takes place. Importantly, the most 'successful' teams – in terms of both grades achieved as well as the less quantifiable but nonetheless important aspects of the activity, such as 'intercultural' communication – are those whose discussion extends beyond the academic focus of the assessment task.

The collaboration provides an opportunity to:

- learn and develop online skills;
- use online technologies from home or work, or another convenient place;
- engage students in other cultures and countries, developing a broader international perspective and addressing institutional internationalization goals;
- intensely examine predefined issues in technology using the literature and perspectives of more than one country;
- build teams across international borders and time zones;
- develop professional relationships leading to exploration of other significant collaborative relationships and activities.

The debate format is particularly useful for developing skills in critical thinking, especially if students are required to argue for a proposition with which they do not agree. Indeed, students who initially feel uncomfortable with the concept of defending an argument that conflicts with their personal position usually agree at the end of the activity that this challenge has in fact provided a more stimulating learning experience than occurs when they are required to articulate a pre-held position. Students are not given a choice of topic, nor are they given a choice of team make-up.

Limitations

A number of students felt that a preliminary training session in a computer lab would have been advantageous. In its first iteration, of the 16 teams 13 worked together productively and successfully (approximately paralleling the 'success/failure' ratio of groups working together face-to-face). The difficulties experienced by the three groups related mainly to absenteeism.

8.4 ONLINE COLLABORATION

Case study from Environmental Psychology (postgraduate)

André Fiedeldey, University of Pretoria, South Africa

The following case study is an edited version of the written and Web site materials that André Fiedeldey provided.

Collaboration between scholars is very definitely enabled by online technologies – indeed it was the driving force behind its inception. The process of producing a common document, whether it be a research report, a conference paper or a journal article is something professionals learn by experience and very rarely through guided support or mentorship. This example not only encourages students to share discussion and ideas but also supports the learning of collaborative publishing skills. The assessment requirements of this unit wholly support all the component skills of collaboration such as sharing information and resources, negotiating content and providing rationales for a common argument.

Context

The MA (Research Psychology) course is a fully and exclusively Web-based programme leading to professional registration in the category of research psychologist with the Professional Board of Psychology in South Africa. Students are mostly selected based on BA (Hons) academic merit and psychological criteria, and are also required to complete an internship and a thesis after successful examination of the first Masters' year of training.

The course has a long reputation of providing hands-on skill, and the aim is to retain that within the Web-based format. Staff who are involved also teach in other under- and postgraduate courses and are not specifically trained in online learning facilitation. Five compulsory subjects are presented at this stage, one of which contains two modules (environmental psychology and systems thinking), within which groupwork assignments are used to evaluate student progress.

The topic for each groupwork assignment is chosen early in the course, and is preceded by individual assignments dealing with *different* aspects of the selected topic. The groupwork assignment provides students with the opportunity of integrating their individual assignment topics into one substantive report reflecting their combined knowledge on and understanding of the subject matter.

Abilities being assessed

Abilities lie on different levels, and consist of:

- ability to share work;
- interpersonal negotiation skills;
- ability to integrate/synthesize own work with that of others.

Assessment tasks

A. Ability to share work

The ability to share work is an important prerequisite in both the virtual domain and in the context of research psychologists' functioning in a work setting, usually within a team context. Because of different capabilities and standards maintained by individual students, this group assignment requires that higher achievers reconcile themselves to the fact that they will have to share their work with others and possibly see it diminished. Lower achievers may be uncomfortable sharing their work with more demanding fellow students.

B. Interpersonal negotiation skills

Because of the points raised under (a), as well as others such as reduction of the content of individual assignments, choice of a single conceptual approach when suitable, delegation of different tasks to group members, etc, the ability to negotiate is essential. Social group processes manifest themselves in the virtual environment as prominently as in direct contact settings, and provide opportunities for typical processes such as conflict resolution, dealing with alliance formation, and establishing overall leadership if so chosen.

C. Ability to integrate/synthesize own work with that of others

This aspect requires that students demonstrate the ability to reduce their own assignment content and adjust the theoretical and methodological orientation of each individual assignment to that chosen by the group for the group assignment. Integrating different areas of content is also required, as the group assignment has to read as if it were written by a single author or at least by a team of experienced authors. All of the above assessment tasks are typical requirements in many research psychology work settings, and this approach provides a thorough training ground for the development of these skills.

Marking

Students are each given a mark for their individual assignment. The group assignment is marked as one submission from all students in each group, and they all receive the same mark. The group assignment mark is allocated for the successful integration of individual assignments into one report (conceptually, methodologically, technically and in terms of literature), the length and technical editing of this report, and for submission by the due date.

Strengths and limitations

Strengths

The strength of this exercise lies in its emphasis on the sharing of individual efforts, effective communication and sustained interactivity via e-mail, conflict resolution skills, and the ability to delegate functions so that the final report is to everyone's satisfaction.

Limitations

A limitation was the absence of peer rating in the first trial. This will be addressed by a requirement that students provide a rating that will contribute towards the final mark obtained by each student for the group assignment. This will allow a differentiation of marks that will reflect individual efforts in the group assignment.

Use of results

The marks for the group assignment contribute 20 per cent to the subject year mark, which counts for half of the final subject mark.

Appendix A

Terms commonly used in assessment

Analyse	Separate or break up a whole into its parts so that you may discover their nature, proportion, function, relationship, etc.
Comment	Make critical observations, even if they are fairly open-ended; however, your texts and lecture and discussion notes should provide sufficient guidelines and your own common sense should prevail.
Compare	Find similarities and differences between two or more ideas, events, interpretations, etc. Ensure you understand exactly what you are being asked to compare. For example, if asked to compare two poems, on which aspects should you focus? Should you be concerned with poetic techniques, philosophy and perspective, or both? Are you expected to include a comparison of personal, social and historical influences that affect the technique and philosophy? If you are unclear about such considerations, find out before you begin the essay.
Contrast	The remarks on 'compare' apply equally to 'contrast'. The difference is that you should concentrate on dissimilarities.
Criticize	Express your judgement regarding the correctness or merit of the factors being considered. Discuss both strong and weak points and give the results of your own analysis.
Define	Provide concise, clear, authoritative meanings. In such statements, details are not necessarily required, but briefly state the boundaries or limitations of the definition. Remember the 'class' to which a thing belongs and whatever differentiates the particular object from all others in that class.
Describe	Recall facts, processes or events. You are not asked to explain or interpret. Try to provide a thorough description, emphasizing the most important points.

Diagram	Present a drawing, chart, plan or graphic representation in your answer. Generally, the student is also expected to label the diagram and a brief explanation or description may be required.
Discuss	Present a point of view. This is likely to need both description and interpretation. Your opinion must be supported by carefully chosen and authoritative evidence.
Enumerate	Provide a list or outline form of reply. In such questions you should recount, one by one, but concisely, the points required.
Evaluate	Present a judgement of an issue stressing both strengths and advantages, and weaknesses and limitations.
Explain	Interpret the facts along the lines of a particular topic. Do not be trapped into describing events or summarizing the plot. Your main focus should be on the 'why' of a particular issue, or on the 'how', with the aim of clarifying reasons, causes and effects. You are being tested on your capacity to think critically, to exercise perception and discernment.
Illustrate	This asks for an explanation; you may clarify your answer to a problem by presenting a figure, picture, diagram or concrete example.
Interpret	Explain the meaning of something and give your own judgement of a situation.
List	Give an itemized series or tabulation; such answers should be concise.
Outline	This asks for an organized description. Give the main points and essential supplementary materials, but omit minor details. Present the information in a systematic arrangement or classification.
Prove	To confirm or verify. You should establish something with certainty by evaluating and citing experimental evidence, or by logical reasoning.
Relate	When showing relationships, your answer should emphasize connections and associations in a descriptive manner.
Review	Re-examine; analyse and comment briefly (in an organized sequence) on the major points of an issue.
State	Express the high points in brief and clear narrative form. Details, and usually illustrations or examples, may be omitted.
Summarize	Provide a brief statement or an account covering the main points; omit details.
Trace	Give the development, process or history of a thing, event or idea, especially by proceeding from the latest to the earliest evidence.

Source: *Guide to Student Assessment,* Southern Cross University, Lismore, NSW, 1996.

Appendix B

Sample marking guide

Consultation and Participation

MN164 external: 1996

Marking sheet and feedback on assignment two
Report on a Plan of a Consultation Process

Student name:

Tutor's name: Grade:

The following marking sheet and feedback relates to the assessment requirements and guidelines that were outlined in your Unit Information Guide.... Feel free to ring if you want any comments clarified. This is your second assignment so you have now received some feedback on your writing and presentation. Note, therefore, that this marking sheet has taken referencing, grammar, expression or presentation into account.

I have circled the number that best describes the extent to which you have met the assessment guidelines. The code for numbering is as follows:

1 = Not at all   2 = Not really   3 = Yes   4 = Yes, well   5 = Yes, very well

Have you provided evidence that you have read the three study modules and the prescribed text, *Processes for Community Consultation*?	1 2 3 4 5
Have you provided clear headings and a structure in a report format?	1 2 3 4 5

Have you provided a clear explanation of your plan, ie have you explained how you will do it by describing the processes or methods you will use?	1	2	3	4	5
Have you anticipated any barriers?	1	2	3	4	5
Have you clearly outlined you strategies for dealing with these barriers?	1	2	3	4	5
Have you provided a clear rationale or justification for: what you want to achieve with your consultation process?	1	2	3	4	5
Have you provided a clear rationale or justification for: what you will do to achieve this?	1	2	3	4	5
Have you provided a clear rationale or justification for: why you think that the process will achieve it?	1	2	3	4	5
Evidence of clear expression?	1	2	3	4	5
Evidence of neat presentation?	1	2	3	4	5

General comments:

This unit advocates good consultation practices so we are keen to practise what we preach. If you strongly disagree with the above judgements I have made, please return your assignment and marking sheet and offer a written argument for changing the grade. Please also include a phone number and a suitable time so that this can be discussed with you.

Be aware that the marking for your final assignment will also relate to the assessment guidelines. Before starting this assignment, refer to your Unit Information Guide for details....

Attachments: leaflets provided by the Learning Assistance Unit (at the LIC, Lismore).

The leaflets noted below have been returned with your assignment because they provide guidance in specific areas that require attention. Remember that the Learning Assistance Unit is available should you need advice on writing or assignment presentation (phone...).

Would you like some help from Learning Assistance? Making your writing clear Assignment questions: what is expected of you? Editing your writing Developing argument in an essay Literature reviews Sentences and clauses Writing sentences Writing paragraphs Punctuation Referencing: bibliographies & reference lists Referencing: footnoting Referencing: Harvard Paraphrasing Reading critically Critical analysis Writing proposals Writing definitions Giving your opinion Success in Tertiary Education – a course in study skills

Source: Lyn Carson, Southern Cross University, Lismore, NSW.

Appendix C

Clinical competence assessment criteria

Description for clinical assessment scale. Criteria for clinical assessment (Key)

Scale	Clinical skill standard	Quality of performance	Assistance
Independent – 5	Safe and accurate each time	Proficient, co-ordinated, confident. Within an expedient time period	Without supporting cues
Supervised – 4	Safe and accurate each time	Competent, co-ordinated, confident. Some expenditure of excess energy. Within a reasonable time period	Occasional supportive cues
Assisted – 3	Safe and accurate each time	Skilful in parts of behaviour. Inefficiency and incoordination. Expends excess energy. Within a delayed time period	Frequent verbal and occasional physical directive cues in addition to supportive ones
Marginal – 2	Safe but not alone. Performs at risk. Not always accurate	Unskilled, inefficient. Considerable expenditure of excess energy. Prolonged time period	Continuous verbal and physical cues
Dependent – 1	Unsafe. Unable to demonstrate behaviour	Unable to demonstrate procedure/behaviour. Lacks confidence, co-ordination, efficiency	Continuous verbal and physical cues

Modified from Benner (1984) and Bondy (1983). *Note*: a score of 3 or above must be achieved for each objective for the learner to be considered competent in performing this clinical skill.

Clinical competency assessment form.
Form A: Procedures

Instructions. The format is on a scale of 1 to 5 with a column for 'not applicable'. For every objective a score must be given or 'not applicable' indicated. Form A should be photocopied for each compulsory skillsheet.

Learner's name...

Clinical skill assessed:	INDEPENDENT	SUPERVISED	ASSISTED	MARGINAL	DEPENDENT	N/A	COMMENTS
	5	4	3	2	1		
The learner has:							
1. Stated the major objectives of the procedure to be undertaken.							
2. Stated expected neonatal outcome.							
3. Identified and prepared resources needed to perform the procedure.							
4. Demonstrated application of theoretical knowledge by outlining the principles in the procedure.							
5. Assessed neonate's condition using a variety of data sources appropriate to the neonate and his/her condition.							
6. Followed nursing procedure (eg recommended guidelines/own or base hospital procedures) to implement the clinical skill.							

7. Provided an adequate explanation to the neonate's parent(s) about the procedure to be undertaken, if appropriate.

8. Described the ongoing care and assessment of the neonate.

9. Identified the differences between actual and expected outcomes.

10. Identified the need for further action.

11. Identified and reported deviations from normal.

12. Accurately documented information relating to the neonate's care on appropriate forms.

13. Demonstrated due care and sensitivity to neonate and parents by responding to their needs.

14. Used verbal and non-verbal communication effectively with neonate, family and other health care members (as appropriate).

15. Identified and minimized actual and potential safety hazards in the work environment.

References

Alexander, S and MacKenzie, J (1998) *Evaluation of Information Technology in University Learning: The CAUT experience*, Australian Government Publishing Service, Canberra

Angelo, T A and Cross K P (1993) *Classroom Assessment Techniques*, Jossey-Bass, San Francisco, CA

Australian Higher Education Council (1992) *Achieving Quality*, Australian Government Publishing Service, Canberra

Ballantyne, R and Packer, J (1995) *Making Connections*, Higher Education Research and Development Society of Australasia, Inc., Canberra

Benner, P (1984) *From Novice to Expert*, Addison Wesley, San Diego, CA

Benson, R (1996) *Assessing Open and Distance Learners: A staff handbook*, Churchill, Centre for Distance Learning, Monash University, Victoria, Australia

Benson, R (1997) Approaches to assessing open and distance learners, in *Research in Distance Education 4*, ed T Evans *et al*, papers from the fourth Research in Distance Education conference, Deakin University Press, Geelong

Benson, R and Rye, O (1996) Visual reports by video: an evaluation, *Distance Education*, **17** (1), pp 117–31

Biggs, J (1992) A qualitative approach to grading students, *HERDSA News*, Volume 14, pp 3–6

Biggs, J (1996) Assessing learning quality: reconciling institutional, staff and educational demands, *Assessment and Evaluation in Higher Education*, **21** (1), pp 5–15

Bondy, K M (1983) Criterion referenced definitions for rating scales in clinical evaluation, *Journal of Nursing Education*, **22** (9), pp 376–81

Boud, D (1986) *Implementing Student Self-assessment*, HERDSA Green Guide No 5, Canberra, ACT

Boud, D (1990) Assessment and the promotion of academic values, *Studies in Higher Education*, **14** (1), pp 20–30

Boud, D (1995) Assessment and learning: contradictory or complementary?, in *Assessment for Learning in Higher Education*, ed P Knight, Kogan Page, London

Bradley, C (1993) Sex bias in student assessment overlooked?, *Assessment and Evaluation in Higher Education*, **18** (1)

Brown, K (1996) The role of internal and external factors in the discontinuation of off-campus students, *Distance Education*, **17** (1), pp 44–71

Brown, S and Knight, S (1994) *Assessing Learners in Higher Education*, Kogan Page, London

Candy, P (1991) *Self-direction for Lifelong Learning*, Jossey-Bass, San Francisco, CA

Carson, L (1997) Assessment in the social sciences: Are we encouraging lifelong learning or essay processing machines?, unpublished assessment seminar paper, Southern Cross University

Chambers, E A (1992) Workload and the quality of student learning, *Studies in Higher Education*, **17** (2), pp 141–52

Chambers, E A (1994) Assessing learners' workload, in *Materials Production in Open and Distance Learning*, ed F Lockwood, Chapman, London

Clanchy, J and Ballard, B (1995) Generic skills in the context of higher education, *Higher Education Research and Development*, **14** (2)

Cowan, J (1996) New thoughts on assessment in open learning, *Open Learning*, June, pp 58–60

Daniel, J and Marquis, C (1979) Interaction and independence: getting the mixture right, *Teaching at a Distance*, **14**, Spring

Day, I (1998) Communication and the media (10701): Report on Web delivery trial, http://www-p.roma.unisa.edu.au/10701/index.htm

Dekkers J *et al* (1992) Use of instructional materials by distance students: patterns and student perceptions, in *Distance Education for the Twenty-first Century*, ed B Scriven, R Lundin and Y Ryan, Conference Papers, International Council of Distance Learning, Brisbane, QUT, pp 378–86

Entwistle, N and Ramsden, P (1983) *Understanding Student Learning*, Croom Helm, Beckenham

Evans, T (1994) *Understanding Learners in Open and Distance Education*, Kogan Page, London

Evans, T and Nation, D (1989) Dialogue in practice, research and theory in distance education, *Open Learning*, **4** (2), pp 37–41

Evans, T, Jakupec, V and Thompson, D (eds) (1997) *Research in Distance Education 4*, revised papers from the fourth Research in Distance Education conference, Deakin University Press, Geelong

Farnes, N (1993) Modes of production and stages of educational development: Fordism and distance education, *Open Learning*, **8** (1)

Garland, M (1993) Student perceptions of the situation, institutional, dispositional and epistemological barriers to persistence, *Distance Education*, **14** (2), pp181–98

Gibbs, G (1992) *Improving the Quality of Student Learning*, Technical and Educational Services Ltd, Bristol

Gibbs, G (1995) *Assessing Student Centred Courses*, Oxford Centre for Staff Development, Oxford Brooks University, Oxford

Gibbs, G, Morgan, A R and Taylor, E (1984) The world of the learner, in *The Experience of Learning*, ed F Marton, N Entwistle and D Housell, Scottish Academic Press, Edinburgh

Habeshaw, S, Gibbs, G and Habeshaw, T (1993) *53 Interesting Ways to Assess Your Students*, Technical and Educational Services Ltd, Bristol

Hager, P, Gonczi, A and Athanasou, J (1994) General issues about assessment of competence, *Assessment and Evaluation in Higher Education*, **19** (1), pp 3–16

Harisim, L (1991) Teaching by computer conferencing, in *Applications of Computer Conferencing to Teacher Education and Human Resource Development*, ed A J Miller, proceedings of an international symposium on computer conferencing, Ohio State University, Ohio

Harisim, L (1992) Foreword, in *From Bulletin Boards to Electronic Universities: Distance education, computer-mediated communication and online education*, M F Paulsen, American Centre for the Study of Distance Education, Philadelphia, PA

Hase, S and Saenger, H (1997) Videomail – a personalised approach to providing feedback on assessment to distance learners, *Distance Education*, **18** (2)

Higher Education Council (October 1992) *Achieving Quality*, Australian Government Publishing Service, Canberra

Holt, D (1997) *Information Technology Enhancement Program*, ITEP Project Report, Deakin University Press, Geelong

Holt, M E *et al* (1998) Evolution of evaluations for critical, reflective and deliberative discourse, National Issues Forums On-Line, http://www.coe.uga.edu/adulted/faculty/mholt/paper1.html

Johnston, S (1996) Using peer support: implications for student and lecturer, in *Implementing Flexible Learning*, Aspects of Educational and Training Technology XXIX, ed C Bell, M Bowden and A Trott, pp 69–75, Kogan Page, London

Juler, P (1990) Promoting interaction, maintaining independence: Swallowing the mixture, *Open Learning*, **5** (2), pp 24–33

Klemm, W R and Snell, J R (1996) Enriching computer-mediated group learning by coupling constructivism with collaborative learning, http://www.usq.edu.au/electpub/e-jist/klemm.htm

Knight, P (ed) (1995) *Assessment for Learning in Higher Education*, Kogan Page, London with Staff and Educational Development Association, UK

Laffey, J and Singer, J (1997) in *Web-based Instruction*, ed B Kahn, pp 357–60, Educational Technology Publications, Englewood Cliffs, NJ

Laurillard, D (1979) The processes of learning, *Higher Education*, **8**, pp 395–409

Laurillard, D (1993) *Rethinking University Teaching*, Routledge, London

Lentell, H (1994) Why is it so hard to hear the tutor in distance education?, *Open Learning*, 9 (3), pp 49–52

Lockwood, F (1992) *Activities in Self-instructional Texts*, Kogan Page, London

Lockwood, F (ed) (1994) *Materials Production in Open and Distance Learning*, Chapman, London

Lockwood, F (1995) Students' perception of, and response to, formative and summative assessment material, in *Open and Distance Learning Today*, ed F Lockwood, Routledge, London

Lockwood, F (1997) Unpublished presentation, *Research in Distance Education 4*, fourth Research in Distance Education conference, Deakin University, Geelong

Marland, P *et al* (1990) Distance learners' interactions with text while studying, *Distance Education*, 11 (1), pp 71–91

Marton, F, Hounsell, D and Entwistle, N (eds) (1984) *The Experience of Learning*, Scottish Academic Press, Edinburgh

Mason, R (1990) Computer conferencing in distance education, in *Media and Technology in European Distance Education*, ed A Bates, pp 221–26, European Association of Distance Teaching Universities, Milton Keynes

Mason, R (1995) Using electronic networking for assessment, in *Open and Distance Learning Today*, ed F Lockwood, Routledge, London

Miller, C and Parlett, M (1974) *Up to the Mark: A study of the examination game*, Society for Research in Higher Education, Guildford

Morgan, A (1990) Whatever happened to the silent revolution? Research, theory and practice in distance education, in *Research in Distance Education 1*, T Evans, papers from the first Research in Distance Education seminar, Deakin University Press, Geelong

Morgan, A (1993) *Improving Your Students' Learning: Reflections on the experience of study*, Kogan Page, London

Morgan, A R (1997) Still seeking the silent revolution? Research, theory and practice in open and distance education, in *Research in Distance Education 4*, ed T Evans *et al*, papers from the fourth Research in Distance Education conference, Deakin University Press, Geelong

Morgan, C J, Dingsdag, D and Saenger, H (1998) Learning strategies for distance learners: Do they help?, *Distance Education*, 19 (1)

National Committee of Inquiry into Higher Education (1997) *Higher Education in the Learning Society* (alternative title: Dearing Report), NCIHE, London

Newstead, S E and Dennis, I (1994) The reliability of exam marking in psychology: Examiners examined, *The Psychologist*, May, pp 216–19

Nightingale, P *et al* (1996) *Assessing Learning in Universities*, Professional Development Centre, University of New South Wales, Sydney

O'Reilly, M and Patterson, K (1998) Assessing learners through the WWW, in *Computer Networks and ISDN Systems*, proceedings of Seventh International World Wide Web Conference, Brisbane, Australia, pp 727–79, Elsevier, Amsterdam

O'Reilly, M, Saenger, H and Brooks, L (1997) Students' responses to optional study activities in distance education materials, in *Research in Distance Education 4*, ed T Evans, V Jakupec, and D Thompson, revised papers from the fourth Research in Distance Education conference, Deakin University Press, Geelong

Parer, M (1988) *Textual Design and Students' Learning*, Centre for Distance Learning, Gippsland Institute, Victoria

Paulsen, M (1995) The online report on pedagogical techniques for computer mediated communication, http://www.nki.no/ morten/

Peters, M (1995) Assessment and the Open University: an alternative view, *Adults Learning*, 7 (2), October

Race, P (1989) *The Open Learning Handbook: Selecting, designing and supporting open learning materials*, Kogan Page, London

Ramsden, P (1992) *Learning to Teach in Higher Education*, Routledge, London

Ramsden, P (1997) The context of learning in academic departments, in *The Experience of Learning*, 2nd edn, Scottish Academic Press, Edinburgh

Rowntree, D (1977) *Assessing Students: How shall we know them?*, Kogan Page, London

Rowntree, D (1990) *Teaching through Self-instruction*, 2nd edn, Kogan Page, London

Rowntree, D (1992) *Exploring Open and Distance Learning*, Kogan Page, London

Shulman, L (1987) Knowledge and teaching: foundations of a new reform, *Harvard Educational Review*, **57** (1), pp 1–3

Siegel, M and Kirkley, S (1997) Moving toward the digital learning environment: the future of Web-based instruction, in *Web-based Instruction*, ed B Kahn, pp 263–70, Educational Technology Publications, Englewood Cliffs, NJ

Taylor, J A (1998) Self test: A flexible self-assessment package for distance and other learners, *Computers and Education*, **31** (3), pp 319–28

Taylor, J A and Morgan, M J (1996) Access to engineering studies: overcoming the mathematical barrier for external students, in *Engineering Mathematics: Research, education and industry linkage*, ed W Y D Yuen, P Broadbridge and J M Steiner, Proceedings of Second Biennial Australian Engineering Mathematics Conference, Sydney

Thorpe, M (1988) *Evaluating Open & Distance Learning*, Longman, Harlow

University of Southern Queensland (1996) *Mathematics Refreshment for Engineering, Science & Technology Students*, Office of Preparatory and Continuing Studies, Toowoomba

University of Sydney (1998) Murder under the microscope: professional challenge, http://www.nettl.usyd.edu.au

Index

Visit Kogan Page on-line

Comprehensive information on
Kogan Page titles

Features include

- complete catalogue listings,
  including book reviews and
  descriptions

- special monthly promotions

- information on NEW titles and
  BESTSELLING titles

- a secure shopping basket facility
  for on-line ordering

PLUS everything you need to know
about KOGAN PAGE

http://www.kogan-page.co.uk